D0146191

Hobbes's political theory

Hobbes's political theory

DEBORAH BAUMGOLD

DEPARTMENT OF POLITICAL SCIENCE
UNIVERSITY OF OREGON

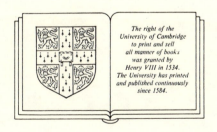

The right of the
University of Cambridge
to print and sell
all manner of books
was granted by
Henry VIII in 1534.
The University has printed
and published continuously
since 1584.

CAMBRIDGE UNIVERSITY PRESS

CAMBRIDGE

NEW YORK   NEW ROCHELLE   MELBOURNE   SYDNEY

Published by the Press Syndicate of the University of Cambridge
The Pitt Building, Trumpington Street, Cambridge CB2 1RP
32 East 57th Street, New York, NY 10022, USA
10 Stamford Road, Oakleigh, Melbourne 3166, Australia

First published 1988

Printed in the United States of America

Library of Congress Cataloging-in-Publication Data
Baumgold, Deborah.
Hobbes's political theory / Deborah Baumgold.
p.   cm.
Bibliography: p.
Includes index.
ISBN 0 521 34125 6
1. Hobbes, Thomas, 1588–1679 – Contributions in political science.
I. Title.
JC153. H66B35   1988
320.1'092'4 – dc19   87–30960
CIP

British Library Cataloging in Publication applied for

For my parents

Contents

Contents

Tables

Acknowledgments

Prefaces are a proper locale for saying something about the "logic of discovery" behind an argument because that process, at least for most people, is a social one. I had the good luck to be taught Hobbes's political theory by Michael Walzer in a seminar at Princeton University in 1973. This book has its roots in a seminar on Hobbes that I led at Oberlin College in the fall of 1979. There developed among us, over the course of the term, a collective sense of some real discrepancy between Hobbism as presented in the secondary literature and the textual political theory. From that group, I have especially to thank David Estrin, who encouraged and chided me in the years since to finish the project. I am grateful to the National Endowment for the Humanities for a fellowship in 1983–84, which funded research for the book. I was fortunate to spend part of that time in the pleasant environment of Clare Hall of the University of Cambridge. James Tully read an earlier version of the manuscript and gave excellent advice concerning revisions. I want to thank, too, Pamela Richards and Lucy Knight for their editorial advice, and Mark Smith for assistance in producing the final manuscript.

Alfonso Damico discussed the project with me literally from beginning to end. He patiently read successive drafts and offered encouragement, suggestions, and useful criticisms. I want particularly to thank him, as well as John Dunn and Jennifer Hochschild. I am grateful for the conversation and friendship of them all. The familiar caveat applies, of course: The arguments of the book are my own.

Chapter 1

Introduction

Hobbes's political doctrine presents the unusual feature that it has given rise to an "official" interpretation, in terms of which, for example, students are expected to show their proficiency in the schools, and at the same time, a general suspicion that the text itself bears only a very approximate relationship to it – a situation which appears to have persisted in spite of the fact that both the "official" interpretation and the grounds of suspicion have changed from time to time.

Howard Warrender, *The Political Philosophy of Hobbes*

Some time ago, Howard Warrender observed that the "official" interpretation of Hobbes's political theory that one learns in school is at odds with the theory actually to be found in *Leviathan*.[1] The present study is inspired by the same suspicion, although my critique encompasses Warrender's own reading. Underlying the various mainstream controversies within Hobbes studies (for example, over the character and cogency of his account of political obligation, or between analytic and historical ways of reading the theory) is a settled opinion that Hobbes is an individualistic political thinker. This is, first of all, a characterization of his reasoning, namely, the view that he deduces political conclusions from premises about the motivation, rights, and duties of abstract individuals. But the opinion involves more. It is reflected in the exegetical interests of commentators, whose attention has been absorbed by Hobbes's accounts of human nature and knowledge in Part I of the theory. Third and most important, the opinion concerns the nature of Hobbes's political under-

1

standing. Based on the assumption that everyman (the abstract individual) is the principal subject of his political analysis, interpreters have attributed to Hobbes the view that the coercive authority of government hinges on the support of ordinary citizens. It follows that political obligation is the controlling problem, and central puzzle, of this political theory. "Elle est un *De Cive* et non pas un *De Principe*," in Raymond Polin's epigrammatic phrase, because it seemed to Hobbes that "the greatest political problem consists in securing the consent and the obedience of citizens."[2]

The present study focuses on the political arguments of the second part of *Leviathan*, and the parallel chapters in the works presenting earlier versions of the theory, *The Elements of Law* and *De Cive*. These arguments are in chapters 17 through 30 of *Leviathan*, starting with the description of the political covenant and concluding with discussion of the duties of the sovereign (see Table 1, later in this introduction). The analysis of politics presented in this, the narrowly political, section of the theory has a different character from Hobbism reconstructed along individualistic lines. The defining problem of the theory is the characteristic problem of weak early-modern states – the need to consolidate coercive national authority. How to erect, in Hobbes's words, "such a Common Power, as may be able to defend them from the invasion of Forraigners, and the injuries of one another."[3] In the orthodox interpretive paradigm, the problem is translated in populist fashion into that of explaining citizens' motivation and duty to cooperate with the state. But Hobbes conceives it differently. He has an elitist and institutional understanding of the principal threat to strong government and the main remedy, that is, the source of coercive authority. He is preoccupied not so much with the *incivisme* of ordinary subjects as with the danger posed by ambitious elites. "Amongst men," *Leviathan* observes, "there are very many, that thinke themselves wiser, and abler to govern the Publique, better than the rest; and these strive to reforme and innovate, one this way, another that way; and thereby bring it into Distraction and Civill warre."[4] Both for the purposes

2

of discouraging bids for power by ambitious elites and to ensure the resources necessary to govern effectively, it is crucial that political authority be properly institutionalized. Among the "infirmities" that cause the dissolution of states, Hobbes "reckon[s] in the first place," in *Leviathan*, "those that arise from an Imperfect Institution," as when "Kings deny themselves some such necessary Power."[5] The defense of absolutism, preferably monarchic absolutism, is therefore central to his theory of politics. To discount this institutional prescription because it is foreign to our own opinions about the best constitution of government, as is so often done, involves a fundamental mistake about the shape of Hobbes's understanding of politics. Because he ascribes central importance to the constitution of sovereign authority, it is a key interpretive task to endeavor to understand the political analysis that made this institutional prescription seem sensible to Hobbes.

His preoccupation with elite conflict and with the institutionalization of political authority had a concrete referent in the current struggle for power between king and Parliament. We will see, more specifically, that Hobbes's political arguments address central issues in the constitutional debates of the 1630s and early 1640s. *The Elements of Law* (1640) and the first edition of *De Cive* (1642) appeared before the outbreak of the Civil War, in a period of "paper war" between royalists and parliamentarians. Some of the revisions to the theory in the second edition of *De Cive* (1647) and in *Leviathan* (1651) reflect the late Civil War period and the postwar Interregnum, respectively, but in the main Hobbes's theoretical understanding of politics was fixed before the war. There is more to his contribution to contemporary constitutional debates than the defense of absolute sovereignty in chapter 18 of *Leviathan*. Hobbes's covenant arguments themselves attack constitutional claims with which parliamentarians justified their cause. The concept of non-resistance is central to the formulation of the political covenant in *The Elements of Law* and *De Cive*, whereas in *Leviathan* Hobbes redescribes the covenant using the idea of authorization. These arguments rebut, first, the parliamentarians' claim of a right of resistance against tyrannous kings and, second, their assertion of royal accountability based on the notion of an authorization relationship between the monarch and the people. In the context of contemporary political debates, in short, Hobbes's covenant arguments bore, in the first instance, on the legitimacy of the parliamentary rebellion – as opposed, that is, to the obligations of ordinary individuals in the abstract. To illustrate just how thoroughly Hobbes was absorbed in contemporary constitutional polemics, I will be comparing his arguments with, in particular, Henry Parker's influential brief for Parliament, *Observations upon some of his Majesties late Answers and Expresses* (London, 1642).[6] Hobbes was not, it scarcely needs saying, an ordinary royalist pamphleteer, nor is the present study simply intended to show that he was engaged in constitutional polemics. Establishing the political significance of Hobbes's arguments is nonetheless essential to appreciating his analysis of politics and to disentangling this from the political understanding that has been attributed to him by twentieth-century commentators.

Hobbes's political arguments are treated in the order in which they appear in the textual theory. In chapter 2 I examine the issues associated with the covenant arguments of *The Elements of Law* and *De Cive*, namely, the doctrine of non-resistance and the related notion of an unalienated individual right of self-defense against violence. Chapter 3 treats *Leviathan*'s formulation of the political covenant, which employs the concepts of authorization and representation, as well as the analysis of political agency that Hobbes developed to rebut the usage of these ideas by the parliamentarians. His constitutional doctrine – the defense of unconditional and unified sovereignty, preferably in the form of monarchy – is the subject of chapter 4. While Hobbesian theology in and of itself lies outside the scope of the present study, his religious arguments will be briefly discussed in this context. These arguments had, and were intended to have, constitutional force, it being Hobbes's purpose to refute religious justifications for resisting rulers and to defend

4

on theological grounds the sovereign's title to supreme ecclesiastical authority. Hobbes's account of obligation, the focus of the reigning "official" interpretive paradigm, is examined in chapter 5. The discussion of the obligation to fight for the state in chapter 21 of *Leviathan* ("Of the LIBERTY of Subjects") is the exemplary case. It manifests a structural, as opposed to individualistic, way of thinking about the performance of civic duties. Rather than discuss the duties of an abstract individual, Hobbes ties obligations to roles, drawing a distinction between the obligations of ordinary subjects and those of soldiers who have enlisted in some more or less voluntary fashion. Hobbes's advice to rulers concerning the exercise of sovereign power is the subject of chapter 6. Hobbism's reputation as a theory licensing tyranny aside, he actually commends good government, conducted according to law. This advice plays a systematic part in the larger theory, complementing his prescription of an absolutist constitution, inasmuch as Hobbes holds that good government enhances rulers' power. The final chapter will examine the deployment of Hobbes's political theory in the Engagement Controversy of the early years of Cromwell's regime, which was the period in which *Leviathan* was published. In this context I offer a concluding assessment of Hobbes's political sensibility.

THE ORTHODOX PARADIGM

Do individuals have instrumental and (or) moral reasons to obey and, beyond that, to cooperate with political authority? The question dominates twentieth-century interpretations of Hobbes's political theory. In the traditional view, put forward by the Utilitarian thinkers who were responsible for reviving interest in Hobbism in the nineteenth century, the political theory is best understood as a deduction from an egoistic psychology.[7] John Plamenatz comments in this vein in *Man and Society:* "Perhaps Hobbes would have done better had he explained political obedience entirely as an effect of self-interest and fear, had he spoken only of maxims of pru-

dence in the state of nature and never of divine laws. . . .
The only ground of obedience would then have been the private interest of the person called upon to obey."[8] A. E. Taylor and, later, Warrender countered with a natural-law interpretation emphasizing the political theory's dependence on
a prior and independent ethical theory. They and others have
argued that Hobbes had a theory of moral duty founded, by
alternative accounts, on the injunction to keep promises or
out of fear of divine punishment.[9] By contrast, it is Michael
Oakeshott's view that political obligations originate in
Hobbesian theory with the institution of a coercive sovereign.[10] Both Warrender's and Oakeshott's interpretations were
rejected by C. B. Macpherson, who revived a sociological
version of the traditional view with the thesis that Hobbes's
explanation of political obedience is a deduction from an account of human behavior in a certain kind of society, a possessive market society.[11] More recently, the traditional case
has been defended, and Warrender criticized, on historical
grounds. According to Quentin Skinner, Hobbes's contemporaries understood the theory to be a defense of obligation
to de facto authority appealing to the rational desire for self-
preservation.[12]

Sharp as the disagreements are among these readers, they
represent quarrels within a school with respect to their common absorption in establishing the foundations of Hobbes's
political theory.[13] So general is this preoccupation that the
classic interpretations can be classified, as W. H. Greenleaf
has done, by the premise to which they give pride of place.
In addition to the traditional view, emphasizing the foundation of Hobbesian theory in an egoistic psychology, and the
contrasting Taylor-Warrender thesis, a third camp emphasizes the philosophical and scientific foundations of the political theory. Michael Oakeshott, for example, insists that
philosophical nominalism is at the root of Hobbes's political
understanding,[14] whereas according to J. W. N. Watkins,
"Hobbes's [resolutive-compositive] method determined the
shape of his civil philosophy."[15] The upshot is to consider
Hobbes's political arguments, presented in Part II of *Levia-*

than, merely as applications of the assumptions laid out in Part I. Watkins's study *Hobbes's System of Ideas* is subtitled, for example, *A Study in the Political Significance of Philosophical Theories*. He explains: "The question it answers is, How much of Hobbes's *political* theory is implied by his *philosophical* ideas? The conclusion it reaches is that the essentials of his political theory are so implied."[16]

It is true that Hobbes hoped to create a unified, deductive science, having three parts – "Of Body," "Of Man," and "Of Body Politic." In the late 1630s, according to the autobiography he wrote in old age, he formed the idea

> . . . of connecting into a whole the knowledge I had gained, so that the conclusions might shine bright in the light of the first principles and the whole argument might have the permanence of a strong chain. From the varieties of motion I passed to the different species of things and the subtleties of matter, to the inner motions of men and the secret places of the mind, and finally to the blessings of Government and Justice. In these studies I buried myself; for three things comprise the whole of philosophy, namely, Body, Man, and the Citizen. I resolved to write three books on these subjects and gathered my material day by day.[17]

How far authorial achievement resembles authorial intention is a matter of dispute: This is the issue contended between psychological and natural-law readings of Hobbes's account of political obligation. Furthermore, there is some consensus, first, that he did not realize the ground plan of deducing psychological theorems from materialist axioms[18] and, second, that psychological arguments become less important, or at least weaker, through the course of the development of the theory. Bernard Gert has shown persuasively that, whereas *The Elements of Law* asserts the "psychological egoist" view that men never act benevolently or from some moral sense, *Leviathan* merely stipulates "tautological egoism," that is, the position that voluntary acts are by definition self-interested.[19] On the other hand, Hobbes also believed the political theory could stand on its own and justified the separate publication of the third section in the form of *De Cive* on this ground:

> My Country some few yeares before the civill Warres did rage, was boyling hot with questions concerning the rights of Dominion, and the obedience due from Subjects, the true forerunners of an approaching War; And was the cause which . . . ripen'd, and pluckt from me this third part. Therefore it happens that what was last in order, is yet come forth first in time, and the rather, because I saw that grounded on its owne principles sufficiently knowne by experience it would not stand in need of the former Sections.[20]

A further feature of the orthodox paradigm is the well-nigh universal assumption that Hobbism exemplifies individualistic political reasoning. Political individualism denotes a style of reasoning translating political issues into questions about the motivation, liberties, and duties of abstract individuals. Scholars frequently cite Hobbism as an exemplar of this kind of political analysis, as Steven Lukes does:

> This abstract way of conceiving the individual is most clear in Hobbes, for whom Leviathan, or the sovereign power, is an artificial contrivance constructed to satisfy the requirements (chief among them survival and security) of the component elements of society – "men as if but even now sprung out of the earth, and suddenly, like mushrooms, come to full maturity, without all kind of engagement to each other."[21]

Since political individualism is a currently fashionable method of analysis, manifested in a fascination with free-rider problems, prisoners' dilemmas, and, generally, problems relating to the fit between individual and collective interest, this characterization of Hobbes's thinking lends the theory some continuing relevance.[22] Michael Walzer, for example, has used *Leviathan* to illustrate the difficulty of justifying an obligation to fight and die for the state, starting from the individualistic, Hobbist premises that human beings are self-interested and possess an unalienated right to defend themselves against violence.[23] Indeed, the Hobbesian assumption of ubiquitous selfishness calls into question altogether individuals' motivation to cooperate with their governors.[24]

The opinion that Hobbes reasons in the fashion of a political individualist is defended on the basis of a second of his scientific intentions: the idea of a "resolutive-compositive" method. The method consists in analyzing a whole into constitutive parts, and deducing from the analysis principles governing the operation of the whole. In virtue of his plan for a deductive science and his philosophical nominalism, commentators take for granted that Hobbes resolved the state to the level of individuals *and* that his analytic recomposition consists in generalizing political conclusions from those individualistic premises.[25]

Regarding the first point, the evidence about Hobbes's intentions is ambiguous. It is notably in *De Cive* (and in a 1655 methodological treatise, *De Corpore*) that individuals are said to be the "constitutive causes" of the state. "Concerning my Method," Hobbes explains in the preface to the second edition of *De Cive:*

> Every thing is best understood by its constitutive causes; for as in a watch, or some such small engine, the matter, figure, and motion of the wheels, cannot well be known, except it be taken in sunder, and viewed in parts; so to make a more curious search into the rights of States, and duties of Subjects, it is necessary, (I say not to take them in sunder, but yet that) they be so considered, as if they were dissolved, (i.e.) that wee rightly understand what the quality of humane nature is, in what matters it is, in what not fit to make up a civill government, and how men must be agreed among themselves, that intend to grow up into a well-grounded State.[26]

That programmatic statement contrasts with the description of the state in the introduction to *Leviathan*. Hobbes re-employs the watch analogy, but here he pictures a political division of labor in which roles and functions are the units of the analysis:

> Why may we not say, that all *Automata* (Engines that move themselves by springs and wheels as doth a watch) have an

9

artificiall life? . . . For by Art is created that great LEVIATHAN called a COMMON-WEALTH, or STATE, . . . which is but an Artificiall Man; . . . in which, the *Soveraignty* is an Artificiall *Soul,* . . . as giving life and motion to the whole body; The *Magistrates,* and other *Officers* of Judicature and Execution, artificiall *Joynts; Reward* and *Punishment* (by which fastned to the seate of the Soveraignty, every joynt and member is moved to performe his duty) are the *Nerves,* that do the same in the Body Naturall; . . . *Counsellors,* by whom all things needfull for it to know, are suggested unto it, are the *Memory; Equity* and *Lawes,* an artificiall *Reason* and *Will.*[27]

To make even *De Cive*'s methodological statement a program for an individualistic political analysis requires assuming, furthermore, the application of the principle of generalizability or universalizability. That is, it requires assuming that Hobbes's political conclusions are derived by generalizing from his premises about human nature. "What if everyone were to exercise the unalienated right of self-defense, or to pursue self-interest?" is a characteristic universalizing question.[28] It remains to the interpretation of Hobbes's political arguments to show that he does not reason in this fashion. His reasoning corresponds, rather, to *Leviathan*'s structural picture of the state. Hobbes presumes a political division of labor and focuses on its constitutive roles and institutions. Fully as much as an individualistic political analysis, a structural analysis of this sort can lay claim to foundation in the "known naturall Inclinations of Mankind."[29] The difference between the two kinds of analysis lies in the way in which questions about human nature and obligation arise within them. We will see that Hobbes situates discussion of individuals' motivation and duties in the context of the roles and institutions they inhabit.

A CONSTITUTIONAL THEORY OF POLITICS

There are three structurally parallel versions of Hobbes's political theory. *The Elements of Law* circulated in manuscript in 1640, before the outbreak of the Civil War, and was published in 1650, although probably without Hobbes's authorization, in two parts (titled *Human Nature* and *De Corpore Politico*). *De Cive* came out in a limited edition in 1642 and in a second, larger edition in 1647. An English translation of the work was published in 1651, and later in the same year *Leviathan* appeared.[30] Table 1 outlines the three versions of the political theory.

The textual political theory more closely resembles a constitutional theory of politics in the traditional Aristotelian style than a model illustration of political individualism. Of course it was Aristotle's theory of politics, above all others in the history of political thought, that Hobbes set out to attack in his work.[31] Hobbesian absolutism is also the antithesis of liberal constitutionalism, the doctrine that political authority should be subject to legal and procedural restraints.[32] "Aristotelian constitutionalism" refers, in a narrowly political sense, to the conviction that the way in which political authority is institutionalized affects the possibility for good political order. In a broader sense, it connotes a social science built around analysis of the constitutive roles and functions of state and society.[33] Hobbes's chapter topics are the customary themes of such constitutional theory: sovereign right; forms of government; comparison of familial, household, and political authority relationships; juridical philosophy; and governmental stability. Notice that the discussion of various aspects of the constitution of state and society and the administration of government is significantly expanded in *Leviathan*. The work includes these new chapters on institutions and roles within the state: Chapter 22 treats subordinate associations within the state, chapter 23 discusses public ministers, and the subject of counsel is covered in chapter 25. The office of the sovereign, encompassing the exercise of power as well as the formal constitution of political authority, is the subject of chapters on political economy (24) and juridical rule (26 through 28). Only in *Leviathan*, as well, is there a chapter specially devoted to the role of ordinary subjects (chapter 21). (Political theology is the other significant area of addition through the several versions of the theory. There are

Table 1. *Political chapters of* The Elements of Law, De Cive, *and* Leviathan *(tables of contents)*

The Elements of Law	De Cive	Leviathan
Part I. Concerning men as persons natural	LIBERTY	Part I. Of Man
xiv. Of the estate and right of nature	i. Of the State of men without civill society	13. Of the Naturall Condition of Mankind . . .
xv. Of the divesting natural right . . .	ii. Of the Law of nature concerning contracts	14. Of the first and second Naturall Lawes . . .
xvi. Some of the laws of nature	iii. Of the other Lawes of nature	15. Of other Lawes of Nature
xvii. Other laws of nature		
xviii. A confirmation . . . out of the Word of God	iv. That the Law of nature is a divine Law	
		16. Of Persons, Authors, and things personated
	EMPIRE	Part II. Of Commonwealth
xix. Of the necessity and definition of a body politic	v. Of the causes, and first Originall, of civill government	17. Of the Causes, Generation, and Definition of a Common-wealth
Part II. Concerning men as a body politic		
i. Of the requisites to the constitution of a commonwealth	vi. Of the right . . . which he hath who is endued with supreme authority	18. Of the Rights of Soveraignes by Institution
ii. Of the three sorts of commonwealth	vii. Of the three kindes of government . . .	(19.)
iii. Of the power of masters	viii. Of the right which Lords and Masters have over their Servants	20. Of Dominion Paternall, and Despoticall
iv. Of the power of fathers, and of patrimonial kingdom	ix. Of the rights which Parents have over their children, . . .	
v. The incommodities of several sorts of government compared	x. A comparison of the three kinds of government . . . according to the inconveniences of each	19. Of severall Kinds of Common-wealth by Institution, and of Succesion . . .
vi–vii. That decision of controversies in religion dependeth on the sovereign power	xi. The places and examples of Scripture concerning the right of government, which make for proof of the foresaid Doctrines	21. Of the Liberty of Subjects

12

Table 1 *(cont.)*

The Elements of Law	De Cive	Leviathan
		22. Of Systemes Subject, Politicall, and Private
		23. Of the Publique Ministers of Soveraign Power
		24. Of the Nutrition, and Procreation of a Common-wealth
		25. Of Counsell
		(26.)
		27. Of Crimes, Excuses, and Extenuations
		28. Of Punishments, and Rewards
viii. Of the causes of rebellion	xii. Of the inward causes which dissolve all civill government	29. Of those things that Weaken, or tend to the Dissolution of a Common-wealth
ix. Of the duty of them that have sovereign power	xiii. Of the duties of those men who sit at the Helm of State	30. Of the Office of the Soveraign Representative
x. Of the nature and kinds of laws	xiv. Of Lawes, and Sinnes	26. Of Civill Lawes

	RELIGION	
	xv. Of Gods government by nature	31. Of the Kingdome of God by Nature
	xvi–xviii.	Part III. Of a Christian Common-wealth
		Part IV. Of the Kingdome of Darknesse
		A Review and Conclusion

Note: The key to the table is *De Cive*, which corresponds to the third (the political) section of Hobbes's plan for a unified science.

four new chapters on these subjects in *De Cive* [15 through 18], which balloon into two parts in *Leviathan.*)

These discussions rely to a large extent on prudential observations and causal generalizations about the dynamics of politics. A notable instance is *Leviathan*'s defense of the need for unified sovereignty, which rests on a causal generalization connecting divided sovereignty, elite conflict, and civil war. In this additional respect, Hobbes's actual political analysis diverges from his scientific intentions, at least according to one of his conceptions of science. This is the equation of science with geometry, that is, formal, axiomatic knowledge, as contrasted with experiential and historical knowledge.[34] *Leviathan's* defense of absolutism corresponds more closely to another Hobbesian definition of science, namely, the view that scientific knowledge consists in knowledge of causes.[35] In light of this latter definition, the pertinent distinction is not between scientific and experiential knowledge but, rather, between two sorts of experiential knowledge: "between," Richard Ashcraft explains, "knowledge derived from experience which is *merely* 'memory' and knowledge derived from experience which explains how and why one fact is dependent upon another."[36] The present study draws attention to the latter, to Hobbes's causal and prudential analyses of politics. The logical edifice of Hobbism as a formal theory has fascinated many readers. I hope to show that he is substantially more political a thinker, and a more interesting political thinker, than is often acknowledged.

There are several caveats to be noted at this point. In characterizing Hobbes's textual political reasoning as a structural analysis of institutions and roles, I do not mean to imply that he attributes ontological reality to social units, independent of the individuals composing them. He does not: Such holist ontology directly contradicts his undoubted commitment to philosophical nominalism, the position that only individuals, particular things, exist.[37] Structural theories, like individualistic doctrines, come in several varieties. Hobbes's political theory illustrates what might be called methodological structuralism, meaning the view that social structure – roles, institutions, and social practices – is the proper level of social and political analysis. Being methodological and not ontological, this approach is consistent with nominalism, and with the "methodological individualist" tenet that statements about groups ought to translate into, ought to permit being translated into, statements about individuals.[38] Within a structural methodology, that is, it is appropriate to ask why individuals should be motivated to perform their role or structural functions (why, in a Hobbesian instance, soldiers should

14

perform their strenuous obligation to fight for the state). What Hobbism is not, I am arguing, is an example of "political individualism," or the view that the significant political unit is the abstract individual. Institutions and roles have intrinsic significance in his discussions of governmental performance and of individuals' political obligations.

In attacking the truism that Hobbism exemplifies individualistic political reasoning, I also do not mean to suggest (as it would be wrong to do) that this is a communitarian political vision. There are other ways of conceiving the relationship between individuals and the state besides the antitheses of instrumental individualism (the state is merely an instrument for the satisfaction of individual purposes) and communitarianism (the view that political membership is crucial to individual identity and development). A structural-functional analysis of constitutive political and social roles is such a way.

Last, consent is the Hobbesian principle of entitlement to roles. This is far different from Aristotle's teleological naturalism, and more congenial to modern sensibilities. *Leviathan*'s "idea of the state," which was quoted earlier, picks out roles and functions of particular salience in the period (e.g., that contentious figure in the early Stuart regimes, the counselor). But the perception of society and polity as a network of roles, which ideally ought to be distributed on the basis of consent, remains a commonplace "amateur" social theory of the relationship between individuals and the whole.[39] The view is closer to ordinary experience, a less abstract way of sorting through connections between oneself and the larger society, than the analytic reductionism of individualistic political reasoning.

TEXTUALISM AND CONTEXTUALISM

For understanding the meaning of a text itself, as opposed to the function ideas have played in history or the ways in which a theory has been received by later audiences, there are three principal interpretive approaches: Biographical interpretations emphasize the author's intention in producing a work; textualist interpretations focus on a work's internal logic; contextual interpretations highlight a work's meaning to contemporary readers.[40] In Hobbes's case, a biographical approach involves peculiar difficulties, for reasons that were discussed.[41] To be sure, a political reading, focused on the arguments of the second section of the theory, corresponds to some of his intentions. Hobbes certainly intended to address the contemporary political crisis, and characterized all three treatises, not only *De Cive*, as "occasioned by the disorders of the present time."[42] On the other hand, the relationship between his program for a scientific analysis of politics and the political theory that he actually wrote is itself a major problem of interpretation. Focusing on that problem distracts attention from his political arguments themselves. In this particular instance, therefore, an interpretive emphasis on the author's understanding of his own enterprise is the least satisfactory avenue of approach.

Textualism and contextualism are often represented as rival approaches to interpretation. In the one, texts are to be considered without regard to external data while the other model equates explaining textual meaning with understanding a work's contextual significance. It is by now also familiar to have pointed out the inadequacies of both models in pure form.[43] The danger of proleptic interpretation, that is, attributing to an author ideas that no one in the period held or even would have understood, attends a purely textualist approach.[44] Contextualist readings are subject to the contrary hazard of reductionism – of depicting masterpieces such as *Leviathan* as no more than examples of ordinary political discourse in their period. Attempting to avoid both shoals, the procedure followed in the present study combines a focus on Hobbes's textual arguments with attention to the contextual significance of the issues these arguments address.

The procedure is inspired by R. G. Collingwood's idea of the "logic of question and answer." To elucidate the meaning and assess the cogency of a proposition, Collingwood argues, it is essential that it be framed in the context of the question – or problem – it addresses. "Whether a given proposition is true or false, significant or meaningless, depends on what question it was meant to answer; and any one who wishes to know whether a given proposition is true or false, significant or meaningless, must find out what question it was meant to answer."[45] Collingwood himself took the logic to entail a biographical approach to interpretation, holding that interpretive understanding requires reconstructing the author's mind and intention.[46] In principle, however, the procedure is adaptable to any of the several approaches to interpretation. Emphasis can be placed on the textual statement of the question on which a given argument bears or on the common understanding in the period of either the question, the answer, or both, as well as on the author's purposes in writing.[47] In this study, I emphasize the textual "logic of question and answer" and, second, the significance for contemporary readers of the problems Hobbes treats.

My disagreement with Collingwood is at the level of statement and not of practice. The procedure I have attempted to follow in reading Hobbes's political theory corresponds to this description by him of interpretive method. "We have to study documents and interpret them. We have to say 'here is a passage of Leibniz; what is it about? what is the problem with which it deals?' "[48] Whatever significance an argument may otherwise have, the least speculative statement of its purpose is the textual statement of the problem on which it bears. Why, for example, does Hobbes introduce the authorization formulation of the political covenant in *Leviathan*? This is a common subject of interpretive speculation, much of which centers on the supposed problem of explaining subjects' motivation to give a Hobbesian sovereign their active support. But we shall see in chapter 5 that the question to which the new covenant supplied the answer is precisely (and differently) defined in *De Cive*. The issue, in brief, concerned subjects' allegiance: Hobbes was intent on rebutting the widespread opinion that in certain circumstances an established government could be deposed.

This political theory lends itself to a textual focus because

Hobbes wrote, over the span of a decade or more, three structurally parallel versions. The internal evidence on the development of his thinking is therefore uniquely abundant. My discussions follow in detail the evolution of his major political arguments – the several versions of the covenant, the argument for absolutism, and Hobbes's advice on the conduct of government. I pay particular attention to his political casuistry, the way he applies principles to cases. This is among the most alien aspects of the theory for a twentieth-century audience. Hobbes distinguishes among cases in a way that baffles readers today.[49] From the stipulation of an unalienated natural right to defend oneself against violence (in *De Cive* and *Leviathan*), it follows in his view, for instance, that subjects do not have to obey a command to commit suicide. But Hobbes does not, as we would expect, deduce from the same principle the absence of an obligation to fight for the state.[50] Exposition of his arguments is accompanied by an effort to reconstruct Hobbes's reasoning. Sometimes – for example, in the discussion of consent in chapter 5 – my interpretation introduces concepts ("prima facie" obligation and "cognitive" consent, in this instance) that are foreign to the textual theory but make sense of particular arguments. Throughout, however, I attempt to keep the analytic reconstruction of Hobbesian logic separate from description of the political arguments themselves.

After the texts, the best guide to Hobbes's topics is their contemporary definition. It is likelier, for instance (and to anticipate chapter 2), that he understood natural-rights arguments as his contemporaries did, as arguments about the constitution of sovereignty and the legitimacy of elite resistance to the throne, than that he assumed (as twentieth-century commentators do) the popular, individualistic force of rights propositions. For understanding the "logic of question and answer" of the theory, the important historical evidence concerns the references of Hobbes's discussions, what someone in that time and place would have imagined them to be about. This appeal to contextualism narrowly privileges contemporary understanding of Hobbes's topics – his "ques-

18

tions," as opposed to contemporary readings of the "answers," the theory itself. How Hobbes handles the issues is another matter. Often the interest of his arguments lies in a critical analysis of the very terms of contemporary polemics. Contemporaries are not necessarily privileged readers for iconoclastic arguments, and may make worse readers of such arguments than a later audience inasmuch as they expect to find familiar opinions expressed and emphasize these. The point, in short, is to avoid depicting Hobbes's political theory as merely another ordinary political tract of the times.

Siting Hobbes's political theory in the context of the prewar constitutional debates contrasts with the historical interpretation Quentin Skinner advances. He associates Hobbism with the Engagement Controversy of 1650–51 over the oath of allegiance demanded by the new regime. All three versions of the political theory appeared for the first time in England and in English in this period. By Skinner's showing, Hobbism was exploited to counsel subjects to "engage" with, and thereby legitimize, Cromwell's government. The reading was originally presented as a historical test of the natural-law interpretation of Hobbes's account of obligation, contrasting that interpretation with the understanding held by contemporary readers.[51] But Skinner has been led to suggest, more strongly, that it captures Hobbes's intentions in writing the theory, or at least some of his main intentions.[52] The upshot is to minimize the significance of Hobbesian constitutional theory and to lend historical support to the familiar interpretive emphasis on his account of obligation.[53]

But when he framed the theory Hobbes could not have had in mind the "engagement" questions of the rights of de facto rulers and subjects' obligations to them. The theory was conceived, and its main outlines settled, before the Civil War. Hobbes would later specifically associate *The Elements of Law* with the debates in the Short Parliament of 1640 over the English constitution:

When the Parliament sat, that began in April 1640, and was dissolved in May following, and in which many points of the

19

regal power, which were necessary for the peace of the kingdom, and the safety of his Majesty's person, were disputed
and denied, Mr. Hobbes wrote a little treatise in English,
wherein he did set forth and demonstrate, that the said power
and rights were inseparably annexed to the sovereignty; which
sovereignty they did not then deny to be in the King; but it
seems understood not, or would not understand that insepa-
rability.[54]

There are in the 1647 edition of *De Cive* and in *Leviathan* some
additions to the theory that make transparent reference to
the Civil War or the early Interregnum, notably, the pointed
treatment in *Leviathan's* "Review and Conclusion" of the
"engagement" issue of when a subject may submit to a conqueror.[55] There is also, however, substantial continuity between the several versions of the theory, as is evident in their
parallel outlines.[56] Indeed, many of the alterations Hobbes
makes to the theory in *Leviathan* continue to address issues
in the earlier constitutional debates. These include the authorization formulation of the political covenant, as well as
the new chapter on subordinate associations within the state,
in which the proper role of a representative assembly under
a monarch is treated at some length. The earlier dating is
therefore more accurate relative to the contours of the theory
as a whole.

Chapter 2

The Hobbesian covenants: rights

To a twentieth-century mind, the social-contract metaphor implies individualistic political thinking. We take for granted that the subject or salient agent in contract arguments is everyman, and the device therefore has popular political force.[1] But it is an error of prolepsis to impute to Hobbes our understanding of the contract metaphor. Propositions about individuals figured in mid–seventeenth-century political arguments differently than in twentieth-century usage. In Henry Parker's *Observations*, for instance, the idea that private individuals have an unalienated natural right of self-defense is used to justify parliamentary resistance against the throne. In particular, Parker means to defend the constitutionally novel Militia Ordinance that was the basis for levying the parliamentary army: "Let the world judge whether this [the king's claim of exclusive prerogative to levy troops] be not contrary to the clearest beames of humaine reason, and the strongest inclinations of nature, for every private man may defend himselfe by force, if assaulted."[2] This compares, for example, with Michael Walzer's exegesis of the contradiction in Hobbism between the right and the obligation to fight for the state. "One man's cowardice kills society," because, Walzer generalizes, "by virtue of the instinct for self-preservation and the fundamental law of nature, all men have a right to be cowards. The very existence of the state seems to require some limit upon the right of self-preservation, and yet the state is nothing more than an instrument designed to fulfill that right."[3] Parker employs the right to deny the king's claim of prerogative over the military and thus legitimize Parliament's army, whereas in Walzer's hands, the right delegitimizes armies *tout court*.

Both Parker and Walzer assimilate public and private realms, reasoning about politics and reasoning about persons. But their patterns of reasoning and political themes differ because they conceive the scale of politics differently. Focusing on elite political and constitutional conflict, Parker uses the individualistic proposition as evidence for an institutional claim. Walzer, putting ordinary subjects at center stage, generalizes political conclusions from the same proposition. The one is reasoning by analogy, from individual to institutional right, whereas the other generalizes from the private right to its potential collective consequences. The two usages reflect, at base, very different political preoccupations. Parker is concerned with the legitimacy of the claims of rival authorities, whereas Walzer takes citizen cooperation with the state to be the problem.

In sixteenth- and seventeenth-century political rhetoric up to the Restoration period, the right of self-defense or resistance connoted a constitutional claim. A corollary of the doctrine of conditional or limited monarchy, the right was understood to legitimize elite opposition to tyrannous kings. It specifically did not carry popular force. Traditional Protestant resistance doctrine taught that superiors may be resisted only by inferior magistrates.[4] The Scottish National Covenant of 1638, a widely circulated protest against Charles I's religious policy, is illustrative. It narrowly referred to elite-led resistance: "In spite of references to 'the people', the covenanters did not believe in a general right of the ordinary people to resist authority on their own initiative. They believed that 'inferior magistrates', those holding authority in the state under the sovereign, had a right and duty to resist and prevent tyranny."[5] In similar vein, monarchomach ("king-killer") constitutional theory located the right of resistance in representative assemblies. These were conceived not simply as agents for the people, but indeed were often equated with the people.[6]

Ideas of genuine popular sovereignty and a popular right of resistance against all tyrannous authorities, including tyrannous parliaments, belong to the later, postwar period.[7] They can be traced back to the late 1640s, in particular to the Levellers' denunciation of parliamentary tyranny and the 1647 Leveller Agreement of the People.[8] But in the political debates of the 1630s and 1640s, populist rights reasoning furnished the stuff of polemical rhetoric. Parliamentarians as well as Levellers were vulnerable to the charge that the rights they advocated, the right to resist tyrants in the one instance and popular political rights in the other, would produce anarchy. While denying that subjects retain a right of resistance, royalist thinkers also exploited the anarchic implications of the parliamentary claim. Parliamentarians reacted defensively by locating themselves on the side of order. An instance of the exchange is the parliamentarian Charles Herle's *Fuller Answer to a Treatise Written by* [the royalist] *Dr. Ferne* (1642):

> A second question begged [by Ferne] is that in case the king and Parliament should neither discharge their trusts, the people might rise and make resistance against them both, a position which no man I know maintains. The Parliament is the people's own consent, which once passed they cannot revoke. He still pursues his own dread of the people's resuming power, whereas we acknowledge no power can be employed but what is reserved and the people have reserved no power in themselves from themselves in Parliament.[9]

In similar vein, Henry Parker declared that someone must rule. The issue was who:

> In policy then, if wee are growne weary of Parliaments, and will dissolve them into nothing, we ought to erect some other Court above them, or in their stead, or else to resigne all into the Kings sole boundlesse discretion, for any forme of Rule is better then none at all; and before we demolish old structures, we ought to be advised of the fashions of new.[10]

Parker also employed an appropriate concept of resistance rights. In an argument recalling Protestant constitutional resistance theory, he spoke of communities' rights against tyrannous rulers – as opposed to individuals' rights against all political authorities.[11] Parliamentarians and Independents, in turn, denounced as subversive the Leveller program for popular political rights. At Putney, Ireton made the famous charge that popular suffrage would "take away all property." "I wish," replied Rainsborough, the Leveller spokesman, "you would not make the world believe that we are for anarchy."[12]

Given the tenor of contemporary debates, there is reason to suppose that the Hobbesian political covenants address constitutional issues, in the first instance. In this and the following chapter, Hobbes's several descriptions of the political covenant are located in the context of contemporary constitutional debates.[13] *The Elements of Law* puts forward the conventional royalist view that subjects have renounced the right of resistance. Polemic becomes philosophy when, in *De Cive*, Hobbes attacks the very terms of contemporary debate. In this work, he grants the opposition's claim of an unalienated right of self-defense. But at the same time Hobbes explains why the right does not legitimize organized resistance to established authority. *Leviathan*'s authorization covenant, which is the subject of the next chapter, carried related constitutional import. The idea of authorization connoted royal accountability, and the associated concept of representation was used to support Parliament's claim to be the agent of the nation. Here again, Hobbes's arguments rebut the parliamentarians. He criticizes the very notion of political accountability, and argues that representation is not a criterion of entitlement to power. The overarching constitutional issue addressed by the three covenant concepts and arguments is conditional sovereignty, referring specifically to the parliamentarians' assertion of the right to hold the king accountable and therefore to the legitimacy of the parliamentary revolt against Charles I.

The present chapter traces the development of Hobbesian rights reasoning from *The Elements of Law* through *Leviathan*. The interest of the arguments lies in the way Hobbes goes about refuting the equation of a right of self-defense with the legitimacy of organized resistance to established authority. His essential move consists in pointing out the political irrelevance of the individual right. Following this observation in *De Cive*, Hobbes recognizes a progressively lengthier series of subjects' freedoms. *Leviathan* is the most libertarian of the three versions of the theory, not in spite of, but because mature Hobbism is not a rights theory of politics. That this seems paradoxical indicates the gap between his and our understandings of rights.

SELF-DEFENSE AND A RIGHT OF RESISTANCE

Let not all resistance to Princes be under one notion confounded.

Henry Parker, *Observations*

Richard Tuck located this aspect of Hobbesian theory in the Grotian tradition of natural-rights theories.[14] It was characteristic of thinkers in this tradition to employ an "active" concept of right as synonymous with liberty – such that conceiving human beings as the bearers of rights implies that we are radically free, even to renounce any and all rights.[15] The tradition came to have two, "conservative" and "radical," branches.[16] Conservatives derived from the principle of the alienability of all rights the idea of a contract renouncing the right of self-defense. This latter idea, Tuck shows, was commonly held by thinkers in the Tew Circle, including John Selden and Dudley Digges, with whom Hobbes associated in the 1630s. The idea supported the royalist constitutional doctrine of non-resistance, or, in the title of Digges's posthumous work, *The Unlawfulnesse of Subjects, Taking up Armes against their Soveraigne* (1644). It was a specific point of this line of argument to rebut Henry Parker's appeal to the private right of self-defense in justification of the parliamentary rebellion.[17] The counter, "radical" school of Grotian thought, to which Parker subscribed, shared the same understanding of rights but appealed to a principle of "interpretive charity" to attack absolutism. Although in principle it is possible to alienate all rights, they argued, it is implausible – "uncharitable" – to assume that subjects have in fact renounced the right to defend themselves against violence.[18]

Tuck shows that Hobbes's contemporaries took *The Elements of Law* to be a standard royalist tract, a defense of the royalist cause on non-resistance grounds.[19] Hobbes describes a political covenant in which individuals collectively renounce the right of resisting the sovereign. Thus sovereign power

> . . . consisteth in the power and the strength that every of the members have transferred to him from themselves, by covenant. And because it is impossible for any man really to transfer his own strength to another, or for that other to receive it; it is to be understood: that to transfer a man's power and strength, is no more but to lay by or relinquish his own right of resisting him to whom he so transferreth it.[20]

Only the stipulation "Covenants bind but to the utmost of our endeavour" tempers this renunciation of right.[21] "No covenant is understood to bind further, than to our best endeavour, either in performance of the thing promised, or in something equivalent."[22]

Reading the covenant in *The Elements* as a constitutional polemic rather than as a piece of individualistic political reasoning resolves an apparent difficulty in Hobbes's argument. The promise of non-resistance does not generate positive duties to cooperate with the sovereign. Subjects have such duties, Hobbes asserts:

> When a man covenanteth to subject his will to the command of another, he obligeth himself to this, that he resign his strength and means to him, whom he covenanteth to obey; and hereby, he that is to command may by the use of all their means and strength, be able by the terror thereof, to frame the will of them all to unity and concord amongst themselves.[23]

But, as he admits in the previously quoted account of sovereign power, the non-resistance formulation really only consists in that, a promise not to resist. Renouncing rights is clearly not the same thing as transferring powers – or, concretely, as promising to fight, to pay taxes, and so forth. "In the last analysis," Sheldon Wolin comments, "the Hobbesian conception of political power was a grossly oversimplified, even hollow, one." Hobbes "ignored the fact that the effective force of the sovereign was crucially dependent on the support of private power. . . . A sovereign who sought to overawe the wealthy by waving the sword conjured up the picture, not of mighty Leviathan, but of a 'mere spit-frog.' "[24]

The equation of transferring rights with transferring powers is a more compelling argument, however, if the topic is institutional prerogative and elite political struggle. This puts the accent on the legitimacy of the claims of rival elites as opposed to the problem of explaining citizen cooperation. Who has the right to command performance of customary political duties? By the terms of the covenant, the right belongs to the sovereign and, by implication, to him alone. As a statement about legitimate authority, the non-resistance covenant bears on citizen cooperation, but the pertinent issue has been misconceived by Hobbes's twentieth-century critics. Legitimation arguments answer the question of who to follow, as contrasted to the obligation question of whether to follow at all.

But there are two other and more pertinent objections to the formulation of the covenant in *The Elements of Law*. These concern the motivation for making and keeping a compact of this sort. They concern, that is to say, the idea of the covenant itself rather than its consequences for everyman's political behavior. On the one hand, we have seen that opponents such as Parker countered this vein of contractarian defense of absolutism with the principle of interpretive charity: It is implausible to assume that individuals have renounced the right of self-defense. The second problem lies in explaining why such a covenant should be honored when it is not in subjects' interest to do so. This latter objection was typically answered with the assertion that God will punish the breaking of a promise: "He that thus violently resists *the powers*, shall *receive to himself damnation*."[25]

In *De Cive*, as in *The Elements of Law*, the political covenant consists in the promise of non-resistance: "Each one of them obligeth himself by contract to every one of the rest, not to resist the *will* of that *one man*, or *counsell*, to which he hath submitted himselfe."[26] But Hobbes introduces this crucial caveat: Each subject "is supposed still to retain a Right of defending himselfe against violence."[27] By admitting that subjects retain the right of self-defense against violence, Hobbes has in effect granted the opposition's claim that it is uncharitable to assume renunciation of this right. Richard Tuck, by contrast, links this admission of unalienated right to the second problem, "Why honor a contract of non-resistance?" Hobbes's religious skepticism, specifically his skepticism about the efficacy of fear of divine punishment in the calculus of interest, made it especially difficult for him to answer this critical query.[28] But the revision is better seen, it seems to me, as a response to the Grotian "radicals' " objection to the very idea of a contract of this sort. Hobbes's explanation for granting an unalienated right of self-defense, it will shortly be seen, echoes their assertion that it is unrealistic to imagine that individuals would make such a contract.

While recognizing self-defense as an unalienated right in *De Cive*, Hobbes continues to insist on the royalist political doctrine of non-resistance. He was enabled to synthesize these seemingly incompatible positions by questioning the assumption common to both "conservative" and "radical" Grotian natural-rights doctrines. Herein lies the philosophical interest of the discussion of resistance rights in *De Cive*. The assumption that Hobbes questions, which is also a presupposition of twentieth-century generalizing rights reasoning, is that private rights have political consequence.

Hobbes's new reasoning is detailed in chapter ii of *De Cive*, defining contracts and covenants generally. He offers, in effect, an internal criticism of the "conservative" Grotian contract of complete non-resistance. Hobbes observes at the start, in the vein of the principle of interpretive charity, that such a contract is unrealistic: "When a man is arriv'd to this degree of fear [mortal fear], we cannot expect but he will provide for himself either by flight, or fight."[29] The argument continues in a realist vein: "They who are brought to punishment, either Capitall, or more gentle, are fettered, or strongly guarded, which is a most certain signe that they seem'd not sufficiently bound from non resistance by their Contracts."[30] Rulers and subjects, this is to say, hardly enact a non-resistance covenant. Besides being implausible, the conservative contract is unnecessary: "Its one thing if I promise thus: If I doe it not at the day appointed, kill me. Another thing if thus: If I doe it not, though you should offer to kill me, I will not resist: All men, if need be, contract the first way; but there is need sometimes. This second way, none, neither is it ever needfull."[31]

What follows is a realist's dissection of the analogy between private and public right.[32] First, the right of self-defense presents an issue only with respect to political relationships. Within organized society, only the state possesses the right to kill, hence the question of individuals' resistance rights narrowly applies to violence from the state.[33] Second, as regards political relationships: "Neither need the Supreme himselfe contract with any man patiently to yeeld to his punishment, but onely this, that no man offer to defend others from him."[34] The last point penetrates the fictions of Grotian conservatives and radicals alike. Of course they only argued as though individual right and individual resistance matter. What they were arguing about, in the early 1640s, was the right "to defend others" from the sovereign, that is, the right to organize and arm against him.[35]

Individualistic readings, focused on the potential collective consequences of a universal, unalienated right of self-preservation, miss the condition on which the right is recognized in Hobbes's theory. He grants it on the condition that the right is politically irrelevant.[36] Not only is it unrealistic to imagine that individuals would forswear the right of self-defense against the sovereign, but more important, it is not "needfull" to imagine that they have done so.

In *De Cive*, chapter vi, the reasoning is applied to cases: "What commands may a subject refuse to obey?" Two seemingly inconsistent principles frame the discussion. On the one hand, Hobbes stipulates that subjects' duties have a consequentialist, as opposed to a contractarian, foundation. "The obligation to performe . . . growes not immediately from that Contract by which we have conveigh'd all our Right on the City, but mediately from hence, That, without obedience, the Cities Right would be frustrate, and by consequence there would be no City constituted." On the other hand, the unalienated right of self-defense also applies: "For it is one thing if I say, I give you Right to Command what you will; another, if I say, I will doe whatsoever you Command; and the Command may be such, as I would rather die then doe it; forasmuch therefore as no man can be bound to will being kill'd, much lesse is he tyed to that, which to him is worse then death."[37] But the cases that are adduced for illustration do not bring the two principles into conflict. These are cases, that is to say, in which exercise of the right of self-defense is politically inconsequential, and Hobbes's explanations make this point. Suicide is the exemplary case. It is unnecessary that I kill myself ("for though I deny to doe it, yet the Right of dominion is not frustrated, since others may be found, who being commanded, will not refuse to doe it"); and I cannot have renounced the right of self-defense ("neither doe I refuse to doe that which I have contracted to doe").[38] Second, subjects may disobey a command to kill their ruler! A covenant to do so is unimaginable. Third, they are excused from commands to execute a parent, "since there are others, who, being commanded, will doe that, and a Son will rather die, then live infamous, and hated of all the world."[39]

In one last respect is the unalienated right of self-defense inconsequential. "For in no case is the Right taken away from him, of slaying those who shall refuse to obey him."[40] Or, as *Leviathan* will stipulate: The "Liberty of the Subject [is] consistent with the unlimited power of the Soveraign."[41] This asymmetry between subjects' and sovereigns' rights reflects the Grotian tradition of rights reasoning within which Hobbes and the parliamentary pamphleteers were working. Hobbes defines right as "liberty to do, or to forbeare."[42] In the Grotian tradition, this is literally all the concept of right signified. It specifically did not involve the notion that rights entail claims or duties on others. In contrast to later rights theories, in which it is assumed that rights entail duties, this sort of rights reasoning is irreducible to a theory of duties.[43] In the politically relevant instance, right-as-liberty does not generate claims on the state. The state does not have a duty to honor subjects' rights.

Leviathan

Hobbes observes in *De Cive*, "He is FREE indeed, who serves his City onely; but a SERVANT is he who also serves his fellow subject: all other liberty is an exemption from the Lawes of the City, and proper only to those that bear Rule."[44] According to the first two versions of the political theory, the "Liberty of Subjects" is almost a contradiction in terms. But this very topic forms a separate chapter in *Leviathan* (21).[45] What changes between *De Cive* and *Leviathan* is not the definition of liberty – absence of external constraint – but Hobbes's understanding of its political application.[46] The contradiction in terms becomes a topic in the political theory when Hobbes sees that subjects' liberties are consistent with the political necessities of a strong state.

The central question of chapter 21, taken over from the discussion of cases in *De Cive*, is "what are the things, which though commanded by the Soveraign, [a subject] may neverthelesse, without Injustice, refuse to do."[47] Here, in the only detailed consideration of military service in the several works, Hobbes recognizes a series of excuses from the obligation to fight for the state. (In *De Cive*, he had declared private judgment about the justness of a war, and therefore about fighting, to be a "sin.")[48] Subjects' obligation and liberty, he begins by stipulating, derive *either* from the "words" of the covenant or from the "End of the Institution of Soveraignty."[49] Suicide, as well as self-incrimination, is placed under the former heading ("Covenants, not to defend a mans own body, are voyd").[50] Then, just at the point at which a rights casuist would deduce the absence of an obligation to fight for the state, Hobbes explains that the right of self-defense does not apply – because fighting is a consequential duty.[51] Precisely in virtue of the unalienated right of self-defense, such duties must be thought about in some other way – namely, in consequentialist terms:

> No man is bound by the words themselves, either to kill him-selfe, or any other man; And consequently, that the Obligation a man may sometimes have, upon the Command of the Sov-eraign to execute any dangerous, or dishonourable Office, de-pendeth not on the Words of our Submission; but on the In-tention; which is to be understood by the End thereof. When therefore our refusall to obey, frustrates the End for which the Soveraignty was ordained; then there is no Liberty to refuse: otherwise there is.[52]

The consequentialist principle admits, on the other hand, of a series of excuses from the duty to fight.[53] A subject may furnish a substitute. Again, as in *De Cive*'s applications of the right of self-defense, this is permissible because the action is politically inconsequential: "for in this case he deserteth not the service of the Common-wealth."[54] Subjects may run from battle if afraid; indeed, cowardice excuses men from fighting altogether. But these excuses are specifically not available to soldiers, a new role category in the theory: "He that inrow-leth himselfe a Souldier, or taketh imprest mony, taketh away the excuse of a timorous nature; and is obliged, not onely to go to the battell, but also not to run from it, without his Cap-taines leave." Only when the defense of the state "requireth at once the help of all that are able to bear Arms" – presum-ably strictly in extremity – must subjects as well as soldiers fight.[55]

In the case of military service, rights casuistry would un-dermine the state. But by treating the issue in terms of ex-cuses from a prima facie obligation, Hobbes balances sub-jects' liberty with the needs of the state.[56] Rights and excuses are both species of liberty, indeed virtually indistinguishable species by Hobbes's definitions of the concepts. "Right," by his definition, "consisteth in liberty to do, or to forbeare," and is the opposite of law.[57] Chapter 27 of *Leviathan* ("Of CRIMES, EXCUSES, and EXTENUATIONS") defines an excuse as "that, which at the same time, taketh away the obligation of the Law."[58] Self-preservation figures in the theory as an excuse as well as a right. It excuses, for instance, stealing food if one is destitute and snatching another man's sword in self-defense. ("If a man by the terrour of present death, be compelled to doe a fact against the Law, he is totally Excused; because no Law can oblige a man to abandon his own preservation.")[59] In Hobbesian political casuistry, the concept of unalienated natural right picks out commands that no one has to obey (e.g., a command to commit suicide). The concept of excuse functions to distinguish among the obligations of different sorts of subjects (some, even most, do not have to fight in most circumstances). Consequentialist reasoning governs the selective deployment of the two concepts. When the liberty in question is politically inconsequential, the unalienated right of self-defense applies. But when the concept of a universal, unalienated right of self-defense would be politically consequential, Hobbes rather frames liberty in terms of excuses.

A DOCTRINE OF INSIGNIFICANT RIGHTS AND SIGNIFICANT EXCUSES

It is obviously a very weak rights theory in which the principle of unalienated natural rights is recognized on the condition that the pertinent right is inconsequential in practice. *De Cive*'s and *Leviathan*'s accounts of subjects' rights and liberties are the mirror opposite of twentieth-century rule-utilitarian defenses of rights. We are accustomed to viewing rights as constitutive principles of a good society. According to this rule-utilitarian line of argument, rights principles then limit the application of consequentialist reasoning to particular cases.[60] Just the reverse of this, Hobbes argues from the *in*consequence of the unalienated right of self-defense to its recognition in principle and its applicability to cases.

Comparison with the rule-utilitarian view brings out the significant features of the Hobbesian argument. To start, consequentialism is an inherently weak foundation for rights theory, because the primacy of utility makes right a less than absolute principle. Hobbes's reverse utilitarian consideration, the *in*consequence of rights, almost entirely undoes the foundation. Precisely what the principle of inconsequential rights does not do is limit the applicability of consequentialist reasoning. (Recall, for example, Hobbes's introduction to the discussion of military service in *Leviathan*. Because states need subjects to fight, the unalienated right of self-defense does not apply.) It is hardly much of a rights theory that thereby avoids the tension between social utility and individual right.

Hobbes's reckoning from the inconsequence of rights reflects a different political estimation of the concept from the rule-utilitarian view. He saw the idea of an unalienated right of self-defense used to justify a civil war. The context was not conducive to confidence that natural-rights principles constitute a good society. Hobbes's reply to that ideological use, his recognition of the right on condition of inconsequence, comes down to the view that some limited natural-rights liberties (and, by extension, some more significant excuses from the performance of political obligations) are consistent with a good society. It is the difference between viewing the principle of liberty as constitutive of a good society, and allowing that some liberties are permissible within, or are not inconsistent with, a good society. The former is less obvious a certitude in circumstances (not limited to Hobbes's England) in which declarations of liberty cloak elite power struggles, conflicts that common people get to fight. On the other hand, Hobbes thought from the first that the public interest included the "harmelesse liberty" of subjects: "There [should] be no restraint of natural liberty, but what is necessary for the good of the commonwealth."[61]

Last, Hobbes was working with a Grotian concept of right.

This concept may be logically stronger than our twentieth-century notion of claim rights,[62] which requires a supplementary account of others' duty to honor rights. But it is politically weaker. Defined as liberties, pure and simple, natural rights do not entail limits on the state. They do not supply, to use Dworkin's well-known metaphor, "trumps" against interference that the state is expected to honor.[63]

Whether a doctrine of inconsequential rights qualifies as a rights theory in any serious sense is doubtful. The weakness of the doctrine shows in the insignificance of rights reasoning within Hobbes's political theory. Chapter 21 of *Leviathan* applies the right of self-defense to exactly three cases: commands to commit suicide, or endure assault; self-accusation; and the liberty to continue defensive resistance once rebellion is initiated.[64] Subjects' liberties primarily consist in excuses from the performance of obligations. *The Elements of Law* had stipulated: "No covenant is understood to bind further, than to our best endeavour."[65] Despite the intervening recognition of an unalienated right of self-defense, the only politically significant alteration in the last version of the theory is that subjects are excused from endeavoring very hard, or at all, to fight. But this argument in *Leviathan* is not made on natural-rights grounds at all. Subjects' liberty in Hobbes's political theory is better identified with his robust account of excuses than with his weak theory of rights.

Chapter 3

The Hobbesian covenants: political agency, representation, and authorization

Hobbes reformulated the political covenant in *Leviathan*. Subjects, he now stipulates, have given the sovereign the authority to act for them. The new covenant oath reads: "I Authorise and give up my Right of Governing my selfe, to this Man, or to this Assembly of men, on this condition, that thou give up thy Right to him, and Authorise all his Actions in like manner."[1] The earlier versions of the political theory had stressed the absence of a contractual relationship between ruler and ruled, by virtue of the fact that the sovereign is not party to the covenant. Although this formal stipulation is reiterated in *Leviathan*, its "authorization" covenant departs from Hobbes's original formulation to posit a direct relationship between the sovereign and each subject. In authorizing the sovereign to act on their behalf, Hobbes explains, subjects individually become responsible for what he does: "Every one [is] to owne, and acknowledge himselfe to be Author of whatsoever he that so beareth their Person, shall Act, or cause to be Acted, in those things which concerne the Common Peace and Safetie."[2] Because the authorization covenant treats a different relationship than the formal proposition, they are not contradictory arguments. The formal proposition rests, it will shortly be seen, on an analysis of the relationship between the sovereign and his subjects as a body, whereas the authorization covenant concerns the relationship between the sovereign and each subject.

Why did Hobbes introduce this new account of political authority in *Leviathan*? An influential interpretation, along individualistic lines, depicts the new covenant as a remedy for the problem of citizen cooperation. Whereas the non-resistance version of the covenant relied on the dubious equation of renouncing rights with transferring powers, the authorization covenant supplies subjects with a positive reason for supporting the sovereign. The reason lies in the stipulation that they are implicated in the sovereign's acts. "Every man is thus evidently involved in society in a positive manner," David Gauthier comments, "for the acts of the sovereign may be considered his own acts."[3] Whether the new covenant succeeds in accounting for civic cooperation is another matter. Particularly in view of Hobbes's pessimistic opinion of human nature, it seems doubtful to suppose that formal responsibility generates a psychological motive sufficient to assure a cooperative citizenry. This is Hanna Pitkin's objection: "The solution is as formal and fictive as before, . . . but it enables Hobbes to avoid the previously troublesome issues: nonresistance, and the transfer of rights or power." "Behind the formal problem," she concludes, "lies the real need to enlist the capacities of citizens for positive political action, the problem of participation, the problem of creating reasons for obedience and cooperation with a government."[4]

Indeed Hobbes asserts in *Leviathan* that "by this Authoritie, given him by every particular man in the Commonwealth," the sovereign "is inabled to forme the wills of them all, to Peace at home, and mutuall ayd against their enemies abroad."[5] It is the obverse proposition – what would disable the sovereign, that is, what is the principal threat to strong government – that is crucial to interpretation of this and all Hobbes's contract arguments. Gauthier and Pitkin import to Hobbesian theory the supposition, characteristic of political individualism as a school of thought, that coercive authority rests in the first instance on civic support. Or, in the negative, a passive citizenry represents the principal threat to strong government. But seventeenth-century Englishmen would rather have assumed that the authorization formulation addressed the parliamentarians' challenge to the throne. Along

with the idea of an unalienated right of self-defense, authorization and the associated concept of representation were key
terms in the constitutional brief with which parliamentarians
justified their cause in the Civil War. To describe the people
as "the Authors, or ends of all power" implied, according to
Henry Parker, a trust relationship between ruler and ruled:
"His interest in the Crown is not absolute, or by a meere
donation of the people, but in part conditionate and fidu-
ciary."[6] It is Parliament to which the king must answer because that institution is "to be accounted by the vertue of
representation, as the whole body of the State."[7] The covenant arguments of *Leviathan* directly attack these parliamentary claims. The idea of authorization, Hobbes stipulates, actually precludes accountability; and representation, far from
being a ground of entitlement to independent authority, is
merely an analytic feature of sovereignty.

    Leviathan's rebuttal to the parliamentarians rests on a con-
ception of political authority having two key features. First,
the sovereign is a "feigned" or "artificial" person, meaning
someone whose words and actions "are considered as representing the words and actions of an other."[8] Hobbes had
not initially described political authority in this way. By the
terms of the original, non-resistance covenant, the sovereign's authority is not given to him by his subjects but, rather,
consists in the rights of nature that he alone retains following
the covenant. The latter argument figures in *Leviathan*, for
example, in explaining the sovereign's right to punish: "For
the Subjects did not give the Soveraign that right; but onely
in laying down theirs, strengthned him to use his own, as he
should think fit, for the preservation of them all."[9] The contrasting idea that the sovereign is a "civil person" appears in
rudimentary form in *The Elements of Law* (a "city" is "a multitude of men, united *as* one person by a common power")[10]
and becomes a central concept in the political theory in *De
Cive*. The work defines a "city" as "one Person, whose will,
by the compact of many men, *is to be received* for the will of
them all."[11] It is this conception of political authority, and
the analysis of social agency on which it rests, that Hobbes

applies in *Leviathan* to dissolve the parliamentarians' claim that their special, representative relationship with the nation entitles them to be the agent of the people.

The second and unique feature of *Leviathan's* account of political authority is the added stipulation of a direct tie between the will of the sovereign and the wills of each of his subjects.[12] "In him consisteth the Essence of the Commonwealth; which (to define it,) is One Person, of whose Acts a great Multitude, by mutuall Covenants one with another, have made themselves every one the Author."[13] It follows, Hobbes explains, that the sovereign is not accountable to his subjects. "Because every Subject is by this Institution Author of all the Actions, and Judgments of the Soveraigne Instituted; it followes, that whatsoever he doth, it can be no injury to any of his Subjects; nor ought he to be by any of them accused of Injustice."[14]

Considered in the abstract, outside the frame of contemporary constitutional polemics, the authorization formulation is, in several respects, a more contentious and less compelling argument than the analysis of political agency advanced in *De Cive*. In the earlier work, the formal proposition that a contract does not pass between the sovereign and the people is supported by an analysis showing the impossibility of such a contract. *Leviathan*, by contrast, posits a political covenant of a specific character. This account of the relationship between the sovereign and each of his subjects is weaker for being merely stipulative, and the stipulated covenant is not itself intuitively persuasive. The assertion that acting by authority precludes accountability runs directly contrary to ideas about delegated authority shared by Henry Parker and very many others, then and now. Last, Hobbes gave readers cause to see in the authorization covenant the lineaments of a Rousseauian general will.[15] He proclaims: "This is more than Consent, or Concord; it is a reall Unitie of them all, in one and the same Person, made by Covenant of every man with every man."[16] Such a notion of an organic community, whose will is the sovereign's will, is at the sharpest odds with the nominalist philosophy to which

Hobbes subscribed.[17] By contrast, the analysis of political agency in *De Cive* reflects a nominalist's incredulity in the idea of natural social agency.

It is a sound maxim of interpretation that "whether a given proposition is true or false, significant or meaningless, depends on what question it was meant to answer; and any one who wishes to know whether a given proposition is true or false, significant or meaningless, must find out what question it was meant to answer."[18] However flawed the authorization formulation considered in the abstract, it was an effort to meet several political arguments supporting the parliamentary cause that previously had not been adequately answered. The larger constitutional issue is sovereign accountability. In this respect, the new formulation supplements Hobbes's original argument. In chapter 18 of *Leviathan* ("Of the RIGHTS of Soveraignes by Institution"), immediately following the political covenant, he turns to a defense of the absolutist constitutional principle of unconditional sovereignty.[19] Hobbes employs for this purpose both the formal proposition that there is not (and cannot be) a contractual relationship between the sovereign and the populace as a body and the stipulation of an authorization relationship between each subject and the sovereign. First, "because the Right of bearing the Person of them all, is given to him they make Soveraigne, by Covenant onely of one to another, and not of him to any of them; there can happen no breach of Covenant on the part of the Soveraigne."[20] Second, the sovereign ought not "to be by any of them accused of Injustice" because every subject is the author of his actions.[21] But under the heading of the principle of unconditional sovereignty, there is a series of subsidiary propositions. The authorization formulation figures in support of the following specific assertions. "The Subjects cannot change the forme of government"; "Soveraigne Power cannot be forfeited"; "The Soveraigns Actions cannot be justly accused by the Subject"; "What soever the Soveraigne doth, is unpunishable by the Subject."[22] These reduce to the twin, negative and positive, propositions that the sovereign is not accountable to his subjects and, more strenuously, has exclusive title to their loyalties. In a monarchy, Hobbes notes very specifically, subjects may not change the form of government or transfer the monarchy to another person; that is, they may not depose or put a ruler to death.[23] It was to defend this latter, strong, proposition, obviously pertinent after the execution of the king in 1649, that Hobbes devised the authorization covenant. At issue, it should be said, was the legitimacy of rebellion, as opposed to the legitimacy of a (Cromwell's) postrebellion government. In *Leviathan*, with arguments that will be examined in the conclusion of the present study, Hobbes otherwise counsels subjects to "engage" with, pledge allegiance to, the Commonwealth of England. Let us turn to an examination of the analysis of political agency in *De Cive* and the authorization covenant of *Leviathan* as political arguments.

HOBBES'S ANALYSIS OF POLITICAL AGENCY

Power and rule are in the first instance terms of agency.
John Dunn, *Western Political Theory in the Face of the Future*

Basic to the analysis of political agency in *De Cive* is a nominalist denial of natural social agency.[24] A "multitude" of persons "cannot promise, contract, acquire Right, conveigh Right, act, have, possesse, and the like, unless it be every one apart, and Man by Man; so as there must be as many promises, compacts, rights, and actions, as Men. Wherefore a Multitude is no naturall Person."[25] It is the function of political rule to provide a corporate will.[26] Hobbes continues:

If the same Multitude doe Contract one with another, that the will of one man, or the agreeing wills of the major part of them, shall be received for the will of all, then it becomes one Person; for it is endu'd with a will, and therefore can doe voluntary actions, such as are Commanding, making Lawes, acquiring and transferring of Right, and so forth; and it is oftner call'd the People, then the Multitude.[27]

41

In short, the "rude multitude" is made one "by vertue of the *supreme command*."[28] "In a *Monarchy*, the Subjects are the *Multitude*, and (however it seeme a Paradox) the King is the *People*," meaning the corporate ego and will.[29]

The observation that the "multitude" lacks a collective will substantiates Hobbes's formal proposition that a contract does not pass between the sovereign and the populace as a body. In *De Cive*, discussing democracy in particular, he makes the point that such a contract is impossible:

> *Democracy* is not framed by contract of particular Persons with the *People*, but by mutuall compacts of single men each with other. But hence it appears in the first place, that the Persons contracting, must be in being before the contract it selfe. But the *People* is not in being before the constitution of government, as not being any Person, but a multitude of single Persons; wherefore there could then no contract passe between the *People* and *the Subject*.[30]

The force of the argument is to distinguish political accountability from individuals' separate evaluations of government. Political accountability, strenuously understood as accountability to a corporate nation, is impossible because the appropriate partner, a national or public will separate from the will of the government, does not and cannot exist.[31]

On the other hand, Hobbes was cognizant that a defense of fundamental popular sovereignty *could* be mounted in nominalist terms. It could be argued that democracy, subjects organized as a corporate body, is the original form of government. Indeed, in *The Elements of Law* he granted that this must be so. "Democracy is by institution the beginning both of aristocracy and monarchy" in the sense that the multitude would have to agree to majority rule in order then to agree on a form of government.[32] But democracy is "annihilated" upon the institution of another form of government. "Who governs" must be decisively (i.e., permanently) settled.[33] Criteria are set out in detail for determining the existing form of government (control of succession, in a monarchy; or for representative democracy, the reservation of future meeting times and places).[34] While describing the process the same way in *De Cive*, Hobbes retreats to the position that the covenant assembly is "almost" a democracy. That assembly, although democratic, is different from a permanent government, which it has the purpose of instituting.[35]

Hobbes's nominalist analysis of corporate agency is more than a philosophical exercise. It first appears in the political theory in rebuttal of several fictitious ideas concerning popular agency and independent parliamentary authority. The notion that rebellions reflect the popular will is wrong, Hobbes observes in *The Elements of Law*. Because a multitude of persons lacks a collective will, there is no difference between rebellion and a mere riot:

> Nor can any action done in a multitude of people met together, be attributed to the multitude, or truly called the action of the multitude, unless every man's hand, and every man's will, (not so much as one excepted) have concurred thereto. For multitude, though in their persons they run together, yet they concur not always in their designs. For even at that time when men are in tumult, though they agree a number of them to one mischief, and a number of them to another; yet, in the whole, they are amongst themselves in the state of hostility, and not of peace; like the seditious Jews besieged in Jerusalem, that could join against their enemies, and yet fight amongst themselves; whensoever therefore any man saith, that a number of men hath done any act: it is to be understood, that every particular man in that number hath consented thereunto, and not the greatest part only.[36]

In similar terms, in the same work, Hobbes attacks the parliamentary pretension that the House of Commons has an independent institutional existence. It is at present a matter of debate among historians whether, in that period, Parliament was regarded as a permanent institution or merely a recurrent series of political assemblies.[37] The latter was Hobbes's position, which he defended using the distinction between institutionalized corporate agency and a multitude. The House of Commons, he argues, has a corporate identity only so long as it is actually in session: "The lower house of parliament is all the commons, as long as they sit there with authority and right thereto; but after they be dissolved, though they remain, they be no more the people, nor the commons, but only the aggregate, or multitude of the particular men there sitting."[38]

In *Leviathan*, this line of analysis is applied to several further parliamentary doctrines.[39] The dictum *rex singulis major, universis minor* was a traditional part of monarchomach and Huguenot resistance theory. It connoted the notion that the community has a fictitious personality and is ultimately sovereign. Henry Parker explains, for example: "Power is but secondary and derivative in Princes, the fountaine and efficient cause is the people, and from hence the inference is just, the King, though he be *singulis Major*, yet he is *universis minor*."[40] The Hobbesian answer attacks the fiction of natural social agency:

> There is little ground for the opinion of them, that say of Soveraign Kings, though they be *singulis majores*, of greater Power than every one of their Subjects, yet they be *Universis minores*, of lesse power than them all together. For if by *all together*, they mean not the collective body as one person, then *all together*, and *every one*, signifie the same; and the speech is absurd. But if by *all together*, they understand them as one Person (which person the Soveraign bears,) then the power of all together, is the same with the Soveraigns power; and so again the speech is absurd: which absurdity they see well enough, when the Soveraignty is in an Assembly of the people; but in a Monarch they see it not; and yet the power of Soveraignty is the same in whomsoever it be placed.[41]

From the proposition that the community is ultimately sovereign, it followed, according to the parliamentarians, that kings are accountable to the political agency of the people, in other words, to Parliament. They conceived the relationship between parliament and people ambiguously, parliaments alternately being figured the agent of or the embodiment of the people. According to Parker, for example, the institution is "to be accounted by the vertue of representation, as the whole body of the State." At other points in the

Observations, the institution is described as "virtually the whole kingdom"; "it is indeed the State it self."[42] But the basic claim is clear. It is the empirical claim that Parliament's special relation to the nation makes it the agent of the people. The development in the period of the idea that Parliament is a representative institution is the subject of a recent study by Derek Hirst. "Perhaps the major theme of Parliament's polemical defence against the King," he concludes, "was its assertion that it represented England."[43] In *Leviathan*, Hobbes applies *De Cive*'s analysis of political agency to the concept of representation to rebut this parliamentary claim.

REPRESENTATION

In *Leviathan*, the idea of representation is introduced to characterize the relationship between the sovereign, figured as an artificial person, and the multitude: "He that acteth another, is said to beare his Person, or act in his name; . . . and is called in diverse occasions diversly; as a *Representer*, or *Representative*, a *Lieutenant*, a *Vicar*, an *Attorney*, a *Deputy* . . . and the like."[44] It is Hobbes's contentious claim, *contra* the parliamentarians, that representation is a necessary feature of sovereign authority. The title "representative" is simply, in other words, a synonym for "sovereign."[45]

> A Multitude of men, are made *One* Person, when they are by one man, or one Person, Represented; so that it be done with the consent of every one of that Multitude in particular. For it is the *Unity* of the Representer, not the *Unity* of the Represented, that maketh the Person *One*. . . . And *Unity*, cannot otherwise be understood in Multitude.[46]

The polemical conclusion is obvious: "The Soveraign, in every Commonwealth, is the absolute Representative of all the subjects."[47] Hobbes admits it is an unconventional truth about the English constitution:

> And I know not how this so manifest a truth, should of late be so little observed; that in a Monarchy, he that had the Sover-

aignty from a descent of 600 years, was alone called Soveraign, had the title of Majesty from every one of his Subjects, and was unquestionably taken by them for their King; was notwithstanding never considered as their Representative; that name without contradiction passing for the title of those men, which at his command were sent up by the people to carry their Petitions, and give him (if he permitted it) their advise.[48]

The Hobbesian argument makes two points against the parliamentarians. First, it is the nature of political rule per se that some person or persons act for, or in the name of, others. Representation is not, in other words, a special relationship, embodied in some political institutions and not in others. The observation effectively strips the concept of representation of legitimizing force: No institution (or, alternately, all political institutions) possesses legitimate authority by virtue of representing the people.[49] Second, the nominalist premise that the multitude lacks a corporate will renders absurd the notion that Parliament represents the "nation." There is no such entity to be represented. Hence it is wrong to conceive political institutions, any political institution, as the institutionalized expression of a prior national community. By Hobbes's account, the state – political organization and specifically political authority – is the condition for the existence of the nation: "It is the *Unity* of the Representer . . . that maketh the Person *One*. . . . And *Unity*, cannot otherwise be understood in Multitude."

Hence the real question presented by the parliamentary doctrine concerns the division of authority among institutional agents. "Where there is already erected a Soveraign Power," Hobbes explains, "there can be no other Representative of the same people, but onely to certain particular ends, by the Soveraign limited. For that were to erect two Soveraigns; and every man to have his person represented by two Actors."[50] That constitutional issue is addressed with an empirical, political argument in Hobbesian theory. To grant that an assembly, under a monarch, has independent authority "must needs divide that Power, which (if men will live in Peace) is indivisible; and thereby reduce the Multitude into the condition of Warre, contrary to the end for which all Sovereignty is instituted."[51] The Hobbesian case for unified sovereignty is examined in the next chapter of the present study.

Hobbes takes the standard royalist view of parliaments in a monarchy. Chapter 22 of *Leviathan* ("Of SYSTEMES Subject, Politicall, and Private") is a classificatory discussion of the various groups and bodies within a commonwealth. In a monarchy, a parliament is a "Bodie Politique for Counsel to be given to the Soveraign."[52] It is the function of parliaments "to enforme him of the condition, and necessities of the Subjects, or to advise with him for the making of good Lawes."[53] But they are subordinate to the monarch, whose right it is to call and dissolve assemblies and to control their deliberations. In short, they are political bodies, agents of the populace, only so long as they are in session, and under the control of the sovereign:

> Such Deputies, having a place and time of meeting assigned them, are there, and at that time, a Body Politique, representing every Subject of that Dominion; but it is onely for such matters as shall be propounded unto them by that Man, or Assembly, that by the Soveraign Authority sent for them; and when it shall be declared that nothing more shall be propounded, nor debated by them, the Body is dissolved.[54]

Representation and accountability

What is it that can be called public, in a civil war, without the King?

Behemoth, Dialogue 3

It has been charged that Hobbes's appeal to representation in *Leviathan* tricks the reader.[55] "By calling the sovereign a representative," Hanna Pitkin explains,

> he implies that the sovereign will in fact represent – take care of, consult – his subjects. True, this implication is vitiated by the authorization definition Hobbes gives, but it is there nevertheless. By labelling his political system representation, Hobbes suggests that it has certain good or desirable attri-

butes. But we should note that this is not a redirection of our attitudes *apart from* the meaning of the concept; quite the opposite, it is *because* we know what representation means that we are attracted to a political system based on it.[56]

With a little less credulity in ordinary, twentieth-century linguistic usage, it can be seen that Hobbes mounts a sensible challenge to any such optimistic opinion of the special virtues of representative government. Far from manipulating ordinary language to benefit his theory, the Hobbesian analysis debunks received ideas about representation, in particular the common wisdom that representation entails accountability.[57]

Hobbes's nominalist account of political agency reduces to the observation that political organization constitutes corporate will. No other truly communal will exists or could exist (assuming natural human diversity, that is). It is a political observation as accurate to our postimperial world as it was to early-modern nation building. Statehood in fact usually is the condition for what is only a fervently hoped for national identity, fervently hoped for and fervently fought over. Extended to the concept of representation, the observation undermines the idea of popular accountability. There is literally no partner – no public, no "general will" distinguishable from rulers' will – to which representative authority could be accountable. In short, accountability is a political fiction, behind which Hobbes would diagnose the reality of a struggle for power.

AUTHORIZATION

The King is a life-renter, not a Lord, or a proprietor of his Kingdome.

Samuel Rutherford, *Lex Rex* (1644)

In contrast to that analytic denial of the possibility of political accountability, the authorization formulation of *Leviathan* is a stipulative argument positing a covenant of a specific character. Each subject contracts "to owne, and acknowl-

48

edge himselfe to be Author of whatsoever he that so beareth their Person, shall Act, or cause to be Acted, in those things which concerne the Common Peace and Safetie."[58] This means, as we have seen, that subjects are responsible for the sovereign's public acts, yet the sovereign is not accountable to them. For example, to depose a ruler is a breach of the covenant promise: "They that have already Instituted a Common-wealth, being thereby bound by Covenant, to own the Actions, and Judgements of one, cannot lawfully make a new Covenant, amongst themselves, to be obedient to any other, in any thing whatsoever, without his permission."[59] "Besides," Hobbes continues, by virtue of the authorization covenant, rebellion is self-contradictory:

> If he that attempteth to depose his Soveraign, be killed, or punished by him for such attempt, he is author of his own punishment, as being by the Institution, Author of all his Soveraign shall do: And because it is injustice for a man to do any thing, for which he may be punished by his own authority, he is also upon that title, unjust.[60]

At the least, this usage of the concepts of authorization and ownership was unusual. The concepts typically figured in the opposition's case. It was monarchomach defenders of ultimate popular sovereignty (independent parliamentary authority) who described the sovereign as the people's agent. Their "ownership" of his actions was taken to imply a trust relationship between monarch and people, and hence his accountability to parliaments, as well as a right of rebellion against tyrants.[61] But Jean Hampton has shown that Hobbes's usage of the concepts was consistent with alternate usages in the period. "Authorization" could also (merely) connote sanctioning or approving authority, and "ownership," submission to authority.[62]

At the outset, I noted that the authorization covenant does not logically contradict Hobbes's previous analysis of political agency. Their topics are different: the relationship between the ruler and each subject versus that between the sovereign and the multitude of the people. Nonetheless, political authority is figured differently in the two accounts. The argument about agency has the point of showing that there cannot be a contractual relationship between ruler and ruled. Authorization identifies subjects' wills with the sovereign's will. It is the difference between willing for us because we cannot will, and being, or standing in for, my will.[63] (Compare, for example, these two accounts of why "Soveraigne Power cannot be forfeited." First, per the account of agency, the sovereign cannot have covenanted "with the whole, as one party, . . . because as yet they are not one Person." But it might be imagined that the sovereign covenants separately with each subject: "If he make so many severall Covenants as there be men, those Covenants after he hath the Soveraignty are voyd, because what act soever can be pretended by any one of them for breach thereof, is the act both of himselfe, and of all the rest, because done in the Person, and by the Right of every one of them in particular.")[64]

The idea that subjects have a covenant obligation to the sovereign is introduced in *De Cive* (chapter vi, on sovereigns' rights). There is a lacuna in the account of political agency, Hobbes observes, namely, the possibility of consensus in the multitude to resist and depose a ruler. Literally, of course, "it is not to be imagined that ever it will happen, that all the subjects together, not so much as one excepted, will combine against the *supreme power*."[65] But most people, he continues, imagine that majority rule is a fundamental, natural principle, and so imagine that merely majority consensus legitimizes rebellion.[66] More to the immediate point, most people imagine that a majority vote in "some great Assembly of Citizens" legitimizes rebellion:

> Now because most men through ignorance esteem not the consent of the major part of Citizens only, but even of a very few, provided *they be of their opinion*, for the consent of the whole *City*, it may very well seem to them, that the *supreme authority* may by right be abrogated, so it be done in some great Assembly of Citizens by the votes of the greater number.[67]

Allowances being made for the loss in translating a hypothetical covenant into practice, the opinion corresponded all too accurately, Hobbes was aware, to his own description of the process of instituting government. "If . . . it were granted," he observes in implicit self-criticism,

> that their [sovereigns'] *Right* depended onely on that contract which each man makes with his fellow-citizen, it might very easily happen, that they might be robbed of that Dominion under pretence of Right; for subjects being called either by the command of the City, or seditiously flocking together, most men think that the consents of all are contained in the votes of the greater part. Which in truth is false.[68]

Is not such an assembly, *mutatis mutandis*, a reenactment of the Hobbesian covenant? As he had described the process in *The Elements of Law* and *De Cive*, the multitude forms itself into a "people," or corporate agent, adopts the principle of majority rule, and on this basis adopts a constitution and institutes a sovereign. Hobbes might have remained content with criticizing the notion that majority rule is a natural principle and the idea that the populace may recover sovereignty at will. It is literally unimaginable that everyone would agree to depose the sovereign, and no group, of whatever size, has the prerogative by nature to act for the whole. He had also explained previously that popular sovereignty is and must be permanently annihilated with the institution of another form of government; that is, the covenant is an irrevocable act. Sovereignty must be permanently settled, and there are criteria for defining the existing form of government.

But he chose to make the further, positive claim that the existing government has exclusive title to its subjects' loyalty:

> But though a government be constituted by the contracts of particular men with particulars, yet its Right depends not on that obligation onely; there is another tye also toward him who commands; . . . that Right which every man had before to use his faculties to his own advantage, is now wholly translated

on some certain man, or Councell, for the common benefit; . . . the government is [therefore] upheld by a double obligation from the Citizens, first that which is due to their fellow citizens, next that which they owe to their Prince. Wherefore no subjects how many soever they be, can with any Right despoyle him who bears the chiefe Rule, of his authority, even without his own consent.[69]

The statement provides a straightforward explanation of the purpose of the authorization formulation of *Leviathan*. By contrast, Hobbes's analysis of political agency, and the corresponding formal proposition that there is not a covenant between ruler and ruled, are technically neutral about the identity of the corporate agent or "civil person." It is one thing to argue, as he had previously, that the constitution of sovereignty is a permanent arrangement, and another, stronger thing to assert that subjects have a positive tie to the government in place, just and simply by virtue of the fact that it is in place.

To describe, in *Leviathan*, the nature of the tie between subject and sovereign, Hobbes translated into individualistic terms two arguments in the earlier texts concerning democratic political responsibility. In the process of instituting a permanent government, the initial, temporary democratic assembly of the people is said, in *De Cive*, to authorize that permanent sovereign. "As an *Aristocratie*, so also a *Monarchy* is derived from the Power of the *People*, transferring its *Right*, (that is) its *Authoritie* on *one man*."[70] *Leviathan*'s authorization formulation avoids the implication of fundamental democratic sovereignty by translating the concept, the "people's authority," into the plural. Subjects severally and individually authorize the sovereign:

And because the Multitude naturally is not *One*, but *Many*; they cannot be understood for one; but many Authors, of every thing their Representative faith, or doth in their name; Every man giving their common Representer, Authority from himselfe in particular; and owning all the actions the Representer doth, in case they give him Authority without stint.[71]

The emphasis correspondingly shifts from depicting the designation of the sovereign as an act of majority will to a focus
on individual agency. In *Leviathan*'s account of the covenant,
the majority does not so much act for the whole as present
individuals with a choice: Either endorse the sovereign chosen by the majority or become an enemy of all.[72]

Second, the stipulation that it is self-contradictory for subjects to accuse the sovereign of injustice originates in a discussion of democracy in *The Elements of Law:*

> How unjust soever the action be, that this sovereign *demus*
> shall do, is done by the will of every particular man subject to
> him, who are therefore guilty of the same. If therefore they
> style it injury, they but accuse themselves. And it is against
> reason for the same man, both to do and complain: implying
> this contradiction, that whereas he first ratified the people's
> acts in general, he now disalloweth some of them in particu-
> lar.[73]

This latter is an un-Hobbesian argument in the first instance,
and he retreats from it in the next paragraph. Only those
who expressly vote for an unjust decree ("any thing contrary
to the law of God or nature"), he specifies, can be held responsible for it. "For a body politic, as it is a fictitious body,
so are the faculties and will thereof fictitious also. But to make
a particular man unjust, which consisteth of a body and soul
natural, there is required a natural and very will."[74] The effort to identify the majority will with the "general will" in a
democracy, such that accountability is nonsensical, requires
precisely some notion (and reality) of communal identity quite
foreign to Hobbes's political vision.[75] Only when subjects really
are rulers, and consciously dedicated to ruling in the common interest, does it make sense to describe accountability
as self-accusation.[76] Outside democracy of that utopian
Rousseauian sort, the description, and the identification of
ruler and ruled on which it is based, are simply incorrect.

We do sometimes remark that nations are responsible for
the governments they get, and citizens therefore simply accuse themselves when they complain of bad government.

53

But these are sensible statements only in a very general way or in very special democratic circumstances. It is one thing to observe, in a most un-Hobbesian way, that a government's actions seem to reflect the national will, meaning that on some occasions a tyrannous government is rightly understood to be acting as the agent of an unjust society. Hobbes would have replied that "to make a particular man unjust . . . there is required a natural and very will." The universalistic assertion that every subject is responsible for public policies is forceful only in the context of strong democracy. Reasoning by analogy, Hobbes asks us to grant that these ideas about the relationship between state and society and about democratic government are accurate to the experience of citizens, individually and universally. At the same time, however, it is the point of the individualistic authorization formulation to avoid admitting fundamental popular sovereignty, and the associated idea that government is the institutional agent of the nation. To defend the title of an established government to the exclusive loyalty of its subjects, Hobbes in effect adapted something very like the parliamentarians' conception of political authority, namely, the idea that rulers are the agents of the people in some real and more than formal sense. But he attempted to strip the conception of critical force by translating it into a stipulation about the necessary character of the relationship between every subject and all governments.

Hobbes's several covenant arguments, we have seen, address a series of ideas supporting the parliamentarians' constitutional doctrine of conditional sovereignty. The concept of an unalienated right of self-defense does not, by his account, legitimize rebellion; political accountability is a fictitious idea, as is the opinion that parliaments, by virtue of representing the people, possess independent political authority. Last, with the authorization formulation, Hobbes took on the idea that a popular majority, meaning specifically a parliamentary majority, might depose and execute a sitting monarch.

In rebutting the parliamentary ideology, to summarize, Hobbes developed three main lines of argument. To counter the "radical" Grotian contractarian defense of a right of rebellion against tyrants, we saw in the preceding chapter, he put forward a consequentialist analysis of the concept of an unalienated natural right of self-defense. It is neither realistic, he granted, nor necessary to suppose that subjects have renounced the said right. It is just, he further argued, that consequentialist considerations narrowly circumscribe the applicability of contractarian reasoning and the unalienated natural right of self-defense. To rebut the notion of a contract between the sovereign and the nation, Hobbes developed, second, a convincing nominalist analysis of social agency. This analysis has the force of showing that political authority is necessarily unconditional, insofar as there is no other agent of the general will to which rulers could be accountable. Third, Hobbes attempted to argue that it is a necessary feature of the relationship between sovereign and subject that subjects owe exclusive allegiance to the sitting government. To make the argument, he drew on ideas that make sense cast in corporate terms and in a democratic context, but that are implausible as stipulations about the necessary character of the relationship between individuals and their government. Hobbes's better answer to the parliamentarians in the current contest for popular allegiance was the contingent and political argument that ordinary people suffer in the conflicts of the great. We take up that argument in the next chapter, which examines the Hobbesian defense of the absolutist constitutional principle of unified sovereignty.

Chapter 4

Hobbesian absolutism

The fate of Hobbesian absolutism in readers' hands resembles the case of the blind men examining the elephant. The doctrine enjoys a varied reputation. One view, put forward by nineteenth-century Utilitarians, is that Hobbesian absolutism offers a sober, realistic account of sovereignty, which contrasts favorably both with romantic Continental imagery of an organic state and with liberal constitutionalism. John Austin, the elder Mill, and William Molesworth, editor of the most complete edition of Hobbes's writings, among others, saw in Hobbes's defense of absolutism a formal account of the necessary structure of all states. For this, and for the allied "command" jurisprudential doctrine that law is simply what the sovereign says it is, they counted the seventeenth-century thinker a prehistoric Utilitarian. Leslie Stephen, for instance, observed this "natural affinity" between Bentham and Hobbes:

> Both thinkers are absolutists in principle, though Hobbes gives to a monarch the power which Bentham gives to a democracy. The attributes remain though their subject is altered. The "sovereign," in fact, is the keystone of the whole Utilitarian system. He represents the ultimate source of all authority and supplies the motive for all obedience. As Hobbes put it, he is a kind of mortal God.[1]

The Utilitarians' interpretation stands in striking contrast to the customary reputation of Hobbesian absolutism. They trivialized the doctrine into a merely analytic statement, whereas

Hobbism has always enjoyed a popular reputation as a constitutional theory licensing tyranny. This latter view dramatizes the potential consequences of a government formed on Hobbist lines. To advocate absolutism, preferably absolute monarchy, in Locke's well-known phrase, "is to think that Men are so foolish that they take care to avoid what Mischiefs may be done them by *Pole-Cats*, or *Foxes*, but are content, nay think it Safety, to be devoured by *Lions*."[2]

Hobbes's response to the latter objection, his discussion of the exercise of power as opposed to the desirable constitution of sovereignty, will be treated in chapter 6. The present chapter examines his constitutional arguments, the case for unconditional and unified sovereignty, preferably in the form of monarchy. The Utilitarians' interpretation directs attention to the main issues, narrow and broad, surrounding Hobbes's discussion. Is it primarily an analytic or a prescriptive argument? As we saw in the preceding chapter, Hobbes does indeed defend the principle of unconditional sovereignty as an analytic truth. His analysis of political agency has the point of showing that sovereignty is necessarily unconditional, meaning, in specific, that popular accountability is impossible. The Utilitarians' observation is therefore accurate only in a weak sense. In this form, analytic absolutism is consistent with opposing constitutional prescriptions, including notably the alternatives of unified sovereignty versus a mixed constitution. In a recent commentary, M. M. Goldsmith maintains that Hobbes's defense of the principle of unified sovereignty is also analytic in character, namely, the argument that sovereignty is necessarily unified or indivisible.[3] The latter is alternately a silly thesis or a purely definitional truth, a matter of labeling a mixed constitution rather a mixed administration.[4] While Hobbes, influenced by Bodin, put forward the strong and implausible analytic thesis in the early versions of the political theory, the claim disappears almost altogether from *Leviathan*. What remains are several far more interesting and prescriptive discussions of the bearing of unified versus divided sovereignty on state power, elite conflict, and social order.

Second, and more fundamentally, the Utilitarians' interpretation misses the significance of political institutions per se in Hobbes's understanding of politics. Their predisposition to discount Hobbes's prescription of an absolutist constitution is traceable to their own view that institutions are not the chief source of political power. It was their opinion that the power of government rests, in the first instance, on a natural habit of obedience among citizens. In light of the ubiquity of government and subjection, the constitution of political authority is a secondary matter.[5] Hobbes was to be applauded for attempting to give a scientific, that is, psychological, account of obedience, as based in self-interest and fear.[6] The obsession in twentieth-century Hobbes studies with reconstructing his account of obligation begins here: Their psychological reading became the traditional view against which later natural-law and contractarian interpretations were directed.[7]

John Plamenatz's critique of Hobbesian absolutism in *Man and Society* illustrates these several assumptions. Unlike Austin and company, Plamenatz understands Hobbesian absolutism to be a prescriptive constitutional theory, resting on an empirical generalization. He paraphrases Hobbes: "The rules governing the use of power are more likely to be respected when they place the final right of decision in all spheres of government (in other words, supreme authority) in the hands of one man or assembly than when they divide it between several."[8] But the proposition is erroneous. The seventeenth-century thinker understandably failed to see that there ordinarily exists a common interest, especially among political elites, in settling political disputes in an orderly, peaceful fashion.[9] This was not true, of course, in Hobbes's England, but Plamenatz does not think the mere presence of a Hobbesian sovereign is likely to deter rebellion in any case. Endorsing a psychological reading of Hobbes's theory of obligation,[10] he offers a populist interpretation of the real source of the sovereign's power: "The sovereign is powerful because he can ordinarily rely on the support of all his subjects except the law-breaker against the law-breaker; his power is not, in the first instance, a cause of trust but an effect of it."[11] "Supreme authority," Plamenatz instructs finally, "can either all be placed in the same hands, or it can be divided between several persons and bodies and rules laid down for settling disputes between them. Which is the better method depends on circumstances."[12] Hobbes, in short, overestimates the importance of political institutions and underestimates the extent to which government in general relies on subjects' interest in and habit of obeying.

It is an exemplary critique. At the same time, Plamenatz makes explicit his disagreement with Hobbes's understanding of politics and gives a fair outline of the latter's thinking. The Hobbesian brief for absolute government rests, first, on an empirical proposition about the consequences of constitutional arrangements for social order. There are actually two main lines of empirical argument in the several versions of the political theory, one emphasizing the proposition that divided sovereignty produces weak government and the other, which is the argument in *Leviathan* that Plamenatz has in mind, treating the connection between constitutional arrangements, elite conflict, and civil war. Hobbes is known for proposing that the division of sovereign authority leads to civil war. This latter hypothesis, Plamenatz observes, presupposes the absence of a shared commitment, among elites and masses, to the peaceful settlement of political conflict. In other words, in effect, it applies only in certain political circumstances. Plamenatz seems to think such circumstances are rare, whereas Hobbes, at the opposite extreme, represents the argument for absolutism as a global prescription. A more reasonable view is that both assessments are faulty. Habitual obedience is less general a phenomenon than the former imagines, and, on the other hand, Hobbes's political analysis has more limited purchase than he recognized. There is, last, the recurring issue of the level of Hobbes's political analysis. Neither does he assume a habit of obedience among citizens, nor, I have been insisting throughout, is he preoccupied in the first instance with popular political behavior. Conceiving politics to be a struggle among elites for power, his arguments for absolutism are directed instead at the dual problems of strengthening the sovereign and discouraging the designs of ambitious rivals.

ABSOLUTISM

Stuart Englishmen's understandings of absolutism have been detailed by James Daly.[13] They inherited a laudatory understanding, born of medieval struggles between king and Papacy, in which "absolute" was equated with "independent." In this sense, "To boast of [the king's] absoluteness was thus to brag about the nation as much as to exalt the ruler."[14] Hobbes's definition of the state, as a distinctive kind of corporate body, plays upon this inherited meaning. Size is the criterion by which he distinguishes states from other societies, for example, families, because the size of the state betokens independence. "A Family," *Leviathan* specifies, "is not properly a Common-wealth; unlesse it be of that power by its own number, or by other opportunities, as not to be subdued without the hazard of war."[15] Hence he criticizes Aristotle and other ancient authorities for the subversive teaching that the term "free state" is a substantive category describing the liberties of individuals in a good society.[16] With respect to states, in the Hobbesian view, "free" is a redundant adjective: a "free state" is simply a synonym for an independent state. It is characteristic of "free Common-wealths" that "their Representative had the Libertie to resist, or invade other people."[17]

Absolutism connoted, second, unconditional or supreme authority, answerable to no other human body. This was a statement about the constitution of sovereignty, as opposed to the exercise of power. Only after 1640, according to Daly, did absolutism take on the further, pejorative connotation of arbitrary government, outside the law.[18] When parliamentarians denied that England was an absolute monarchy, they typically had in mind the royalist doctrine of non-resistance. "They wished above all to deny," Daly observes, "that the king had an absolute claim on their obedience, or even their passive disobedience."[19] In chapter 18 of *Leviathan*, concerning the rights of sovereignty, Hobbes states the principle of unconditional sovereignty in this fashion, as a proposition about subjects' obligations.[20] The first five rights of sovereignty are various specifications of the doctrine of non-resistance: "1. The Subjects cannot change the forme of government"; "2. Soveraigne Power cannot be forfeited"; "3. No man can without injustice protest against the Institution of the Soveraigne declared by the major part"; "4. The Soveraigns Actions cannot be justly accused by the Subject"; "5. What soever the Soveraigne doth, is unpunishable by the Subject."[21]

Third, absolutism was a constitutional doctrine concerning the scope of sovereign powers, referring both to unified control of specifically enumerated powers and to general discretionary prerogative.[22] Hobbes's basic list of essential sovereign powers is identical in the three versions of the political theory, with the notable addition in the last two versions of the power of censorship. "It is annexed to the Soveraignty," by *Leviathan*'s account, to have legislative, judicial and penal, and war-making authority; and to have the rights to censor public speeches and books, to appoint counselors and ministers, and to bestow titles.[23] Discretionary ("arbitrary") authority is included under the heading of the right of punishment, but this is a minor feature of Hobbesian constitutional theory and, as will be seen in chapter 6, he recommends against governing on this basis.[24]

Analytic versus prescriptive absolutism

The importance of this distinction becomes evident on considering how often in sociology or political science it is left unclear whether a statement is to be understood as a definitional truth, i.e. as an analytic statement, or as an empirical statement to which evidence is relevant, i.e. as a synthetic statement.

Alan Ryan, *The Philosophy of the Social Sciences*

Absolute power is explicitly defined by Hobbes only in *De Cive*. The definition narrowly refers to supreme authority. Someone or some body, Hobbes asserts, always holds ultimate authority:

> It is most manifest by what hath been said, That in every perfect City (that is, where no Citizen hath *Right* to use his faculties, at his owne discretion, for the preservation of himselfe, or where the *Right of the private Sword* is excluded) there is a *Supreme power* in some one, greater then which cannot by Right be conferr'd by men, or greater then which no mortall man can have over himself. But that power, greater then which cannot by men, be conveigh'd on a man, we call ABSOLUTE.[25]

In this form, analytic absolutism is a weak doctrine, contentious principally for denying "constitutionalism,"[26] the view that law should be sovereign.[27] Otherwise, the claim is compatible with a variety of constitutional doctrines, most notably with the parliamentary doctrine of a mixed constitution.[28] Henry Parker, for example, agreed that "there is an Arbitrary power in every State somewhere tis true, tis necessary, and no inconvenience follows upon it."[29] Parker and Hobbes held different ideas, of course, about who should be supreme.[30] But Parker could reconcile the analytic claim with the traditional parliamentary ideology of divided powers by endorsing a balanced constitutional scheme in which Parliament holds the position of ultimate "umpire."[31]

Analytic absolutism is a strong – exclusive – doctrine only as a claim about the scope of sovereign powers; to wit, sovereignty is necessarily indivisible. This view is the logical antithesis of a functional argument for unified sovereignty, or the prescription that one master ought to control all major state powers. M. M. Goldsmith takes Hobbes to be committed to the strong analytic view:

> Hobbes was not trying to show that it was practically better not to divide sovereignty. When he uses that type of empirical argument he signals it. . . . Hobbes's argument for the indivisibility of sovereign powers is couched in no such empirical

terms. The rights of sovereignty are "incommunicable and inseparable." . . . Thus the concept of sovereignty is used in an all or nothing way: either there is a sovereign possessing all these powers or there is none.[32]

Such claims indeed figure in *The Elements of Law* and *De Cive*. It was unusual for Hobbes to invoke authority, but these early versions of the political theory cite and actually paraphrase Bodin's *Republique* on the point.[33] Bodin held both that sovereignty is necessarily indivisible and that it ought to be unified.[34] In *The Elements of Law*, the topic is seditious opinions:

> The third opinion: that the sovereign power may be divided, is no less an error than the former, as hath been proved, Part II. chap. I, sect. 15. And if there were a commonwealth, wherein the rights of sovereignty were divided, we must confess with Bodin, Lib. II, chap. I. *De Republica*, that they are not rightly to be called commonwealths, but the corruption of commonwealths. . . . But the truth is, that the right of sovereignty is such, as he or they that have it, cannot, though they would, give away any part thereof, and retain the rest.[35]

The confusing Bodinian conflation of prescriptive and analytic theses is reiterated in *De Cive*. A mixed monarchy, Hobbes declares, "would no whit advantage the liberty of the subject," and, in any case, "there can be no such kind of Government."[36] It follows from the latter claim that civil war is by definition the only circumstance in which sovereignty is divided: "ever there is such a [Chief] Command, and alwayes exercis'd, except in the time of Sedition, and Civill War, and then there are two *Chiefe Commands* made out of one."[37]

The analytic view had to be carefully qualified to meet the obvious empirical objection. Echoing Bodin, Hobbes explains that states appearing to have mixed constitutions really have mixed administrations.[38] Functional authority may be delegated by the sovereign to other agents.[39] It is a distinction without a difference. To admit that in a peaceful commonwealth political authority may be divided, although sovereignty cannot be, effectively reduces strong analytic absolutism into the weaker proposition that there must be a human *"terminus ultimus"* of power.[40] An analysis in *The Elements of Law* of the constitution of Venice is illustrative:

> As if a man should think, because the great council of Venice doth nothing ordinarily but choose magistrates, ministers of state, captains, and governors of towns, ambassadors, counsellors, and the like; that therefore their part of the sovereignty is only choosing of magistrates; and that the making of war, and peace, and laws, were not theirs, but the part of such councillors as they appointed thereto; whereas it is the part of these to do it but subordinately, the supreme authority thereof being in the great council that choose them.[41]

But the strong analytic claim is smuggled back into the argument through the enumeration of multiple marks of supreme sovereignty. Given the empirical possibility of a mixed "administration," it becomes crucial to identify the powers denoting supremacy. In *The Elements of Law*, discussing the issue in the abstract, Hobbes lists the following: the power to punish individuals and, the institutional equivalent, the power to dissolve assemblies; legislative authority; the right to appoint magistrates, judges, counselors, and ministers of state; and, last, autonomous authority.[42] Stipulation of such a lengthy list elides the distinction between supreme and unified sovereignty. This was done to counter the kind of constitutional argument put forward in Parker's *Observations:* the case for a mixed constitution in which one branch possesses supreme, but not unified, sovereignty. The obfuscation persists in *Leviathan*, where the enumeration of essential sovereign powers concludes with the statement: "These are the Rights, which make the Essence of Soveraignty; and which are the markes, whereby a man may discern in what Man, or Assembly of men, the Soveraign Power is placed, and resideth. For these are incommunicable, and inseparable."[43]

Prescriptive absolutism

Amongst the *Infirmities* therefore of a Common-wealth, I will reckon in the first place, those that arise from an Imperfect

Institution. . . . Of which, this is one, *That a man to obtain a Kingdome, is sometimes content with lesse Power, than to the Peace, and defence of the Common-wealth is necessarily required.*

Leviathan, chapter 29

Why are the essential rights of sovereignty "incommunicable and inseparable"? This is the central issue distinguishing strong analytic absolutism from the prescriptive argument that sovereign powers ought to be controlled by a single body. In contrast to the Bodinian thesis that sovereignty is necessarily indivisible, the enumeration of essential rights of sovereignty in chapter 18 of *Leviathan* opens with the statement that the purposes, or "end," of the state require unified sovereignty:[44]

Because the End of this Institution, is the Peace and Defence of them all; and whosoever has right to the End, has right to the Means; it belongeth of Right, to whatsoever Man, or Assembly that hath the Soveraignty, to be Judge both of the meanes of Peace and Defence; and also of the hindrances, and disturbances of the same; and to do whatsoever he shall think necessary to be done, both before hand, for the preserving of Peace and Security, by prevention of Discord at home and Hostility from abroad; and, when Peace and Security are lost, for the recovery of the same. And therefore, . . .[45]

Admittedly, lingering remnants of the strong analytic claim are to be found in *Leviathan*. Besides the confusing equation of essential powers with marks of sovereignty, the notable instance is a statement prefacing discussion in the next chapter (19) of forms of government: "Other kind of Commonwealth [besides monarchy, aristocracy, and democracy] there can be none: for either One, or More, or All must have the Soveraign Power (which I have shewn to be indivisible) entire."[46] But the prescriptive claim that the purposes of the state require unified sovereignty is more accurately ascribed not only to the arguments of *Leviathan* but also to Hobbes's arguments in the earlier versions. Rhetorical flourishes aside, his defense of the principle of unified sovereignty consists in a series of related discussions of the political desirability of central control of major state powers.

These arguments merit close attention in their own right and because the terms of Hobbes's brief are crucial to ideas about his fundamental understanding of politics. In the early versions of the theory, Hobbes follows Bodin in emphasizing the deleterious effects of divided sovereignty on state power. Under a mixed constitution, Bodin had observed, the several branches of government possess veto power over one another's actions. Hobbes paraphrases in *The Elements of Law:*

> If one part should have power to make the laws for all, they would by their laws, at their pleasure, forbid others to make peace or war, to levy taxes, or to yield fealty and homage without their leave; and they that had the right to make peace and war, and command the militia, would forbid the making of other laws, than what themselves liked.[47]

Put more generally, it is the proposition that divided sovereignty produces impotent government. In *Leviathan,* this line of argument is augmented with an elaboration of the bearing of constitutional arrangements on elite conflict and social disorder.

Strictly speaking, the strong analytic thesis that sovereignty is necessarily indivisible renders superfluous an enumeration of essential powers (versus marks) of sovereignty. But in *The Elements of Law* and *De Cive,* as well as in *Leviathan,* Hobbes details these powers and explains the need for unified control of them. Basic are the "swords" of justice and war, meaning coercive authority at home and war-making authority. *De Cive* states, "This right (which we may call the *Sword of Warre*) belongs to the same *Man,* or *Counsell,* to whom the *Sword of Justice* belongs; for no Man can by Right compell Citizens to take up armes, and be at the expences of Warre, but he who by Right can punish him who doth not obey."[48] To separate judicial or legislative authority from these carries the danger of political stalemate. First, "if the *power of judging* were in one, and the power of executing in another, nothing would be done."[49] Second, the authority to make laws "must of right belong to him that hath the power of the sword, by which men are compelled to observe them; for otherwise they should be made in vain."[50] In turn, judicial authority entails the power of appointing magistrates and other public ministers.[51] In *De Cive* and *Leviathan*, censorship of opinions and doctrines, notably constitutional and religious doctrines, is counted a further essential right of sovereignty: "For the Actions of men proceed from their Opinions; and in the wel governing of Opinions, consisteth the well governing of mens Actions, in order to their Peace, and Concord."[52]

Of special concern to Hobbes are the powers contested by king and Parliament – namely, taxation, command of the military, and the authority to call and dissolve parliaments. Divided control of the former, he contends, can be fatal to the state. In *The Elements of Law*, the topic is that most contentious issue in the period of "personal rule" by Charles I (1629–40), constitutional limitations on the sovereign's power to raise revenue. Hobbes has in mind both the parliamentary demand of no taxation without consent and the conservative, backward-looking idea that supply should be provided through a fixed allotment of land and taxes.[53] If "the revenue is limited,"

> so must also be the forces; but limited forces, against the power of an enemy, which we cannot limit, are unsufficient. Whensoever therefore there happeneth an invasion greater than those forces are able to resist, and there be no other right to levy more, then is every man, by necessity of nature, allowed to make the best provision he can for himself; and thus is the private sword, and the estate of war again reduced.

"Revenue, without the right of commanding men," he continues, "is of no use."[54] The parliamentarians' pretension to independent taxation authority is the obvious target, again, in *De Cive:*

> There are also some who divide the Supreme Authority so as to allow the power of War, and Peace, unto one, (whom they call a *Monarch*) but the right of raising Monies they give to some others, and not to him: But because monies are the sin-

ewes of War, and Peace, they who thus divide the Authority, doe either really not divide it at all, but place it wholly in them, in whose power the money is, but give the name of it to another, or if they doe really divide it, they dissolve the Government: for neither upon necessity can War be waged, nor can the publique Peace be preserved without Money.[55]

Hobbes emphasizes, third, the importance of the right to call and dissolve representative assemblies. This right was the subject of the Triennial Act of 1641, which required that a Parliament be called at least every three years. He often designates this single right the key mark of supreme sovereignty. Occasionally, as in the just-quoted passage, taxation or, alternatively, control of the military is so designated.[56] But more commonly Hobbes defines supreme sovereignty in terms of procedural rather than substantive authority. Who will be sovereign in the future? Control of the succession to the throne is the mark of an absolute monarchy, whereas legislation making Parliament a permanent institution, assembling at recurrent intervals, marks the sovereignty of that branch:

> That they may therefore avoyd this kind of *supreme authority*, some of them will have a City well enough constituted, if they who shall be the Citizens convening, doe agree concerning certaine Articles . . . [and] they appoint a certain and limited return, with this condition, that if that suffice not, they may call a new convention of estates. Who sees not in a City thus constituted, that the Assembly who prescribed those things had an *absolute power?* If therefore the *Assembly* continue, or from time to time have a certain day, and a place of meeting, that *power* will be perpetuall.

If the Assembly "wholly dissolve[s]," the passage concludes, either the state dissolves or else, necessarily, there is another, real sovereign.[57] This specification of a single, procedural mark of "absolute" power avoids conflating essential sovereign powers with marks of supreme sovereignty. The more firmly Hobbes has his eyes set on the exigencies of government in the real world, it seems fair to say, the less expansive are his claims regarding the necessity of unified sovereignty.

Leviathan

Divided sovereignty, Hobbes reiterates in *Leviathan*, is likely to produce impotent government. If the sovereign "transferre the *Militia*, he retains the Judicature in vain, for want of execution of the Lawes":

> Or if he grant away the Power of raising Mony; the *Militia* is in vain: or if he give away the government of Doctrines, men will be frighted into rebellion with the feare of Spirits. And so if we consider any one of the said Rights, we shall presently see, that the holding of all the rest, will produce no effect, in the conservation of Peace and Justice, the end for which all Common-wealths are Instituted.[58]

In this context, he makes what is a minor admission from a political standpoint, but a rather more major admission in analytic terms. Some trivial rights of sovereignty may be transferred: "The Power to coyn Mony; to dispose of the estate and persons of Infant heires; to have præemption in Markets; and all other Statute Prærogatives, *may be transferred by the Soveraign; and yet the Power to protect his Subjects be retained.*"[59] Minor though the latter powers are in comparison with war-making and taxation authority, the admission belies the suggestion that indivisible sovereignty is a logical proposition in mature Hobbesian theory.[60]

Emphasis is laid in *Leviathan* on a second critique of divided sovereignty.[61] Looking back on the experience of the last decade, Hobbes discerns a causal connection between divided sovereignty and civil war:

> And this division is it, whereof it is said, *a Kingdome divided in it selfe cannot stand:* For unless this division precede, division into opposite Armies can never happen. If there had not first been an opinion received of the greatest part of *England,* that these Powers were divided between the King, and the Lords, and the House of Commons, the people had never been divided, and fallen into this Civill Warre; first between those

that disagreed in Politiques; and after between the Dissenters
about the liberty of Religion.[62]

Hobbes does not specify the empirical hypothesis with the
exactitude of a modern logician, and it is therefore not entirely clear what the falsifying case would be. This passage
implies the view that divided sovereignty is a necessary condition of civil war – absent divided sovereignty, civil war will
not occur – and therefore the falsifying case would be civil
war in an absolutist state.[63] In the passage quoted in the next
paragraph, he rather implies that divided sovereignty is a
sufficient condition for the occurrence of civil war, a hypothesis that is falsified by the example of a peaceful society with
a mixed constitution. But the general proposition is clear
enough: Divided sovereignty leads to civil war. Most readers
have not found the hypothesis convincing. According to
Goldsmith, for example, "Hobbes needs to prove that the
division of sovereign powers always leads to disagreement
among those who hold them and that disagreement cannot
be resolved peacefully – it must always lead to contention."
Which he does not do: "All that Hobbes actually shows is
that not dividing sovereign power cannot lead to disagreement (and contention) among the holders of the power while
division may lead to contention."[64]

It is worth inquiring why Hobbes thought divided sovereignty leads to civil war. What, in his view, is the causal
mechanism? To divide sovereignty between a king and Parliament, he explains in chapter 19,

> were to erect two Soveraigns; and every man to have his per-
> son represented by two Actors, that by opposing one another,
> must needs divide that Power, which (if men will live in Peace)
> is indivisible; and thereby reduce the Multitude into the con-
> dition of Warre, contrary to the end for which all Soveraignty
> is instituted.[65]

In other words, divided sovereignty fosters elite conflict and
this in turn tends to spread into civil war as elites mobilize
the people to fight on their behalf. It is a trivial truth to ob-

serve that divided sovereignty institutionalizes elite conflict, but this is less banal if emphasis is laid on the somewhat different point that divided sovereignty lends constitutional legitimacy to bids for power by ambitious elites. In the immediate circumstance, the ideology of a mixed constitution legitimized parliamentary resistance to the throne: It gave parliamentarians a rightful claim to the loyalties of ordinary Englishmen.

A similar analysis is elaborated in *Behemoth*, the history of the Civil War that Hobbes wrote after the Restoration. The war issued from the constitutional struggle between Parliament and king, in which "the true meaning of the Parliament was, that not the King, but they themselves, should have the absolute government."[66] But "ambition can do little without hands,"[67] and the support of common people hinges on their believing that those ambitious of power have legitimate title to it. The ideology of a mixed constitution, together with pernicious religious doctrines, justified Parliament's claim that it, not the king, should be master:

> For those that by ambition were once set upon the enterprise of changing the government, they cared not much what was reason and justice in the cause, but what strength they might procure by seducing the multitude with remonstrances from the Parliament House, or by sermons in the churches.[68]

The people, in short, were "carried into" rebellion by the arguments of an "impudent" Parliament.[69]

As both Goldsmith and Plamenatz point out, the causal analysis presupposes a further necessary condition: Elites and masses must share the opinion that it is permissible to fight political disputes on the battlefield.[70] Hobbes observes in this vein in *Leviathan:* Men that dare "take up Armes, to defend, or introduce an Opinion, are still in Warre; and their condition not Peace, but only a Cessation of Armes for feare of one another; and they live as it were, in the procincts of battaile continually."[71] He may be faulted, as he is by Plamenatz, for failing fully to imagine other circumstances, in which there is a settled procedure for resolving disputes, and therefore for overgeneralizing his defense of absolutism.[72] Hobbes surely hoped his theory would help create the happier circumstance in which political disputes are not fought out on the battlefield, but he is perhaps to be excused for failing to envision that circumstance very clearly.

Hobbes was well aware, on the other hand, that political ambition can find other rationalizations besides divided sovereignty, although it was not his concern to describe the variety of rationales that have been or may be given for rebellion. Religion furnished the principal alternative rationalization in the present case. He devoted increasing attention to religious argument through the several versions of the theory, appending a four-chapter section on the subject to the political theory in *De Cive*, which expands into two parts in *Leviathan*.[73] Hobbesian theology is not separate from, but is another aspect of, his defense of absolutism as his arguments have as their principal themes the doctrines of non-resistance and unified sovereignty. To attack the defense of resistance on religious grounds,[74] he put forward a minimalist interpretation of essential Christian doctrine. All that is necessary for salvation is the belief that Jesus is Christ.[75] This theological position reduces religious controversies to essential insignificance and strips the issue of conflicting religious and political duties of any real practical significance. The specific tenets of various Christian denominations do not, Hobbes maintains, bear on the one consideration that would give devout Christians good cause to resist political authority, their fate in the next life.[76] Rather, "in most controversies the contention is about humane Soveraignty; in some, matter of gain, and profit; in others, the glory of Wits."[77] Only in the hypothetical – for Hobbes's readers – circumstance of subjection to an infidel might there arise a genuine conflict between religious and political duty. Hobbes counsels the choice of martyrdom in such circumstance, as opposed to resistance, and in *Leviathan* specifies even more narrowly that only missionaries ("such as are sent to the conversion of Infidels") have the duty to martyr themselves.[78]

For the Erastian doctrine that the sovereign should possess supreme ecclesiastical authority, he offers a theological proof to complement the prudential argument that peace requires unified temporal and spiritual authority. This is the subject of Part III of *Leviathan*, "Of A CHRISTIAN COMMON-WEALTH," which focuses in particular on the claims of the Papacy.[79] The question is: "Whether Christian Kings, and the Soveraigne Assemblies in Christian Common-wealths, be absolute in their own Territories, immediately under God; or subject to one Vicar of Christ, constituted over the Universall Church."[80] On the one hand, the

> . . . Governor must be one; or else there must needs follow Faction, and Civil war in the Common-wealth, between the *Church* and *State*; between *Spiritualists*, and *Temporalists*; between the *Sword of Justice*, and the *Shield of Faith*; and (which is more) in every Christian mans own brest, between the *Christian*, and the *Man*.[81]

Hobbes's theological proof for the proposition takes the form of a "Holy History."[82] From the covenant with Abraham, he traces forward through the Old Testament the thesis that secular and religious authority were always united in the kingdom of Israel.[83] Neither is divided sovereignty legitimized by the New Testament. Because the kingdom of Christ is not of this world, spiritual leaders have the function merely of teaching religious doctrine and do not have the right to rule or to demand obedience.[84] Rather, "they who have sovereign power, are immediate rulers of the church under Christ, and all others but subordinate to them"; they are God's "vice-gods, or lieutenants here on earth."[85]

It is commonly said, especially with reference to *Behemoth*, that Hobbes gave an ideological explanation of the Civil War.[86] This is correct as far as it goes. "What civill war was there ever in the Christian world," Hobbes asks rhetorically in *De Cive*, "which did not either grow from, or was nourisht by this Root [of subversive doctrines]?"[87] But an emphasis on ideas as causes can be misleading and, in any case, gives an incomplete picture of Hobbes's political understanding. In one sense, to be sure, *Leviathan*'s hypothesis that divided sovereignty is a necessary condition of civil war resolves into an ideological explanation. In a case in which the constitution is unwritten, it is especially transparent that institutions are constituted in some large measure by popularly held beliefs about them.[88] Something stronger is usually intended, however, in identifying ideas as causes. An ideological explanation implies an ideological characterization of the nature of the conflict itself; for example, the Civil War really was a contest over political and religious doctrines.[89] Hobbes most certainly did not think this to be the case. His narrowly political and religious arguments have the twin purposes, throughout, of rebutting the various ideologies used to justify rebellion and, further, of exposing these as pretexts for a struggle for power. "Those seditious persons who dispute against absolute Authority, doe not so much care to destroy it," he put the point succinctly in *De Cive*, "as to conveigh it on others."[90] So in a real sense, ideas are epiphenomena in a Hobbist analysis, although ideology is nonetheless central to the causation of civil war. Political ambition needs the legitimation provided by "pernicious" doctrines, "such are those, which . . . require obedience to be given to others beside them to whom the supreme authority is committed."[91]

Hobbes did not fear subversive ideas writ large or ambition in and of itself. He always asked whose interest ideas served, and he always answered the question in terms of concrete institutions, for example, notably Parliament and the Papacy. Institutionalized political ambition – that was what he feared: ambition cloaked in claims of institutional prerogative and responsibility, and furnished with the support of institutional organization. His preoccupation with the constitution of sovereignty and constitutional doctrines, broadly conceived, recalls traditional resistance doctrine, which taught that rebellion is legitimate only when initiated by parliaments or other inferior magistrates, such as religious leaders. Hobbes, of course, meant to deny that as a normative doctrine. But the political analysis underlying *Leviathan*'s hypothesis consists in the equivalent empirical proposition. Rebellions are the product of political ambition provided with an institutional home and hence a claim on the allegiance of ordinary people.

Leviathan's hypothesis that divided sovereignty leads to civil war fits within a broader analysis of the causation and deterrence of rebellion to which we will return in chapter 6. The subject of the chapter is Hobbes's advice on the exercise of sovereign power, the art of government. This advice complements his constitutional doctrine. He appreciated, as his many readers who equate Hobbesian absolutism with a license for tyranny have ignored, that the conduct of government has some connection with the likelihood of rebellion.

THE ARGUMENT FOR MONARCHY

And therefore no great Popular Common-wealth was ever kept up; but either by a forraign Enemy that united them; or by the reputation of some one eminent Man amongst them; or by the secret Counsell of a few; or by the mutuall feare of equall factions; and not by the open Consultations of the Assembly.

Leviathan, chapter 26

Of his preference for monarchy, Hobbes wrote in the preface to the 1647 edition of *De Cive*, it is the weakest part of the political theory: *"which one thing alone I confesse in this whole book not to be demonstrated, but only probably stated."*[92] In view of its date, too much should not be made of the remark. It may be less a statement of his own considered judgment than a passing opinion mirroring the current political climate. In this late Civil War period, there was widespread among Englishmen a mood of indifference to the constitution of government, a mood born of the experience of civil war, and quite the opposite of the fervent constitutional debates of the prewar period.[93] Earlier, Hobbes had praised monarchy extravagantly, alleging (in the first edition of *De Cive*): "Nor doe we readily meet with any example that shewes us when any subject, without any default of his own, hath by his Prince been despoiled of his life, or goods, through the sole licenciousnesse of his Authority."[94]

75

His defense of monarchy runs along the same lines as the defense of unified sovereignty in *Leviathan*.[95] The emphasis is on the inferiority of the salient alternative, parliamentary government.[96] Of the several "inconveniences" of the latter, its worst feature is the institutionalization of elite conflict and the threat that poses to public order. Secondarily, Hobbes also makes the positive assertion that "the publique and private interest are most closely united" in monarchy. Monarchs in particular, he claims, have an interest in governing well.[97] This latter argument will be treated in chapter 6, in connection with the larger Hobbesian theme that it serves rulers' interest to govern well.

Theology and history, in Hobbes's view, support a general preference for monarchic rule. Nonetheless, a reasoned defense of monarchy requires showing that this form of government is suited to the particular kind of association that is the state.[98] The relevant characteristic is the purpose of the association. In chapter 22 of *Leviathan*, he compares associations characterized by collective goods, for example, states, with associations dedicated to the private interests of the membership, such as bodies of merchants.[99] For the latter, an assembly is the best form of government:

> The end then of these Bodies of Merchants, being not a Common benefit to the whole Body, . . . but the particular gaine of every adventurer, it is reason that every one be acquainted with the employment of his own; that is, that every one be of the Assembly, that shall have the power to order the same; and be acquainted with their accounts.[100]

The corresponding question is which form of government best serves the purpose of the state, namely, "the Peace, and Security of the people."[101] Or, to put the question in more characteristically Hobbesian fashion: Which form of government is least "inconvenient" to that purpose?

In *The Elements of Law*, Hobbes addresses several common criticisms of monarchy: On each score, parliamentary government would be worse. "First it seemeth inconvenient, there should be committed so great a power to one man" because "the monarch may be swayed to use that power amiss."[102] Passion poses more political danger, however, when policy is decided in great assemblies because "the passions of many men be more violent when they are assembled together" – "even as a great many coals, though but warm asunder, being put together inflame one another." "There is no doubt," Hobbes explains,

> when things are debated in great assemblies, but every man delivering his opinion at large, without interruption, endeavoureth to make whatsoever he is to set forth for good, better; and what he would have apprehended as evil, worse, as much as is possible; to the end his counsel may take place; which counsel also is never without aim at his own benefit, or honour: every man's end being some good to himself. Now this cannot be done without working upon the passions of the rest. And thus the passions of those that are singly moderate, are altogether vehement.[103]

"Another inconvenience of monarchy" is avarice. In this case the larger number of rulers in a parliamentary government in and of itself exacerbates the inconvenience. Hobbes has in mind this imaginative quantification of corruption potential, "whereas the Favorites of Monarchs, are few, and they have none els to advance but their owne Kindred; the Favorites of an Assembly, are many; and the Kindred much more numerous, than of any Monarch."[104] In a similar vein, the greater the number of rulers, the larger ranks the problem of partiality in the administration of justice: "In aristocracies, not only one, but many have power of taking men out of the hands of justice."[105] A fourth inconvenience of monarchy is inconstancy in lawmaking, that is, frequent alteration of the laws. This is more apt to occur under parliamentary government, however, because the legislators are more numerous and because assemblies are easily swayed one way and another by persuasive oratory and by factions. Under that form of government, "the Laws do flote here, and there, as it were upon the waters."[106]

In the main, the case for king over Parliament is a critique of the politics of assembly government. Answering the criticism that monarchy suffers infant and mad rulers, Hobbes bluntly charges in *Leviathan:* "There is no great Commonwealth, the Soveraignty whereof is in a great Assembly, which is not, as to consultations of Peace, and Warre, and making of Lawes, in the same condition, as if the Government were in a Child."[107] Parliamentary government not only involves a larger body of imperfect human rulers than monarchy; the process of policy-making in an assembly is flawed in a number of respects. For example, just as children are unable to evaluate the counsel they are given, "an Assembly wanteth the liberty, to dissent from the counsell of the major part, be it good, or bad."[108] Hobbes harps on the theme that the forum encourages persuasive oratory to the detriment of "right reason" in policy-making;[109] he charges, furthermore, that assemblies tend to act slowly[110] and that few in an assembly are likely to possess the knowledge necessary for domestic and foreign policy-making.[111]

But there is a worse flaw in assembly government. Like divided sovereignty, the parliamentary form of government has an "aptitude to dissolve into civil war."[112] "A Monarch cannot disagree with himselfe, out of envy, or interest; but an Assembly may; and that to such a height, as may produce a Civill Warre."[113] At root, Hobbes dislikes parliamentary government because he mistrusts all institutional arrangements that give encouragement to political ambition. The menace of ambitious elites – their proclivity to "attempt by force of armes" "what they cannot obtain by craft, and language" – forms a principal theme of Hobbes's constitutional doctrines throughout.[114]

So the case for unified sovereignty and that for monarchy are of a piece: Absolute monarchy is a prophylactic against the menace of political ambition. As Hobbes put it in *The Elements of Law:* "The greatest inconvenience that can happen to a commonwealth, is the aptitude to dissolve into civil war; and to this are monarchies much less subject, than any other governments."[115] This translates into the positive thesis that absolute monarchy serves the interest of ordinary people: "Whosoever therefore in a *Monarchy* will lead a retired life, let him be what he will that Reignes, he is out of danger: for the ambitious onely suffer, the rest are protected from the injuries of the more potent."[116]

Empathy with ordinary subjects, I will argue in the concluding chapter, is at the root of Hobbes's political vision. This is different from the customary view that subjects' motivation and duties are the principal topic of the political theory. The recommendation of absolute monarchy on the ground of its benefit for ordinary subjects runs directly counter to our own received ideas about absolutism and about the kind of political institutions that best protect common people against political endangerment. Appreciating Hobbes's political understanding requires, and evokes, an appreciation for the variety of forms of political endangerment there are and have been. "No man can be a Polititian, except he be first an Historian or a Traveller," James Harrington observed in *Oceana*. "For except he can see what Must be, or May be, he is no Polititian: Now if he have no knowledge in story, he cannot tell what hath been; and if he hath not been a Traveller, he cannot tell what is: but he that neither knoweth what hath been, nor what is; can never tell what must be, or what may be."[117] The menace on which Hobbes focused, the momentous consequences for ordinary people of political ambition, did not disappear from the world after the English Civil War.

Chapter 5

Hobbesian roles

For by Art is created that great LEVIATHAN called a COMMON-WEALTH . . . in which, the *Soveraignty* is an Artificiall *Soul*, as giving life and motion to the whole body; The *Magistrates*, and other *Officers* of Judicature and Execution, artificiall *Joynts*; *Reward* and *Punishment* (by which fastned to the seate of the Soveraignty, every joynt and member is moved to performe his duty) are the *Nerves*, that do the same in the Body Naturall; . . . *Counsellors*, by whom all things needfull for it to know, are suggested unto it, are the *Memory*; *Equity* and *Lawes*, an artificiall *Reason* and *Will*.

Leviathan, "Introduction"

The familiar picture of Hobbes's state has an awesome ruler looming over an undifferentiated mass of subjects. In fact, a variety of persons and institutions inhabit the Hobbesian commonwealth. Besides simple subjects and the sovereign, there are soldiers, public ministers, counselors, judges, spies, and traitors, as well as masters, servants, and children. The *Leviathan*-state incorporates subordinate political bodies including representative assemblies called to counsel the sovereign; colonial, local, and university governments; private bodies, such as the family; and unorganized assemblies, such as markets and shows.

Reflecting the customary preoccupation with the foundations of Hobbes's political theory, as opposed to the theory itself, the kinds of distinctions among Hobbesian persons that have interested twentieth-century commentators are psychological, sociological, and moral distinctions. J. W. N.

Watkins and M. M. Goldsmith, for example, debate the question whether or not Hobbes assumes uniformity in human nature. According to the former: "For Hobbes to admit that men may be differently motivated would have been fatal to his project of a political science deduced from universal psychological principles."[1] Goldsmith does not think Hobbes supposed, or needed to suppose, that men have similar desires; the theory merely requires the supposition that all men have desires, are motivated.[2] A sociological school grants limited, social-psychological relevance to Hobbes's social imagination. In C. B. Macpherson's well-known view, the theory presupposes a model of man formed along bourgeois lines. "The postulate of innate desire of all men for more power without limit is only apparently tenable about men who are already in a universally competitive society."[3] While agreeing that bourgeois man is the predominant character type in the Hobbesian landscape, Michael Oakeshott suggests that the theory depends for the "first performance" of political obligations on that contrasting sociological figure, the courageous aristocrat.[4] Classes of moral agents are the salient distinction in Howard Warrender's reconstruction of Hobbes's theory of obligation. Security, he argues, is the central "validating condition" in the theory for the obligation to keep promises, an obligation that has, however, independent foundation in natural law.[5] Specifically, Warrender distinguishes the performance obligations of citizens from the weaker, merely prima facie, obligations of individuals in conditions of insecurity, notably, the state of nature.[6]

On the other hand, there is a general lack of interest in Hobbes's own complex idea of the state, yet another consequence of the reigning orthodoxy that this is an individualistic political theory. In virtue of the assumption that everyman is the principal subject of Hobbes's arguments, and the related notion that the power of a Hobbesian sovereign hinges, in the first instance, on the support of ordinary citizens, Hobbism becomes first and foremost a theory about the obligations and motivation of individuals more or less abstractly conceived. Hence the various institutions and roles he describes, as well as the distinction between elite politics and mass behavior that informs his political arguments, are essentially trivial details in the portrait of the *Leviathan*-state. Upon noticing that the pertinent chapters of *Leviathan* (22 through 25, and 28) "are commonly neglected by Hobbes's critics," Gauthier comments, for example, "No doubt a detailed analysis of their arguments is unnecessary to an understanding of the structure of Hobbes's political theory, [although] their general character casts an important light on what Hobbes deemed to be the nature of the society to which his theory applied."[7]

Precisely to the contrary, to understand the logic of Hobbes's theory of politics it is necessary to examine his discussions of the constitutive roles, as well as institutions, of political society. This will show, first of all, that obligation and consent are lesser themes in the political theory than is commonly supposed. Hobbes treats the problem of generating and maintaining coercive authority as a constitutional problem, centering on the need to structure sovereignty in such a way as to deter elite conflict: The argument for absolute monarchy was the subject of the preceding chapter. Second, he counts on special offices, or roles, for the performance of civic functions. In the notable instance, only soldiers, those who have enlisted or taken impressment money, have a strong obligation to fight for the state. Only about some political roles (e.g., the soldier) is the juridical casuistry of consent and obligation the significant consideration. Regarding others, character is the salient issue: Cowardice, for example, excuses a subject from having to fight. With respect to the sovereign, as we shall see in the next chapter, Hobbes appeals to the interests attaching to the role to explain why rulers ought to govern according to law. In short, consent, though the primary principle in Hobbes's account of civic duty, is nonetheless a local, not a comprehensive, consideration.

It is also a different political casuistry of consent and obligation from that presumed by commentaries in the individualistic genre. These concepts attach to roles in Hobbes's political arguments. The duties of individuals are defined with respect to their roles in the state, the obligation to fight for the state being the crucial case. Correspondingly, Hobbes describes consent differently with respect to various authority relationships, namely, household and parental authority, as well as political subjection. Interpretations of Hobbes's theory of obligation typically reconstruct that theory along individualistic lines, deducing from Hobbesian premises the conclusions that ought to follow for the duties of individuals in the abstract. By contrast, the following exegesis offers a reconstruction of his logic based on the actual accounts of role obligations given in the textual political theory. My reconstruction resembles Warrender's interpretation in distinguishing prima facie from strong obligations. Unlike Warrender, however, I maintain that the distinction applies within civil society to individuals as the occupants of roles.

COMPOSITION OF SOCIETY AND THE STATE

Having spoken of the Generation, Forme, and Power of a Common-wealth, I am in order to speak next of the parts thereof.

Leviathan, chapter 22

After discussing sovereigns' rights, Hobbes turns to the traditional Aristotelian theme of comparing various authority relationships. *The Elements of Law* and *De Cive* devote separate chapters to household authority (masters, servants, and slaves) and to parental dominion, which are summarized in a single chapter in *Leviathan*, 20, "Of Dominion PATERNALL, and DESPOTICALL."[8] Although these discussions have primarily comparative significance, for understanding political authority and its basis in consent (see the final section of this chapter), the earlier versions treat in some detail the hierarchy of authority relationships in a feudal society. (For example: "But servants subordinate, though manumitted by their immediate lord, are not thereby discharged of subjection to their lord paramount; . . . Nor if the chief lord should manumit his immediate servant, doth he thereby release the servants of their obligation to him that is so manumitted.")[9] The feudal detail is omitted from *Leviathan*,[10] where Hobbes more narrowly focuses on the composition of the state. At the same time, his description of the constitutive parts of the state – institutions, roles, groups, and offices – greatly expands in this work. It has new chapters on the "liberty of subjects" (21), subordinate associations or "subject systems" (22), public ministers (23), and on counsel (25).

Chapter 22 of *Leviathan*, "Of SYSTEMES Subject, Politicall, and Private," classifies various institutions and groups within the state on the basis of two criteria: (1) organization and agency and (2) public authorization. Organized bodies with a corporate agent are "regular" systems (thus the state, e.g., is an "absolute" and "independent" "regular" system). "Irregular" systems, such as markets, lack authority and organization. Corporate bodies that have been authorized by the sovereign are termed "political" systems: These include subordinate representative assemblies, the governments of colonies and of towns, universities, colleges, and churches. Bodies created by subjects or by a foreign power are "private" systems, such as the family, which is the principal lawful private system.[11]

The three "regular" and "political" bodies of concern to Hobbes are parliaments, colonial governments, and merchant companies. He comments on their functions, the appropriate form of government for each,[12] and on the financial liabilities of their membership.[13] It is here that Hobbes specifies and details the limited powers of subordinate representative assemblies: they are governed by the sovereign's instructions in letters patent and are subject to the law of the land.[14] He reiterates the standard royalist position that parliaments have the function, merely, of counseling the sovereign and that he controls their assembly and considerations; . in other words, they are "temporary" as opposed to "permanent" political bodies.[15]

The "private," or unauthorized, systems that occupy

Hobbes's attention, not surprisingly, are leagues of subjects – factions, conspiracies, cabals, and the like.[16] He warns, "Leagues of Subjects . . . are . . . for the most part unnecessary, and savour of unlawfull designe. . . . For all uniting of strength by private men, is, if for evill intent, unjust; if for intent unknown, dangerous to the Publique"; and cautions in particular about family feuds ("Factions for Kindred"), religious leagues, and political parties ("Factions for Government of Religion . . . or of State").[17] In *De Cive*, discussing the causes of rebellion (chapter xii), he had described the operation of seditious factions. Leaders assemble the "ill affected" to "deliberate of such things whereby the present government may be reformed," and simultaneously (shades of Lenin) develop a secret organization:[18]

And thus when they have gotten a faction big enough, in which they may rule by their eloquence, they move it to take upon it the managing of affaires; and thus they sometimes oppresse the Common-wealth, namely where there is no other faction to oppose them, but for the most part they rend it, and introduce a civill warre.[19]

The next chapter in *Leviathan* (23) enumerates various kinds of public ministers, who are defined as agents of the sovereign in his political capacity.[20] They are classed by the scope and nature of their authority. There are "Ministers for the generall Administration" of an entire commonwealth, such as regents for an infant king; governors of provinces; and, third, ministers in charge of "some speciall businesse."[21] The enumeration of the last corresponds to the essential powers of sovereignty. Hobbes mentions economic ministers, with responsibility for the public revenue; military authorities; those with authority to instruct the people; judges and other officers in the criminal justice system; and ambassadors. His discussion carefully distinguishes public from private actors, based on the source of their authority and the nature of their business.[22] (Spies are difficult to classify in this scheme. Although their authority and business are public, they pretend to be merely private citizens, and Hobbes therefore terms them "private ministers"!)[23] Throughout, as well, he emphasizes the subordination of public ministers to the sovereign.[24]

Discussing two subordinate offices, counselor and judge, Hobbes details the character and knowledge requisite for each position. In the "paper war" of the early 1640s, parliamentarians avoided attacking Charles I by blaming "evil counselors" for his regime.[25] *Leviathan* devotes chapter 25 to counsel;[26] here, as well as in the discussion of sovereigns' duties in chapter 30, Hobbes instructs on the qualities of good counselors. "The most able Counsellours, are they that have least hope of benefit by giving evill Counsell, and most knowledge of those things that conduce to the Peace, and Defence of the Common-wealth."[27] More specifically, counselors' interests should not be inconsistent with the interests of those whom they counsel; advice should be expressed in calm, reasoned fashion; and counsel requires long experience in public affairs.[28] Against the claim that Parliament (a "great Assembly") provides the best counsel, Hobbes expressly warns that the publicity of their proceedings, together with the "contrary" interests of some members, makes such groups bad counselors; it is better to hear advisers individually, in private.[29] Regarding judges, he explains in the chapter on law (26), it is more important that they be fair than that they possess a scholarly knowledge of law. The office requires men contemptuous of great wealth and status, capable of dispassionate judgment; and, last, it requires a patient temperament.[30]

Hobbes's discussions of subjects' obligations and liberties are properly seen against the background of this complex idea of the state. Elite political actors, including public officials, are the primary figures on the Hobbesian stage; and his political analysis ranges beyond the formalities of consensual obligation to take into account more prudential considerations of motivation, character, and knowledge.

POLITICAL DUTIES:
THE CASE OF FIGHTING FOR THE STATE

Those who are paid for the performance of their duties, *Leviathan* states, have a strong obligation to perform them: "When the Soveraign of a Common-wealth appointeth a Salary to any publique Office, he that receiveth it, is bound in Justice to performe his office; otherwise, he is bound onely in honour, to acknowledgement, and an endeavour of requitall."[31] C. B. Macpherson would have us understand such statements as indicative of the bourgeois character of Hobbes's social imagination.[32] More concerned to elaborate his own conception of the significance of Hobbes's reliance on wage relationships than with understanding Hobbes's conception of their significance, Macpherson ignores the role played by employment in the textual arguments. He also makes the orthodox assumption that the principal problem confronting Hobbes and his interpreters is explaining the motivation of ordinary subjects to support the sovereign.[33] Employment figures importantly in *Leviathan*'s account of political obligation, and it is therefore a different account of such obligation than Macpherson imagines. On this basis, as the quotation states, Hobbes distinguishes the special political duties of some individuals, and these are the individuals on whom he counts for the performance of politically necessary functions.

Basic to Hobbesian reasoning is a distinction between performance and obligation. Employment entails a strong obligation to perform the duties attached to an office, whereas those who are simply commanded to serve are bound only to "acknowledgement, and an endeavour of requitall" of their duties. The difference between the military obligations of soldiers and simple subjects is the illustrative and notable case on which the following discussion will focus. Soldiers, in this respect, are more akin to public ministers than to ordinary citizens, "insomuch as the most common Souldier, may demand the wages of his warrefare, as a debt."[34] In this same passage in *Leviathan*, Hobbes elaborates regarding ordinary subjects: "For though men have no lawfull remedy, when they be commanded to quit their private businesse, to serve the publique, without Reward, or Salary; yet they are not bound thereto, by the Law of Nature, nor by the Institution of the Common-wealth, unlesse the service cannot otherwise be done."[35] Let us begin with the latter, his account of the obligations of simple subjects.

Although both the stipulation concerning the strenuous obligation of paid employees and the discussion of the special role of the soldier are new arguments in *Leviathan*, the just-quoted description of subjects' obligations is consistent with previous discussions. The Hobbesian covenants, in all three versions, have primarily negative force, their essential point being to deny legitimacy to political resistance against established authority. Subjects, ordinary subjects and grandees, are obligated to passive obedience to the sitting government.

But Hobbes always also stipulated that, in virtue of the covenant, the sovereign "may use the strength and means of them all, as he shall think expedient, for their Peace and Common Defence."[36] Possibly because cooperation came to be something of a problem during the Civil War, *Leviathan* adds several specific injunctions about subjects' positive duties. (In the Civil War, some localities organized to keep both sides in the fighting away; this was known as the "Clubmen" movement.)[37] *Leviathan*'s "Review and Conclusion" adds this law of nature regarding the duty to fight for the state: "Every man is bound by Nature, as much as in him lieth, to protect in Warre, the Authority, by which he is himself protected in time of Peace."[38] In a similar vein, this work strengthens the obligation of subjects to assist the sovereign in the execution of justice. In *De Cive*, it will be recalled from chapter 2, when Hobbes grants subjects' unalienated right of self-defense, he does so with the proviso "that no man offer to defend others" from the sovereign.[39] That work specified: "Every man Contracts not to assist him who is to be punished."[40] *Leviathan*'s account of punishment puts a positive duty on subjects: "In the making of a Common-wealth, every man giveth away the right of defending another; but not of defending himselfe. Also he obligeth himselfe, to assist him that hath the Soveraignty, in the Punishing of another; but of himselfe not."[41]

On the other hand, all three versions of the theory also only require of subjects the "endeavour of requitall" of positive duties. According to *The Elements of Law*, "No covenant is understood to bind further, than to our best endeavour, either in performance of the thing promised, or in something equivalent."[42] The limits of subjects' obligations were detailed in chapter 2 of this volume.[43] In *Leviathan*, to recall, Hobbes excuses cowardly subjects from the obligation to fight for the state, as well as those who furnish a substitute soldier. Ordinary subjects must fight only when the aid of all is immediately necessary to the defense of the state.

In contrast, Hobbes details in several places in *Leviathan* soldiers' strenuous duty to fight for the state. Chapter 21 stipulates: "He that inrowleth himselfe a Souldier, or taketh imprest mony, taketh away the excuse of a timorous nature; and is obliged, not onely to go to the battell, but also not to run from it, without his Captaines leave."[44] Furthermore, the distinction extends beyond the battlefield. An ordinary subject may submit to a conqueror "when the means of his life is within the Guards and Garrisons of the Enemy."[45] "But if a man, besides the obligation of a Subject, hath taken upon him a new obligation of a Souldier, then he hath not the liberty to submit to a new Power, as long as the old one keeps the field, and giveth him means of subsistence, either in his Armies, or Garrisons."[46]

Last, he marks the limits of soldiers' obligation. Whereas simple subjects may submit when their lives are in jeopardy, soldiers' obligations hinge on their army's condition. When an army no longer keeps the field or supplies its soldiers, "a Souldier also may seek his Protection wheresoever he has most hope to have it; and may lawfully submit himself to his new Master."[47] When the organization fails, in other words, so end the obligations of the role. Elsewhere, Hobbes notes along these lines that the size of military units matters:

> For where a number of men are manifestly too weak to defend themselves united, every one may use his own reason in time of danger, to save his own life, either by flight, or by submission to the enemy, as hee shall think best; in the same manner as a very small company of souldiers, surprised by an army, may cast down their armes, and demand quarter, or run away, rather than be put to the sword.[48]

These qualifications concerning the limits of soldiers' obligations may have been suggested to Hobbes by Anthony Ascham's Engagement treatise, *Of the Confusions and Revolutions of Governments* (1649). Similarities between this work and *Leviathan's* "Review and Conclusion," including this point, will be discussed in chapter 7.

Prima facie and strong obligations

Leviathan's treatment of military service bears some resemblance to Howard Warrender's reconstruction of Hobbes's account of *moral* obligation, although Warrender, in my view, nevertheless gives a mistaken interpretation of Hobbes's account of *political* obligation. He is concerned to show that moral obligation is pervasive in the theory: The state of nature is not a "moral vacuum"; rather, the obligation to keep valid covenants precedes the institution of the sovereign.[49] To make this case, Warrender distinguishes the ground or source of obligation (which in his view is natural, finally divine, law) from the "validating conditions" of obligation. The latter specify the conditions under which obligations are operative, which is to say, they specify the classes of persons to whom obligations apply.[50] "*Grounds* of obligation specify 'a', the type of action. *Validating Conditions* specify 'p', the class of persons."[51] Security, according to Warrender, is the central Hobbesian validating condition for natural-law obligations. Thus men in the insecure state of nature have (for the most part) "suspended obligations" because the validating condition is absent, in contrast to the strong obligations of citizens who enjoy the security provided by the state.[52]

Although the principal contrast is between moral agency in the state of nature and that in civil society, Warrender's interpretation has obvious bearing on citizens' obligation to perform dangerous duties. He revises Hobbes's arguments to show how the seventeenth-century thinker should have applied the premises of his moral theory, in particular the premise of an absolute natural right of self-defense.[53] Warrender notices that Hobbes, in *De Cive* and *Leviathan*, frames positive duties under a consequentialist appeal to the "intention" of the covenant.[54] Still, "in view of what Hobbes says elsewhere, it is unlikely that he intended his argument concerning the frustration of the purpose of the covenant to cover the subject in mortal danger."[55] The right of self-defense – which "appears to be absolute, and to provide an argument for the individual more ultimate than the preservation of civil society itself" – precludes a strong obligation to risk death for the state. Warrender suggests, therefore, that the consequentialist argument only applies to and justifies duties carrying "smaller degrees of danger or dishonour, such as killing others or taking risks."[56] The estimation of mortal danger must be left to the individual, however.[57] Finally, therefore, the extent of subjects' liberty and duty is vague; and the class of "insecure" citizens, indeterminate: "In some circumstances only he [the subject] can know what his duties are."[58]

This quite orthodox reconstruction of Hobbist logic imports two assumptions foreign to the actual textual arguments. Hobbes does not, we saw in chapter 2, share this strong understanding of the force of natural-rights principles, nor are individuals in the abstract the subject of his discussion of political obligation. A more accurate interpretation of his account of political obligation would follow the lines of Warrender's exegesis of his moral theory. Hobbes asserts a universal obligation to assist the sovereign, covering specifically (in *Leviathan*) the duty to fight for the state and to assist in catching criminals. But for ordinary subjects, this turns out to be a weak – merely prima facie – duty, requiring only "acknowledgement, and an endeavour of re-quitall."[59] While appeal to the consequentialist consideration of the needs of the state underpins the assertion that subjects have political obligations,[60] this same consideration also limits their actual (strong) duties. Only when "the service cannot otherwise be done" is their performance obligatory; for example, "when the Defence of the Common-wealth, requireth at once the help of all that are able to bear Arms, every one is obliged."[61] This understanding of subjects' duties is applied to particulars in the enumeration of insignificant exercises of the unalienated right of self-defense (not including military service) and of valid excuses from fighting, detailed in chapter 2 of this volume. With respect to ordinary subjects, there is a "mutuall Relation between Protection and Obedience,"[62] but only in extremity is there also a mutual relationship between protection and the performance of civic duties.

On the other hand, *Leviathan* stipulates a class of persons with a strenuous duty to fight for the state. The role of the soldier resembles a "validating condition" inasmuch as it is the circumstance in which the obligation to perform military service becomes fully operative. Hobbes's role casuistry has the important advantage of avoiding the problems of subjectivism and indeterminacy that afflict Warrender's reconstructed logic. *Leviathan*'s arguments precisely distinguish the group of persons under a strenuous obligation to fight for the state from the group having a merely prima facie obligation to do so.

Taking Hobbes's role casuistry seriously, it is apparent that commentaries in the individualistic mold misconceptualize the problem of explaining citizen cooperation. Defined in Hobbesian terms, the problem is not that of explaining the motivation and duty of individuals in the abstract to perform civic duties. What needs to be made plain is individuals' motivation and duty to perform their role responsibilities. These issues arise for treatment in Hobbes's discussions of social authority relationships, namely, those involving the roles of master, servant, slave, parent, and child. His discussions of

consent in the context of these several role relationships suggest the contours of a moral psychology consonant with the
distinction between (subjects') prima facie and (e.g., soldiers') strong obligations.

THE NATURE OF CONSENT: SERVANTS, CHILDREN, SUBJECTS, AND SOLDIERS

It is manifest that the *Children* are no lesse subject to those by
whom they are nourisht, and brought up, then *Servants* to their
Lords, and *Subjects* to him who beares the *Supreme Rule*.
De Cive, chapter ix, section seven

Hobbes's account of consent is one of the more curious
features of his theory. He attempted to assimilate all authority relationships under the rubric of consent, an especially
counterintuitive idea in the case of parental authority. His
consent accounts of household and parental authority have
the primary purpose of establishing the similarity of "sovereignty by acquisition," meaning conquest, to "sovereignty
by institution," that is, the covenant story.[63] With respect
both to the rights of dominion and to the condition of subjection, Hobbes asserts, all authority is essentially the same.[64]
Furthermore, he is known for arguing a particularly expansive definition of consent, which extends the concept of voluntary action to include coerced acts, in particular acts motivated by fear. "Feare and Liberty are consistent," *Leviathan*
explains, "as when a man throweth his goods into the Sea
for *feare* the ship should sink, he doth it neverthelesse very
willingly, and may refuse to doe it if he will: It is therefore
the action, of one that was *free*."[65] The political force of the
claim is to forestall the objection that neither variety of political subjection is truly voluntary because both are motivated
by fear. In the case of "sovereignty by institution," it is individuals' fear of one another in the state of nature, whereas
"sovereignty by acquisition" originates in fear of the conqueror.[66]

On the other hand, Hobbes is also attentive to variations

in the character of consent. He draws the familiar distinction between express and tacit consent, defined as the difference between an oath and a promise conveyed by "other sufficient signes of the Will":[67] "As for example, a man that hath not been called to make such an expresse Promise, (because he is one whose power perhaps is not considerable;) yet if he live under their Protection openly, hee is understood to submit himselfe to the Government."[68] Second, he recognizes that authority is acquired in different ways. While insisting that consent is the source of all legitimate authority among human beings, Hobbes distinguishes between dominion that is brought about by conquest (household authority and "sovereignty by acquisition"); by generation (parental authority); and by "consent," referring narrowly to "sovereignty by institution" of the political covenant.[69] The following analysis focuses on his elaborations of the principle of consent in connection with household authority (meaning the relationship of master, servant, and slave) and parental authority. In these discussions can be found, I think, inklings of another distinction, besides that between tacit and express consent, which is pertinent to the contrast between prima facie and strong obligations. This is the distinction between "cognitive" and "voluntary" consent: between acknowledging a role and choosing one. "Where the ends of the self are given in advance," Michael Sandel explains in *Liberalism and the Limits of Justice,*

> the relevant agency is not voluntarist but cognitive, since the subject achieves self-command not by choosing that which is already given (this would be unintelligible) but by reflecting on itself and inquiring into its constituent nature, discerning its laws and imperatives, and acknowledging its purposes as its own.[70]

The key points in Hobbes's discussions, in this regard, are his concern with power and with the consequences of consent. Who controls the relationship and what duties does consent entail? In the case of servants and children, like "conquered" subjects (whose condition reflects, as the hypothetical contract does not, the reality that citizenship is most often a role "given in advance"), the primary agent in the relationship is their superior. In all instances, by Hobbes's account, subordinates are obliged to acknowledge their position and not harm their masters.

Masters, servants, and slaves

"Every one that is taken in the War . . . is not suppos'd to have Contracted with his *Lord*." Slaves, meaning those who are subsequently imprisoned or kept in chains, have not; only servants, who enjoy corporal liberty, have entered into a consensual authority relationship with their masters.[71] "The obligation of a Servant," Hobbes states in *De Cive*, "ariseth from that freedome which is granted him by his Lord."[72] Liberty marks the consensual nature of their relationship because trust is a necessary condition of contracts:

> The obligation therefore of a *Servant* to his *Lord* ariseth not
> from a simple grant of his life, but from hence rather, That he
> keeps him not bound, or imprison'd, for all obligation derives
> from Contract; but where's no trust, there can be no Contract,
> as appears by the 2. Chap. Artic. 9. where a Compact is de-
> fin'd to be the promise of him who is trusted.[73]

By extension, the contractual relationship and therefore a servant's obligations end should the master return him to chains or otherwise deprive him of corporal liberty.[74]

Hobbes offers several descriptions of the compact between master and servant, which differ in the emphasis placed on the servant's choice in the matter. In *The Elements of Law*, he speaks of "a supposed covenant, without which the master had no reason to trust them."[75] That a servant is permitted liberty implies, in other words, the passage of a covenant with the master. Alternately, *De Cive* emphasizes that the contract between master and servant involves an exchange of benefits: "The good which the vanquisht, or inferiour, in strength doth receive, is the grant of his life, which by the Right of War in the naturall state of men he might have de-priv'd him of, but the good which he promises, is his service

95

and obedience."[76] In *Leviathan*, the accent is on the servant's choice. "Nor is he obliged," Hobbes states, "because he is Conquered; . . . but because he commeth in, and submitteth to the Victor."[77]

The key actor in the relationship is not the conquered, however, nor is his consent, whether tacit or express, the controlling factor. The master, not the servant, decides whether the relationship is to be one of authority or one of force, whether, that is, the conquered is to be servant or slave. In the first instance, the nature of the relationship hinges on the master's decision whether to trust the subordinate with liberty. According to *Leviathan*, "Nor is the Victor obliged by an enemies rendring himselfe, (without promise of life,) to spare him for this his yeelding to discretion; which obliges not the Victor longer, than in his own discretion hee shall think fit."[78] Furthermore, it serves the master's interest to trust the conquered with liberty. Masters, by Hobbes's account, have the same rights of dominion over both servants and slaves, specifically the rights to their property and to "dispose of the *Person*."[79] On the other hand, servants, as opposed to slaves, are obliged not to harm their masters. Absent a contractual authority relationship, slaves are at liberty to kill their masters: "Such men . . . have no obligation at all; but may break their bonds, or the prison; and kill, or carry away captive their Master, justly." Conquerors, then, have some incentive to allow freedom to their prisoners: Servants, Hobbes stipulates, enjoy liberty and trust "upon promise not to run away, nor to do violence to his Master."[80]

In respect to the recognition that power (and powerlessness) matters, Hobbes's acccount of the relationship of master, servant, and slave is a realistic representation of the way in which roles figure in much of ordinary life. In large measure, our parts are apportioned and not actively chosen, apportioned by virtue of the structure of the society within which we live and by circumstance. This affects the quality of consent. The ambiguity in Hobbes's several accounts of the compact between master and servant, between "supposing" the latter's tacit consent and stipulating an express promise, reflects an existential ambiguity. It is a familiar feature of everyday subordination relationships for it to be unclear even, or sometimes especially, to the parties whether service is voluntary or a matter of "going along" in expected fashion. Last, Hobbes's accent on servants' negative duty not to kill their masters corresponds, albeit as an extreme example, to the ordinary intuition that when consent is ambiguous, duties ought to be lesser.

Parent and child

It would seem to strain the idea of consent beyond meaning to imagine that the subjection of childhood is voluntary.[81] In this case, subjection really is entirely the decision of others. Hobbes nonetheless attempted to give a consensual account of parental authority. We can make sense of the account using the concept of cognitive consent, that is, the idea that acknowledging a role represents a kind of consent.[82]

"Paternall" dominion, *Leviathan* declares, "is not . . . derived from the Generation, as if therefore the Parent had Dominion over his Child because he begat him; but from the Childs Consent, either expresse, or by other sufficient arguments declared."[83] The latter – tacit consent – is obviously the operative concept, and in this instance it is linked to preservation. "It is to be presumed, that he which giveth sustenance to another, whereby to strengthen him, hath received a promise of obedience in consideration thereof."[84] Although the benefit implying tacit consent is different, as must needs be, from that of servants' liberty, the consequence is similar. One of the two questions Hobbes finds curious about parenthood is why anyone should nurture a potential enemy. Describing theirs as a contractual relationship meets the danger, just as the servant's consent protects the master. This is the passage in *The Elements of Law* in which the just-quoted account of the child's tacit consent appears:

And though the child thus preserved, do in time acquire strength, whereby he might pretend equality with him or her that hath preserved him, yet shall that pretence be thought unreasonable, both because his strength was the gift of him, against whom he pretendeth; and also because it is to be presumed, that he which giveth sustenance to another, whereby to strengthen him, hath received a promise of obedience in consideration thereof. For else it would be wisdom in men, rather to let their children perish, while they are infants, than to live in their danger or subjection, when they are grown.[85]

(The other question that preoccupies Hobbes is which parent has dominion. By nature, he decides, it is the mother, though civil law usually transfers the right to fathers.[86] His insistence that only one parent can have dominion is consistent with his account of political agency. It is impossible, *Leviathan* explains, for children to be subject equally to both parents, "for no man can obey two Masters.")[87]

Children are positively obliged to obedience and to acknowledge the benefit of parental care:

> And because the first instruction of Children, dependeth on the care of their Parents; it is necessary that they should be obedient to them, whilest they are under their tuition; and not onely so, but that also afterwards (as gratitude requireth,) they acknowledge the benefit of their education, by externall signes of honour.[88]

The latter duty – to acknowledge benefit by actions in adulthood – is suggestive of the idea of "cognitive" consent. These actions evidence a moral choice, and hence are indicative of consent, because they are counterfactual. Just as he puzzles why people should choose to parent, Hobbes also puzzles why children should honor their parents. Honor means "the estimation of anothers power."[89] But parents lose their power advantage as children grow.[90] Acknowledging the latter role means acting as though that were not so. "He who is freed from subjection, whether he be a *servant, sonne*, or some *colony*, doth promise all those externall signes, at least whereby *Superiours* used to be *Honour'd* by their inferiors."[91] As with children, servants' consent is evidenced by how they later treat their former masters. These roles have a bearing on hu-

man relationships that extends beyond the term of their existence; and in reverse, later actions show whether or not
they were consensual relationships in the first instance.

Childhood, service, and political subjection have several
parallel features. In each instance, to varying degree, the roles
are more given than actively chosen. Hobbes's consent accounts of the several roles correspond to common moral sense
in two significant respects. In all instances, the primary duties are negative: Subjects are enjoined against political resistance, servants may not kill their masters, nor children turn
on their parents. Second, positive duty consists specifically
in acknowledgment, which is the feature captured by the
concept of cognitive consent. Children ought to "acknowledge the benefit of their education, by externall signes of
honour"; a subject "is bound onely in honour, to acknowledgement, and an endeavour of requitall" of the sovereign's
commands. We commonly think that given roles require less,
only negative and limited positive duties, as Hobbes specifies, than roles that are undertaken in some more expressly
voluntary fashion, such as *Leviathan*'s soldier.

In sum, Hobbes treats the problem of citizen cooperation differently, and it is a lesser problem than individualistic commentaries presume. It is not his problem to explain why ordinary subjects should find it in their interest or (for the most
part) feel obliged to perform political duties because he rather
counts for political performance on special roles. Hence the
theory is a poor illustration of the characteristic problematic
of individualistic political thinking, public goods and the free
rider. Ordinary Hobbesian subjects have a strong obligation
to serve the community only when they are uniquely capable
of some specific service (when "the service cannot otherwise
be done," in Hobbes's words). Unlike public-goods dilemmas, these are situations in which it is not permissible for
anyone to free ride. Which is to say that the theory narrowly
limits instances of potential conflict between individuals' interest and state need. Such instances are limited by the
weakness of the obligations of simple subjects; and they are

limited, in the main, to individuals such as soldiers who have specially consented to serve and therefore have more reason to (be expected to) disregard self-interest.

Hobbes was not especially imaginative in describing the structure of society and the state, nor was he especially concerned with legitimizing a particular set of role and authority relationships.[92] His idea of the *Leviathan*-state, and the principal political actors therein, replicates the composition of the Stuart commonwealth, while his discussions of social-authority relationships rather evidently take their inspiration from Aristotle's classic comparisons in the *Politics*. Still, *Leviathan*'s addition of the role of the soldier evinces a recognition of the plasticity, the malleability, of political roles.[93] Perhaps the addition reflects a prudential estimation, born of the Civil War, of the greater reliability of a professional army as compared to armies raised on feudal lines.[94] In theoretical terms, the addition spells the recognition that roles can in some measure be manipulated by the state. There is more than one way to provide for necessary state functions.

At a more abstract level, Hobbes seems to have held the view that hierarchical authority per se is altogether necessary to social peace. "Each man," he remarks in *De Cive* in the course of discussing parental authority, "is an enemy to that other whom he neither obeys nor commands."[95] *Contra* the Aristotelian appeal to natural inequality to justify inegalitarian social and political relationships, and consonant with his own insistence that consent is the foundation of all legitimate authority, Hobbes locates the source of present inequalities in civil law.[96] To define the scope of subjection, he appeals to the principle of social utility. In the notable instance, political subjection is defined this way: "There is so much obedience joyn'd to this absolute Right of the Chief Ruler, as is necessarily requir'd for the Government of the City, that is to say, so much as that Right of his may not be granted in vaine."[97] This is as far as Hobbes goes, I think, toward moralizing the structural relationships constitutive of the *Leviathan*-state.

Chapter 6

The art of government

As if when Men quitting the State of Nature entered into Society, they agreed that all of them but one, should be under
the restraint of Laws, but that he should still retain all the Liberty of the State of Nature, increased with Power, and made
licentious by Impunity. This is to think that Men are so foolish
that they take care to avoid what Mischiefs may be done them
by *Pole-Cats*, or *Foxes*, but are content, nay think it Safety, to
be devoured by *Lions*.

John Locke, *The Second Treatise of Government*, section 93

In popular imagination, Hobbism has come to be identified with arbitrary despotism, even with twentieth-century
totalitarianism.[1] To be sure, Hobbes denies in principle the
distinction between good and bad government, describing
"tyranny" as but the term for monarchy misliked.[2] His formal permission of arbitrary rule inspires images of political
horror, like this picture of a mad king. "The citizen of
Hobbes's leviathan state is . . . faced with the terrifying ab-
surdity of finding himself totally obligated to obey an insane
individual who will not listen to Parliament's advice or seek
its assent, and who may be utterly incapable of protecting
and governing himself, much less the commonwealth."[3] But
more careful readers notice that Hobbes commends fair and
lawful government, directed to the common interest.[4] Chapter 30 of *Leviathan*, "Of the OFFICE of the Soveraign Representative," enjoins concern for the people's safety and prosperity, political education, promulgation of good laws, equal
justice and taxation, fair execution of punishments and re-

wards, and the discriminating choice of counselors and military commanders.

Noticing Hobbes's preference for good government is one thing; it is another thing to account this counsel an integral and significant part of the larger theory. The latter view faces several objections. On the supposition that Hobbism is a theory of obligation, which locates the source of state power in a supportive citizenry, his advice regarding the exercise of sovereignty has to be seen as a secondary part of the theory, tangential to the main account of the generation of sovereign power.[5] This first objection merely reflects the familiar bias of orthodox Hobbes studies. Second, there is a common inclination to juxtapose Hobbes's discussion of sovereigns' duties against his account of their rights, and to give the latter much more importance than the former. Mario Cattaneo, for instance, whose commentaries on Hobbes's juridical doctrine emphasize the "liberal" character of this part of the theory, nonetheless concedes there is a "contradiction between the absolute power of the prince and the principle of legality for the protection of the subject."[6] But this is erroneous. Hobbes intended his discussion of rulers' duties to complement the prescription of an absolutist constitution. The enumeration of sovereigns' duties in chapter 30 of *Leviathan* corresponds, as Table 2 shows, to the enumeration of sovereigns' rights in chapter 18.[7] The correspondence is illustrative of an appreciation for the bearing of the conduct of government, as well as its constitution, on the possibility of good political order.

The last and strongest objection to taking seriously Hobbes's recommendation of good government is simply that it seems implausible to expect a ruler possessing unconditional authority to heed the counsel. As the duty to govern well cannot be enforced by any human agency, it seems unlikely it would count for much in the calculations of a Hobbesian sovereign.[8] Thus the counsel stands as no more than a pious supplement to a theory that truly licenses tyranny. This is Locke's objection, and Hobbes himself took it seriously. He states the objection in *De Cive:* "If any man had

Table 2. *Sovereigns' rights and duties in* Leviathan

Chapter 18 "Of the RIGHTS of Soveraignes by Institution"	Chapter 30 "Of the OFFICE of the Soveraign Representative"
1. Foundation of the rights of sovereignty (p. 229) Applications of the principle of unconditional sovereignty (pp. 229–32)	1. Duty to maintain the essential rights of sovereignty (pp. 376–77)
2. Right to "Judge of what Doctrines are fit to be taught them" (p. 233)	2. Duty to teach the people (pp. 377–85): "The Essentiall Rights of Soveraignty" "Not to affect change of Government" "Nor adhere (against the Soveraign) to Popular men" "Nor to Dispute the Soveraign Power" "And to Honour their Parents" "And to avoyd doing of Injury" "And to do all this sincerely from the heart"
3. Right of legislating (p. 234)	3. Duty to make good, i.e., necessary and perspicuous, laws (pp. 387–89)
4. "Right of Judicature" (p. 234)	4. Duty to administer equal justice (p. 385)
5. "Right of making War, and Peace"; of levying money for armies; and of being chief commander (pp. 234–35)	5. Duty to tax equally (pp. 386–87); and to choose good – loyal and popular – army commanders (pp. 393–94)
6. Right of "choosing all Councellours, Ministers, Magistrates, and Officers" (p. 235)	6. Duty "to choose good Counsellours; I mean such" as cannot benefit from evil counsel, and are knowledgeable (pp. 391–93)
7. Power of reward and punishment (p. 235)	7. Duty "to make a right application of Punishments, and Rewards" (pp. 389–91)
8. Right of appointing "Lawes of Honour," e.g., titles (pp. 235–36)	8. Rulers should not show partiality toward "the great," as doing so encourages rebellion (pp. 385–86)

such a Right [of "Absolute Command"], the condition of the Citizens would be miserable: For thus they think, He will take all, spoil all, kill all; and every man counts it his onely happinesse that he is not already spoil'd and kill'd."⁹

There are three Hobbesian replies, the first of which is a negative argument weighing the hazard of wicked rule against the calamity of civil war:

The Power in all formes [of government], *if they be perfect enough to protect them,* is the same; not considering that the estate of

Man can never be without some incommodity or other; and that the greatest, that in any forme of Government can possibly happen to the people in generall, is scarce sensible, in respect of the miseries, and horrible calamities, that accompany a Civill Warre; or that dissolute condition of masterlesse men, without subjection to Lawes, and a coërcive Power to tye their hands from rapine, and revenge.[10]

There is more here than the cynical observation that government per se is a necessary evil in virtue of man's antisocial nature. Hobbes is making a narrower observation about the benefit of an absolutist constitution (i.e., a constitution in which "the [sovereign's] Power . . . is perfect enough to protect them") as a deterrent to civil war. The benefit outweighs the attendant danger of bad government: "He that hath strength enough to protect all, wants not sufficiency to oppresse all."[11] In the first instance, then, Hobbes grants that tyranny is a danger inherent to an absolutist constitution, but a risk to be accepted because the constitution deters the greater evil of civil war.

He also thinks, however, that rulers have moral and instrumental reasons for governing well. This is the root issue between Hobbes and constitutionalist thinkers. In the latter's view, legal restraint and popular accountability – the antitheses of unconditional sovereignty – are requisites of good rule. Absolutism is therefore rightly equated with arbitrary government. Hobbes, in this respect typical of royalists in the early Stuart period, distinguishes between the structure of sovereign authority and the conduct of government, "between the *Right*, and the *exercise* of supreme authority."[12] Ruling well is a natural-law duty for which rulers are accountable to God.[13] "And therefore," according to *De Cive*, "there is some security for Subjects in the Oaths which Princes take."[14] But Hobbesian skepticism about the tenets of positive religion precludes attaching strong weight to this consideration.[15] Whereas constitutionalist thinkers favor procedural mechanisms to promote good government, Hobbes counts on sovereigns' interest in ruling well. Duty coheres with interest: "For the duty of a sovereign consisteth in the good government of the people. . . . And as the art and duty of sovereigns consist in the same acts, so also doth their profit."[16]

The argument concerning interest attaches to the role or office of the sovereign, the "politique Person" as opposed to the natural man.[17] Hobbes is therefore only committed to showing that ruling well really is in sovereigns' interest, not to a strong assertion about the propensities of actual rulers. He draws the distinction as between reason and passion, attributing bad rule to "the affections and passions which reign in every one, as well monarch as subject; by which the monarch may be swayed to use that power amiss."[18] In context, which is the comparison of forms of government, this is less than the damaging admission that rationality is unlikely in rulers. Hobbes's immediate point is the greater likelihood of rational rule in a monarchy than in any other form of government. "Where the publique and private interest are most closely united," *Leviathan* claims, "there is the publique most advanced. Now in Monarchy, the private interest is the same with the publique."[19] Why this should be so, regarding hereditary monarchies at least, is suggested in *De Cive*. When the state is rulers' patrimony, there is dynastic reason for identifying personal with state interest: "We cannot on better condition be subject to any, then one whose interest depends upon our safety, and welfare; and this then comes to passe when we are the inheritance of the Ruler; for every man of his own accord endeavours the preservation of his inheritance."[20]

It improves the motivational plausibility of the role argument that the operative interest is the ubiquitous human passion of desire for power.[21] The secular motive is expressly contrasted, in *A Dialogue . . . of the Common Laws of England*, with the less certain constraint of divine punishment:

> For if, say they, the King may notwithstanding the law do what he please, and nothing to restrain him but the fear of punishment in the world to come, then, in case there come a king that fears no such punishment, he may take away from us, not only our lands, goods, and liberties, but our lives also

if he will. And they say true; but they have no reason to think he will, unless it be for his own profit; which cannot be, for he loves his own power; and what becomes of his power when his subjects are destroyed or weakened, by whose multitude and strength he enjoys his power, and every one of his subjects his fortune?[22]

The proposition that Hobbes must establish is that ruling in the public interest and according to law enhances sovereign power. Good government is also powerful government. Right makes might. Contrary to Cattaneo's view, the same desideratum governs Hobbes's consideration of the exercise of power as guides the argument for absolutism. Good rule, in the framework of unified, unconditional sovereign right, provides twin prescriptions for generating coercive authority. Hobbes's "art of government" is the antipode of Machiavellian statecraft. Both are preoccupied with the very real problems for early-modern rulers of consolidating central authority and controlling ambitious rivals. Only Hobbes holds that lawful, fair rule enhances power, while it is Machiavelli who endorses arbitrariness (arguing that for princes it is better to be unpredictable and feared than to be known and loved).[23] They also conceive the problem of good rule differently, Machiavelli focusing on rulers' personal characteristics, their *virtù*, and Hobbes on the incentives of the role.

THE GOVERNMENTAL ART

Having hitherto set forth how a body politic is made, and how it may be destroyed, this place requireth to say something concerning the preservation of the same. Not purposing to enter into the particulars of the art of government, but to sum up the general heads, wherein such art is to be employed, and in which consisteth the duty of him or them that have the sovereign power.

The Elements of Law, Part II, chapter ix, section 2

Like the arguments for absolutism, those concerning the exercise of power treat the problem from two sides: on the one hand, the positive prerequisites of power and, on the other, measures deterring challenges to sitting authority. Specifically, Hobbes holds that rulers have a positive interest in their subjects' well-being, and second, that good rule deters elite conflict and rebellion.

"If you be rich I cannot be poor." James I's well-known statement to Parliament is a Hobbesian argument.[24] *Salus populi* is the supreme law and duty of political rule, "by which must be understood, not the mere preservation of their lives, but generally their benefit and good."[25] Caring for the common good, meaning specifically the common wealth, also profits rulers. Hobbes has in mind the dependence of the state, and therefore the sovereign, on social prosperity. "The riches, power, and honour of a Monarch," *Leviathan* observes, "arise onely from the riches, strength and reputation of his Subjects. For no King can be rich, nor glorious, nor secure; whose Subjects are either poore, or contemptible, or too weak through want, or dissention, to maintain a war against their enemies."[26] Taxation, the state's supply, is the pertinent issue. "If therefore," Hobbes explains in *The Elements of Law*,

> the sovereign provide not so as that particular men may have means, both to preserve themselves, and also to preserve the public; the common or sovereign treasure can be none. And on the other side, if it were not for a common and public treasure belonging to the sovereign power, men's private riches would sooner serve to put them into confusion and war, than to secure or maintain them.[27]

Second, there is much that rulers can do to strengthen their position, and provide for public order, by way of deterring rebellion and elite conflict. The list of rulers' duties, which in *Leviathan* is framed to correspond to the list of sovereigns' rights, appears in the earlier versions of the political theory as a series of remedies to the causes of rebellion, although Hobbes's counsel remains substantially the same throughout.[28] According to *De Cive*, "Many things are required to the conservation of inward Peace, because many things concur (as hath been shewed in the foregoing Chapter) to its pertur-bation."[29] Specifically, Hobbes lists these "concurring" causes of rebellion: popular discontent, ambitious elites, ideological justification, and political organization.[30] Correspondingly, he commends equal taxation, as an antidote to discontent.[31] Equal justice, or the "constant application of rewards, and punishments," deters the ambitious.[32] Rulers ought also to root out false opinions and attack subversive factions.[33]

The following discussion focuses on two Hobbesian poli-cies, rule according to law and equal taxation. The first is crucial to the fearsome image of the *Leviathan*-state. The sec-ond addresses an essential constituent of coercive authority – supply, with an army, being the foundation of state and rulers' power.[34]

JURIDICAL RULE AND COERCIVE AUTHORITY

For the Ruler (as such) provides no otherwise for the safety of his people, then by his Lawes, which are universall; and there-fore he hath fully *discharged* himselfe, if he have thoroughly endeavoured by wholesome constitutions, to establish the welfare of the most part, and made it as lasting as may be.

De Cive, chapter xiii, section 3

Hobbes's political theory treats both jurisprudence, what law is, and juridical rule, the exercise of legislative and penal authority. Like his defense of absolutism, Hobbesian juris-prudence attacks parliamentary constitutional doctrine. In this instance, his target is the common-law doctrine that law is customary, made by judges, and Parliament is its guardian.[35] At issue, fundamentally, is "whose Reason it is, that shall be received for Law."[36] Against Coke's representation of the common law as the embodiment of an "Artificiall perfection of Reason," Hobbes insists that law must be authoritatively settled.[37] "But this is certain, seeing right reason is not exis-tent, the reason of some man, or men, must supply the place thereof; and that man, or men, is he or they, that have the sovereign power."[38] Law, then, is what the sovereign, in his public capacity, commands.[39]

As opposed to jurisprudence, our topic is juridical rule – why rule according to law is preferable to personal rule, and how juridical authority should be exercised. It is the difference between the *Dialogue . . . of the Common Laws*, a treatise on law, and the political treatises. A critique of common-law jurisprudence, the 1666, posthumously published *Dialogue* elaborates Hobbes's "command" theory of law into an analysis of the criminal justice system. Hobbes surveys kinds of courts, arguing that the king has authority over them all;[40] emphasizes the statutory definition of crime (with the exception of treason);[41] and catalogs punishments, again with an emphasis on the authority of the sovereign.[42] In the political treatises, the jurisprudential doctrine is accompanied by psychological and sociological discussions of the function of law and punishment. (Compare, for example, the accounts of punishment in the *Dialogue* and *Leviathan*. The former emphasizes the sovereign's penal authority, reiterating the familiar argument that punishment is an essential right of sovereignty.[43] *Leviathan*'s definition of punishment states, further, the purpose of punishment: "A PUNISHMENT, is an Evill inflicted by publique Authority, on him that hath done, or omitted that which is Judged by the same Authority to be a Transgression of the Law; to the end that the will of men may thereby the better be disposed to obedience.")[44]

Hobbes's political discussions of juridical rule have two themes, general conditions of social order and, more specifically, the art of deterring ambitious rivals. Under the former heading, he explains why government according to law is preferable to arbitrary rule, and offers standards of good lawmaking. It is in connection with the latter that Hobbes sanctions selective justice, meaning the discriminating – but not capricious – exercise of juridical authority.

"Arbitrary" rule usually refers, in Hobbesian usage, to personal rule and is the opposite of rule according to law (e.g., a punishment is "arbitrary" that has not been defined in law).[45] To start, Hobbes's critique of Coke implies a preference for rule by law. Because men naturally disagree and are therefore in conflict, "it was necessary there should be a

common measure of all things that might fall in controversy."[46] For the sovereign's judgments to function as that
common measure, a settled standard, they must take the form
of codified law. *De Cive* justifies legislative authority as an
essential sovereign right in these terms:

> Furthermore, since it no lesse, nay it much more conduceth to
> Peace to prevent brawles from arising, then to appease them
> being risen; and that all controversies are bred from hence,
> that the opinions of men differ concerning Meum & Tuum,
> just and unjust, profitable and unprofitable, good and evill,
> honest and dishonest, and the like, which every man esteems
> according to his own judgement; it belongs to the same chiefe
> power to make some common Rules for all men, and to declare
> them publiquely, by which every man may know what may
> be called his, what anothers, what just, what unjust. . . . But
> those Rules and measures are usually called the civill Lawes,
> or the Lawes of the City, as being the Commands of him who
> hath the supreme power in the City.[47]

The explanation of the bearing of law on social order hinges
on the deterrence proposition:"It much more conduceth to
Peace to prevent brawles from arising, then to appease them
being risen." Hobbes has in mind the idea that laws, with
appointed punishments, are efficacious in and of themselves
in controlling behavior. Action is governed, generally, by expectations and opinions ("the will of doing, or omitting ought,
depends on the opinion of the *good* and *evill* of the *reward*, or
punishment, which a man conceives he shall receive by the
act, or omission; so as the actions of all men are ruled by the
opinions of each").[48] Under this general psychological principle, juridical rule provides one way of manipulating opinion,[49] and political education is another.[50] Laws, *The Elements*
explains, supply a reason for action, distinct from calculations about the utility of an act. Whereas the latter reasoning
is appropriate to covenants ("in simple covenants the action
to be done, or not done, is first limited and made known,
and then followeth the promise to do or not do"),[51] in the
case of laws, "the command [itself] is the reason we have of
doing the action commanded."[52]

There are two motivations, by Hobbes's account, for obedience to law: the prior promise to obey the legislator (that is, the political covenant) and fear of punishment. The first is the formal ground of the obligation (according to *De Cive*, for example, "the *Law* holds the party obliged by vertue of the universall *Contract* of yeelding obedience");[53] the second supplies a prudential motive for obedience ("the Law . . . compells him to make good his promise, for fear of the punishment appointed by the Law").[54] Thus, unlike John Selden, another member of the Tew Circle, Hobbes does not conflate the obligatoriness of law with the sanction of punishment. In Selden's view, " 'The idea of a law carrying obligation irrespective of any punishment annexed to the violation of it . . . is no more comprehensible to the human mind than the idea of a father without a child' – i.e. [Richard Tuck comments] it is a logical and not contingent connexion."[55]

Still, Hobbes's position is virtually the same as Selden's inasmuch as he holds that it is fear of punishment that makes laws effectual. "Of all Passions, that which enclineth men least to break the Lawes, is Fear. Nay, (excepting some generous natures,) it is the onely thing, (when there is apparence of profit, or pleasure by breaking the Lawes,) that makes men keep them."[56] "Vindicative" – penal – sanctions are therefore an essential part of law. "In vain therefore is the Law, unlesse it contain both parts, that which *forbids* injuries to be done, and that which *punisheth* the doers of them."[57] In addition, the punishments appointed by law must be sufficient to the purpose of deterring crime. "We must therefore provide for our security, not by *Compacts*, but by *Punishments.*" According to *De Cive:*

> And there is then sufficient provision made, when there are so great punishments appointed for every injury, as apparently it prove a greater evil to have done it, then not to have done it: for all men, by a necessity of nature, chuse that which *to them appears to be the lesse evill.*[58]

However, the sanction is not always explicitly included in the law, and is then either "implicit," based on prior instances of punishment, or "arbitrary," dependent on the sovereign's will.[59]

"To the care of the Soveraign, belongeth the making of Good Lawes. But what is a good Law? By a Good Law, I mean not a Just Law: for no Law can be Unjust."[60] From the first proposition, the need for common rules of property and justice, nothing follows about the quality of law. But the accompanying psychological account of the bearing of laws and punishments on expectations, and therefore action, generates criteria for good law and the "right application" of punishment.[61] "A good law is that, which is *Needfull*, for the *Good of the People*, and withall *Perspicuous*."[62] It encourages obedience to limit legislation, as subjects are apt to forget or ignore laws when they are overabundant or otherwise obscure.[63] According to *De Cive*, the policy also encourages private enterprise: "As water inclosed on all hands with banks, stands still and corrupts . . . so subjects, if they might doe nothing without the commands of the Law would grow dull, and unwildly."[64] Brevity is similarly a virtue of good law, aiding understanding and deterring unnecessary litigation.[65] The third criterion falls under the larger claim that rulers have a stake in their subjects' well-being. It cannot be, *Leviathan* explains, that a good law benefits a ruler but not the ruled, "for the good of the Soveraign and People, cannot be separated."[66]

It is further necessary that penal authority be properly exercised because "the fear whereby men are deterred from doing evil, ariseth not from hence, namely, because penalties are set, but because they are executed; for we esteeme the future by what is past, seldome expecting what seldome happens."[67] *Leviathan*'s definition of punishment (quoted earlier) includes the stipulation that punishment should regard the future good (as opposed to the past evil, meaning punishment for revenge).[68] There follow a series of discriminations between acts of punishment and acts of "hostility." All "evil" inflicted without the intention or possibility of encouraging obedience is simply "hostility," including retribution in excess of penalties set by law. Inadequate penalties also fail to qualify, because then the penalty is rather the price for obtaining the benefit of the crime.[69] When a punishment is not specified in law, and is therefore "arbitrary," it should reflect the same policy of encouraging service to the state and deterring disobedience.[70]

Politic justice

Hobbes's preoccupation with discouraging those ambitious of political power enters into his discussion of juridical rule. All three works recommend the policy of "equal justice" as a means, specifically, "for the keeping under of those, that are disposed to rebellion by ambition."[71] The consistent execution of punishments helps control political ambition: "By constant application of rewards, and punishments, they may so order it, that men may know that the way to honour is, not by contempt of the present government, nor by factions, and the popular ayre, but by the contraries."[72] In reverse, Hobbes warns against rewarding popular and ambitious subjects, seeking to buy their adherence with money or flattery.[73] Partiality toward the "great" encourages insolence, which encourages hatred, which brings rebellion and the ruin of the state.[74]

Going along with this special emphasis on "constant severity in punishing" great and ambitious subjects, Hobbes recognizes and commends a series of politic discriminations in the administration of justice.[75] "Seeing the end of punishing is not revenge, and discharge of choler; but correction, either of the offender, or of others by his example; the severest Punishments are to be inflicted for those Crimes, that are of most Danger to the Publique."[76] The political criterion of punishment has wide-ranging application – to causes, persons, and crimes and their effects. Crimes that proceed from "malice to the Government established" and "contempt of Justice" are worse than "Crimes of Infirmity; such as are those which proceed from great provocation, from great fear, great need, or from ignorance."[77] Prominent persons, who teach and serve as examples to others, bear responsibility for the crimes they encourage, and therefore should be more severely treated:

> The Punishment of the Leaders, and teachers in a Commotion; not the poore seduced People, when they are punished, can profit the Common-wealth by their example. To be severe to the People, is to punish that ignorance, which may in great part be imputed to the Soveraign, whose fault it was, they were no better instructed.[78]

More generally, crimes by the vainglorious great, those who assume that wit, blood, or riches exempt them from punishment, "are not extenuated, but aggravated by the greatnesse of their persons; because they have least need to commit them."[79] Political crimes, for example, assassination attempts and giving secrets to the enemy, are more serious than crimes against private persons; accepting a bribe to perjure oneself is more serious than simple stealing, as are also robbing the public treasury and counterfeiting.[80] In short, the utilitarian principle applies: "The same fact, when it redounds to the dammage of many, is greater, than when it redounds to the hurt of few."[81] These distinctions technically concern the degree of responsibility for crime, excuses from crime, and extenuating circumstances.[82] But they introduce into Hobbesian theory, under the heading of the administration of justice, a substantive legal policy, a policy with more content than the criteria of good law associated with the general deterrent psychology of juridical rule.

Whereas Hobbesian absolutism and jurisprudence, his formal doctrines of sovereign right, license arbitrary rule and iniquitous law,[83] Hobbes's art of government is a normative account of the exercise of coercive and legislative authority. Rule according to law is preferable to personal rule, however fair, because laws and legally appointed punishments deter disobedience. Substantive criteria for legal policy, absent from Hobbesian jurisprudence, follow from that deterrent psychology and from its extension into a policy of discriminating, politic justice.

EQUAL TAXATION

To Equall Justice, appertaineth also the Equall imposition of Taxes.

Leviathan, chapter 30

Hobbes counts burdensome and inequitable taxation as one of the chief causes of popular discontent.[84] Prudence, as well as justice, therefore dictates equal taxation: "To remove . . . all just complaint, its the interest of the publique quiet, and by consequence it concernes the duty of the Magistrate, to see that the publique burthens be equally born."[85]

In this instance, the opinion, or perception, of fairness is a key prudential consideration,[86] and the first matter is the fairness of taxation itself. Among the seditious doctrines, commonly used to justify rebellion, is the claim that subjects have absolute dominion over their property – "by which they would pretend to contribute nothing to the public, but what they please."[87] Public revenue is an essential requisite for the performance of the sovereign's office, and taxation authority is therefore an essential right of sovereignty.[88] In *Leviathan*, commenting on the pretense that subjects have an exclusive property right, Hobbes offers what is evidently a report, an interested report, on Charles I's problems raising taxes: "From whence it commeth to passe, that the Soveraign Power, which foreseeth the necessities and dangers of the Common-wealth, (finding the passage of mony to the publique Treasure obstructed, by the tenacity of the people,) whereas it ought to extend it selfe, to encounter, and prevent such dangers in their beginnings, contracteth it selfe as long as it can, and when it cannot longer, struggles with the people by stratagems of Law, to obtain little summes."[89]

But why should every subject feel obliged to contribute to the public treasury? To answer the latter question, Hobbes casts taxation as a matter of individual benefit and debt. On one account, taxes are a debt owed rulers for the service of providing security; alternately, they are rulers' wages for the same.[90] What is fair taxation policy follows: "Seeing then the benefit that every one receiveth thereby, is the enjoyment of life, which is equally dear to poor, and rich; the debt which a poor man oweth them that defend his life, is the same which a rich man oweth for the defence of his."[91]

But Hobbes does not actually have in mind equal assessments, but rather "equal" taxation on consumption.[92] He defends the policy as both equitable and prudential. In the latter regard, it encourages private virtues that serve the public interest, namely, work and thrift:

> The Equality of Imposition, consisteth rather in the Equality of that which is consumed, than of the riches of the persons that consume the same. For what reason is there, that he which laboureth much, and sparing the fruits of his labour, consumeth little, should be more charged, then he that living idlely, getteth little, and spendeth all he gets; seeing the one hath no more protection from the Common-wealth, then the other? But when the Impositions, are layd upon those things which men consume, every man payeth Equally for what he useth: Nor is the Common-wealth defrauded, by the luxurious waste of private men.[93]

Finally, and perhaps most important, consumption taxes seem "least to trouble the mind of them that pay."[94]

However strained the connections between the several points in Hobbes's argument, the translation of the injunction to tax equally into the stipulation of equal indebtedness and that into the recommendation of taxing consumption, he presents the policy as one exemplifying the unity of duty, art, and profit in governing. The policy is fair; it eliminates a major source of popular discontent; and by encouraging private industry, it indirectly as well as directly benefits the public treasury.

CONCLUSION

Something striking follows from Hobbes's prudential accounts of the bearing of the conduct of government on the reality of political power. He holds rulers responsible for their fate and for their societies' character:

> This same *supreme command*, and *absolute power*, seems so harsh to the greatest part of men, as they hate the very naming of them; which happens chiefly through want of knowledge, what *humane nature*, and the *civill Lawes* are, and *partly also through their default, who when they are invested with so great authority, abuse their power to their own lust*.[95]

Political responsibility, of course, is the topic, as opposed to the formal accountability denied by the absolutist constitution. Still, Hobbes describes rebellion as the "naturall punishment" of negligent government.[96] Furthermore, the "poore seduced People" in a rebellion ought not to be punished severely inasmuch as the sovereign is also at fault for not better instructing them.[97] Short of rebellion, subjects' crimes are extenuated by inconsistent punishment or tacit approval (e.g., duels) on the sovereign's part. In such cases, too, the sovereign "is in part a cause of the transgression"; he "hath his part in the offence."[98] Last, if "the Legislator doth set a lesse penalty on a crime, then will make our feare more considerable with us, then our lust; that excesse of lust above the feare of punishment, whereby sinne is committed, is to be attributed to the Legislator (that is to say) to the supreme";[99] or, as *Leviathan* puts it, such law is an "invitement" to crime.[100]

Assigning responsibility to rulers – to government – is a classic political response to individualistic, moral and psychological, treatments of public goods. The view is articulated by the figure of the "Defaulter" in Colin Strang's dialogue on the principle of universalization (viz., the moral argument that individuals must ask themselves what would happen if everyone acted as they proposed to act):

> If anyone is to blame it is the person whose job it is to circumvent [e.g.,tax] evasion. If too few people vote, then it should be made illegal not to vote. If too few people volunteer, then you must introduce conscription. If too many people evade taxes, then you must tighten up your system of enforcement.

My answer to your "If everyone did that" is "Then someone had jolly well better see to it that they don't."[101]

Hobbes states the same proposition in *Leviathan*'s introductory, metaphorical description of the commonwealth: "*Reward* and *Punishment* (by which fastned to the seate of the Soveraignty, every joynt and member is moved to performe his duty) are the *Nerves*, that do the same in the Body Naturall."[102] From the introduction of conscription in *Leviathan* to furnish an army, through the recommendation of a tax policy that will "least . . . trouble the mind of them that pay," and the recommendation that juridical rule promotes obedience and order, Hobbes translates political and social problems into problems of governmental policy. This of course does not commit him to the strong negative proposition that rulers bear exclusive responsibility.[103] At issue are the relative significance of governmental versus civic virtue in Hobbes's political understanding and the way in which he thinks about subjects' duties.[104] In this chapter and the preceding one, I have argued that Hobbes reflects first on governmental policy – how civic performance can be structured and encouraged by the state – and only secondarily calculates in terms of citizens' virtue and self-interest.

Last, Hobbes supplies good reasons why rulers ought to govern well, and defines good rule, which is different from and lesser than a defense of the proposition that good rule is expectable. The stronger claim, about the benevolence of Hobbesian absolutism, depends on the plausibility of the identification of role and personal interests. Although an interest in coercive authority may be inherent to the office of the sovereign, this does not assure that actual rulers may not desire other goods more than power, or may not perceive some discrepancy between the pursuit of power for themselves and the requisites of a strong state.[105] It is an objection that Hobbes both grants (e.g., "all the acts of *Nero* are not essentiall to Monarchie")[106] and discounts, especially with regard to this relatively best form of government. The problem of translating institutional roles into descriptions of role occupants' intentions is a characteristic problem of structural political analyses.[107] For all that, it is one thing to charge, with Locke, that a benevolent *Leviathan*-state is implausible, and another to dismiss Hobbes's art of government as a trivial part of the political theory.

Chapter 7

Hobbes's political sensibility

Hobbes's seventeenth-century audience, familiar with Scripture, would have readily understood the title imagery of *Leviathan* and *Behemoth*.[1] These are sea and land monsters in the Biblical story of Job. Leviathan and behemoth were popular symbols of the great and mighty of the world.[2] As emblems for the subject matter of writings on politics, they telegraph an elitist conception of the political world, an analysis trained on rulers and would-be rulers. But leviathan and behemoth are also characters in the tale of a victim. Job is an ordinary and innocent man made to suffer by an omnipotent God. The Epicurean mood of the story, a fatalistic sense that common people are pawns and victims of fortune, was prevalent in England during the late Civil War and early Interregnum periods.[3] Hobbes's political sensibility has this second side, which complements his preoccupation with elite politics and the constitution of sovereign authority. He identifies with ordinary subjects, and thinks an absolutist constitution serves their interest. Figuratively, the political theory is about leviathan and behemoth, but it speaks to Job.

Leviathan and behemoth are made to stand for the central institutions on the Hobbesian political landscape, a strong state and an ambitious Parliament. The introduction to *Leviathan* famously identifies the sea monster with the state: "For by Art is created that great LEVIATHAN called a COMMONWEALTH."[4] The art Hobbes has in mind is human artifice, especially his own political theory. He says of the work's political covenant that it describes "the Generation of . . . that

Mortall God, to which wee owe under the *Immortall God*, our peace and defence."[5] Toward the conclusion of Part II, he again compares the power of the state to the power of leviathan:

> Hitherto I have set forth the nature of Man, (whose Pride and other Passions have compelled him to submit himselfe to Government;) together with the great power of his Governour, whom I compared to *Leviathan*, taking that comparison out of the two last verses of the one and fortieth of *Job;* where God having set forth the great power of *Leviathan*, called him King of the Proud. *There is nothing*, saith he, *on earth, to be compared with him. He is made so as not to be afraid. Hee seeth every high thing below him; and is King of all the children of pride.*[6]

Continuing the allusion, Hobbes gave the title *Behemoth or The Long Parliament* to the history of the Civil War that he wrote after the Restoration.[7] He did not intend it to be a descriptive history of the war, but only meant to tell the story of the "injustice, impudence, and hypocrisy," the "knavery, and folly" of that Parliament. These were men "resolved to acknowledge for law nothing that was against their design of abolishing monarchy, and placing a sovereign and absolute arbitrary power in the House of Commons."[8]

This description of *Behemoth* gives concrete political meaning to *Leviathan*'s image of the state as "King of the Proud."[9] Earlier chapters of the present study have detailed the complexity of Hobbes's idea of the state. He sees a network of roles and offices (chapter 5) and distinguishes, more informally, great from ordinary subjects (chapter 6). In the world of politics as Hobbes conceives it, elite actors are the principal figures. Ordinary subjects are subordinate figures on the landscape, followers who "receive their motion" from rulers and those who would be rulers. In these terms, he warns in *Leviathan*:

> The Popularity of a potent Subject . . . is a dangerous Disease; because the people (which should receive their motion from the Authority of the Soveraign,) by the flattery, and by the

reputation of an ambitious man, are drawn away from their obedience to the Lawes.[10]

It ignores Hobbes's elite frame of reference to suppose that he thinks about politics in the fashion of a political individualist, generalizing political conclusions from propositions about the rights, obligations, and motivation of subjects in the abstract. To his mind, ambitious elites such as the membership of the Long Parliament pose the principal threat to a strong, a leviathan-like, state. "Those men are of most trouble to the Republique," he writes in *De Cive*, "who have most leasure to be idle; for they use not to contend for publique places before they have gotten the victory over hunger, and cold."[11] Political ambition, as opposed to political obligation, is the central problem of the political theory. Controlling political ambition is the theme of Hobbes's theoretical analysis of politics, just as it was also his more immediate, polemical purpose to fight the current outbreak of political ambition. The Hobbesian case for absolutism, specifically monarchic absolutism, as the best form of government in general rests on the claim that the constitution deters elite power struggles. *Leviathan's* warning about the menace of popular "potent Subject[s]" continues, for example, with a typical comparison between constitutions: "And this is commonly of more danger in a Popular Government, than in a Monarchy; because an Army is of so great force, and multitude, as it may easily be made believe, they are the People."[12] Hobbes obviously has Cromwell in mind. We have seen that his arguments, about rights, authorization, and representation, as well as his narrowly constitutional arguments, refute ideologies used to justify the present rebellion.

But it is Job's tale in the end. Hobbes tells the Biblical story in *De Cive* and *Leviathan*. Its topic, he begins by observing, is that ancient moral question, "Why Evill men often Prosper, and Good men suffer Adversity."[13] There are two ways of viewing the question, through the eyes of God and from Job's perspective. On the one hand, "This question in the case of *Job*, is decided by God himselfe, not by arguments derived from *Job's* Sinne, but his own Power."[14] The immediate point to telling the story is the peculiar nature of divine sovereignty. Whereas political authority must be created by the artifice of consent, God and God alone possesses sufficient natural power to rule solely on this basis.[15] But Job's suffering has another moral, besides divine omnipotence. Seen from the perspective of the victim, it is a tale of injustice and the irrationality of fortune. "How bitterly did *Job* expostulate with God, that being *just*, he should yet be afflicted with so many calamities."[16]

By 1647 at the latest, Hobbes had come to see that the political theory takes Job's side.[17] The preface to the second edition of *De Cive* addresses the work to ordinary subjects.[18] Understand, Hobbes says, that you are victimized by elite power struggles. In the conflicts of the great, common people suffer. The moral is the quietistic injunction to refuse to follow:

> Weighing the justice of those things you are about, not by the perswasion and advise of private men, but by the Lawes of the Realme, you will no longer suffer ambitious men through the streames of your blood to wade to their owne power; . . . you will esteeme it better to enjoy your selves in the present state though perhaps not the best, then by waging Warre, indeavour to procure a reformation for other men in another age, your selves in the meane while either kill'd, or consumed with age.[19]

Similar sentiments are expressed in *Leviathan*, in portions of the theory that were likely written after 1647. The "Review and Conclusion" recommends the teaching of the theory in university: "By that means the most men, knowing their Duties, will be the less subject to serve the Ambition of a few discontented persons, in their purposes against the State; and be the lesse grieved with the Contributions necessary for their Peace, and Defence."[20]

Claiming that this political theory serves the interest of common people means claiming, in specific, that an absolutist constitution benefits them. In one of his last works, the

Dialogue . . . of the Common Laws, Hobbes left the following autobiographical statement. In it, he identifies with ordinary subjects and pleads his and their interest in absolute monarchy:

> I [the "Philosopher"] am one of the common people, and one of that almost infinite number of men, for whose welfare Kings and other sovereigns were by God ordained: for God made Kings for the people, and not people for Kings. How shall I be defended from the domineering of proud and insolent strangers that speak another language, that scorn us, that seek to make us slaves, or how shall I avoid the destruction that may arise from the cruelty of factions in a civil war, unless the King, to whom alone, you say, belongeth the right of levying and disposing of the militia by which only it can be prevented, have ready money, upon all occasions, to arm and pay as many soldiers, as for the present defence, or the peace of the people, shall be necessary? Shall not I, and you, and every man be undone?[21]

The statement can serve to summarize the two sides of Hobbes's political vision. On the one hand, there is his constitutional and elitist political analysis, which treats the political dynamics attending absolute and divided sovereignty and focuses on elite political actors. On the other hand, Hobbes identifies with, and appeals to, ordinary subjects. They are secondary figures in the political analysis, but his advice to them complements that analysis and serves the aim of controlling political ambition. Ordinary people ought to recognize they are best off under absolute monarchy. "Whosoever . . . in a *Monarchy* will lead a retired life, let him be what he will that Reignes, he is out of danger: for the ambitious onely suffer, the rest are protected from the injuries of the more potent."[22] They ought not "suffer ambitious men through the streames of your blood to wade to their owne power."

THE ENGAGEMENT CONTROVERSY

After the war, in the early years of the Interregnum, Hobbes's theory was deployed in, and adapted to, a political debate

about subjects' obligations. In October 1649, following the
execution of the king, abolition of the House of Lords, and
establishment of the Commonwealth of England, the Rump
Parliament exacted an oath of allegiance from most literate
Englishmen. The oath, to be "true and faithful to the Commonwealth of England, as it is now Established, without a
King or House of Lords," was extended, the following January, to apply to all adult male citizens eighteen years of age
and older.[23] The Engagement Oath posed for subjects the
problem of resolving their political loyalties and obligations,
but what was at stake was the legitimacy of the new regime.
In the period in which the oath was promulgated, Cromwell's government was threatened both by Leveller agitation
for more radical change and by the danger of continued royalist resistance.[24] Similar in this respect to the prewar constitutional debates, the ensuing Engagement Controversy was
a debate about whose leadership to follow in confusing political circumstances.

All three versions of Hobbes's political theory appeared in
print, in English, in this period: *The Elements of Law* was published in the spring of 1650; an English translation of *De Cive*
came out in March 1651, and *Leviathan* was published soon
thereafter.[25] Furthermore, apologists for the Commonwealth
invoked Hobbes's authority, the two notable instances being
Anthony Ascham's *Of the Confusions and Revolutions of Governments* (1649) and Marchamont Nedham's *The Case of the
Commonwealth of England, Stated* (1650).[26] Describing Hobbes
as an authority among royalists, Nedham excerpted *De Corpore Politico* (the second section of *The Elements of Law*) in an
appendix to the second edition of his work. He meant to
"foil our adversaries with weapons of their own approba-
tion."[27] It was an application of the theory that Hobbes himself endorsed in *Leviathan*'s "Review and Conclusion." Making explicit reference to the current situation, the chapter treats
the engagement questions, "What point of time it is, that a
Subject becomes obliged to the Conqueror; . . . how it comes
about, that it obliges men to obey his Laws."[28] Hobbes's short
answer, ignoring differences in the obligations attaching to

various roles, is a maxim that figured prominently in the Engagers' case: there is a "mutuall Relation between Protection and Obedience."[29]

It seems paradoxical that a political theory framed in denunciation of the parliamentary rebellion, and offering a sustained critique of the parliamentarians' constitutional ideology, should have been used after the war to support the new regime. The explanation lies in understanding the nature of the latter context. It was the terms of the Engagers' case that made Hobbesian arguments useful and relevant. A dominant theme, the theme of Ascham's and Nedham's treatises, was the proposition that obedience is owed de facto authority.[30] This was something less, to say the least, than an ardent republican defense of the Commonwealth. By contrast, the "official" theory of the Commonwealth, put forward in a parliamentary *Declaration* of March 1649, and defended by John Goodwin and in Milton's *Tenure of Kings and Magistrates* (1649), reiterated the traditional parliamentary ideology of ultimate popular sovereignty and royal accountability.[31] Hobbism could never have been fitted to that official constitutional doctrine. The theory was also inimical to a third strand of engagement argument, in this instance by virtue of Hobbes's "atheistic" skepticism of all specific accounts of Christian doctrine. Francis Rous, John Dury, and others recommended submission to the present government on providential grounds.[32] Appealing to the authority of Romans 13, a classic text in non-resistance doctrines, they defended the view that God ordains the powers that be.[33] What lent Hobbes's theory to the Engagers' position was its Epicurean themes, as opposed to its constitutional and religious arguments.

To see Hobbism through the filter of the Engagement Controversy, compare the preface to the 1647 edition of *De Cive* and *Leviathan*'s "Review and Conclusion" with Ascham's *Confusions and Revolutions of Governments* and Nedham's *Case of the Commonwealth*. These sections of Hobbes's theory make evident, and at some points explicit, reference to the parochial context of the late Civil War and early Interregnum period. The comparison shows how the two sides of Hobbes's political vision came to be separated in the Engagement Controversy. His appeal to common people to obey present powers was pertinent; not so the Hobbesian political analysis justifying an absolutist state.

There is a great similarity in temper between the *De Cive* preface and Ascham's work, both of which date from the late Civil War period. (The second edition of *De Cive* appeared early in 1647; Ascham's *Discourse*, the first edition of his work, in the summer of 1648.)[34] Hobbes, at the beginning of the preface, reiterates his usual attack on the parliamentary doctrine of conditional sovereignty,[35] but the accent is on that other quintessential Hobbesian theme: "The greatest inconvenience that can happen to a commonwealth, is the aptitude to dissolve into civil war."[36] Noting his "grief for the present calamities of his country," he asks readers to consider *De Cive*'s arguments in a non-partisan spirit, "since they are not so much spoken for the maintenance of parties, as the establishment of peace."[37] Ascham had the opposite partisan sympathies. He was to become the representative of the Commonwealth in Spain, where he would be assassinated by royalists in June 1650.[38] But the *Confusions and Revolutions of Governments* is not written in a partisan spirit.[39] The introduction rules out questions about the just causes for civil war on the ground that these pertain to the beginning stages of a war. Ascham means to focus on issues that arise later on, namely, "how farre a man may lawfully submit to, and obey opposite parties, during the confusions of War actually formed and introduced" and "what may be lawfull for a man to submit to upon the issue of a Warre, which may end to the advantage of him who by unjust force hath possest himselfe of anothers right."[40]

The calamity of civil war, hatred of political ambition, empathy for the suffering of ordinary people – these themes of Hobbes's preface are also Ascham's themes. Common people, the latter puts it, are not "the first movers of . . . calamitous confusions" but are "afterwards by a strict necessity involv'd in them."[41] Echoing Hobbes's appeal for political quiescence, Ascham asks ordinary people to see that they are victimized by the power struggles of the great. Civil war, he writes, "disorders all the other relations of Justice":

> The worst of all this is, that many times ambitious or angry men forme subtilties and pretences, and afterwards the poore people (who understand them not) are taken out of their houses . . . to fight and maintaine them at the perils of one anothers lives; and such Wars not being of their Interest, they are sure to reap nothing but desolation by them.[42]

The sensibility that Hobbes and Ascham, and many others, shared is beautifully described by John M. Wallace in the first chapter of his study of Andrew Marvell, *Destiny His Choice.* Beginning in the late Civil War period but especially after the execution of the king in 1649, an Epicurean mood in the vein of the tale of Job swept the country.[43] The opposite of exultation for a victorious cause, what prevailed was a somber awareness of the destruction wrought by the Civil War and an overwhelming desire for peace. Wallace labels the mood "loyalist," a loyalist being the opposite of a partisan, and the term referring especially to those many Englishmen who, like Hobbes, supported whichever side held power because it was peace they wanted above all else.[44] Hobbes could, in *Leviathan*, endorse the use of his theory to justify Cromwell's regime, and himself come home and swear the Engagement Oath, for the same reason that Ascham forswore trumpeting the success of his cause, out of the shared knowledge that civil war is the worst evil, and peace the most desirable thing.[45]

At the heart of the secular case for engagement was a simple answer to Ascham's question "What may be lawfull for a man to submit to upon the issue of a Warre?" Protection entails obedience.[46] Ascham, Nedham, and Hobbes in *Leviathan's* "Review and Conclusion" state the principle in virtually identical terms: "Protection infers publique obedience"; "protection implies a return of obedience and friendship from the persons protected to those that protect them"; there is a "mutuall Relation between Protection and Obedience."[47] While supplying a straightforward answer to the immediate question whether the Engagement Oath should be sworn, the general principle was ambiguous in two notable respects: How extensive are subjects' obligations? Second, does de facto power imply a right to rule? Does might make right?

The strongest evidence of a reciprocal influence between Hobbes and Ascham lies in their similar treatments, in the *Confusions and Revolutions of Governments* and *Leviathan*'s "Review and Conclusion," of the scope of subjects' obligations.[48] On the one hand, Ascham marks the limits of their obligations with a familiar Hobbesian principle: "A man cannot by oath, or any other way be oblig'd further to any power, then to do his utmost in the behalfe thereof."[49] For example, he continues:

> In an Army each man is or may be oblig'd by oath to lose his life for the Prince whose Army it is, rather then turn back or avoid any danger; such an oath is call'd *Sacramentum militare;* This Army after having done its utmost, is beaten, and now the Souldiers can do no more for their Prince then die, which indeed is to do nothing at all, but to cease from ever doing any thing, either for him or themselves. In these streights therefore it is not repugnant to their oath to aske quarter or a new life; and having taken it, they are bound in a new, and a just obligation of fidelity to those whom they were bound to kill few hours before.[50]

This assertion that a soldier's obligations end when his army is beaten anticipates *Leviathan*'s "Review and Conclusion." There, to recall, Hobbes stipulates that a soldier is obliged to fight as long as his army "keeps the field, and giveth him means of subsistence," but "when that also failes, a Souldier also may seek his Protection wheresoever he has most hope to have it; and may lawfully submit himself to his new Master."[51] In the same context, Hobbes also paraphrases a rationalization for submission by the propertied to the present government that had been suggested by Ascham: "Besides, if a man consider that they who submit, assist the Enemy but with part of their estates, whereas they that refuse, assist him with the whole, there is no reason to call their Submission, or Composition an Assistance, but rather a Detriment to the Enemy."[52] In Ascham's words: "If they refuse to submit in such a case, then they doe that which advantages their Enemies: Because at that time they will take all, whereas in case of submission they aske but a part."[53]

More generally, Ascham's discussions of subjects' obligations employ a distinction between passive and active obedience that is similar to the distinction in Hobbesian casuistry between prima facie and strong obligations. In Ascham's usage, passive obedience means more than non-resistance, and includes paying taxes and fighting when pressed into military service, whereas active obedience includes serving in government and swearing to a regime's legitimacy.[54] This concept of passive obedience parallels the Hobbesian assumption (as I have labeled it) of prima facie obligation. Both Ascham and Hobbes, that is to say, assume certain essential forms of civic cooperation, namely, paying taxes and fighting for the state. Furthermore, Ascham offers a Hobbist rationale for the assumption: "Security or Protection being here the chief end, it is suppos'd always that we must contribute our obedience and riches so farre as may best conduce to the security both of our owne persons and estates, and of theirs also who command us, without which contributions, it were not called Society."[55] On the other side, both distinguish passive obedience or prima facie obligation from active cooperation, the latter encompassing governmental service and the special military obligation of soldiers.

In this way, the principle "Protection entails obedience" rationalized cooperation with the new regime in the performance of customary political duties. It also addressed the threat of continued resistance from royalists and others. In this vein, the second part of Nedham's *Case* surveys the designs of various discontented parties – royalists, Scots, Presbyterians, and Levellers. In all cases, he argues, their plans are unlikely to succeed and inconvenient to the nation.[56] But the principle left open the important question of the legitimacy of the Commonwealth. And regarding this question, Ascham and Nedham conspicuously disagreed. Insisting that discussion of subjects' duties be separated from debate over the rights of various parties to rule, the former meant only to show that obedience is due de facto authority.[57] Nedham intended the stronger claim that might makes right: "The present prevailing party in England have a right and just title to be our governors."[58] It was an issue on which Hobbes contradicted himself in *Leviathan* and *Behemoth*. *Leviathan*'s "Review and Conclusion" endorses Nedham's position. In virtue of the express or tacit consent of the conquered, Hobbes argues, conquest yields a right to sovereignty: "So that *Conquest* (to define it) is the Acquiring of the Right of Soveraignty by Victory. Which Right, is acquired, in the peoples Submission, by which they contract with the Victor, promising Obedience, for Life and Liberty."[59] But in *Behemoth*, written after the Restoration, he would distinguish between the right to sovereign power and its exercise, and insist that the Stuarts retained the right of sovereignty throughout the Civil War period.[60]

But if there was much about Hobbism that was congenial to the Engagers' case, his constitutional doctrine was not. Ascham preached indifference to the form of government: "Wee can turne to no sort of government which hath not in the very constitution of it a power to wrong us in all the parts of Distributive Justice, Reward, and Punishment."[61] For the lives of ordinary men, it does not matter who governs. "Forsomuch therefore as concernes this anxious life of ours, which is begun and ended in very few dayes, what matters it under whose government we, who are thus hourely expiring, Live, if they, (who ere they be that rule over us) command us not Impious things?"[62] In the late war period, this fatalistic stance held some attraction for Hobbes. The 1647 preface to *De Cive* advises subjects, in Ascham's vein, "Esteeme it better to enjoy your selves in the present state though perhaps not the best, then by waging Warre, indeavour to procure a reformation for other men in another age, your selves in the meane while either kill'd, or consumed with age."[63] It is here, as well, that Hobbes professes uncertainty about his proof of the superiority of monarchy.[64] But alongside the counsel of political quietism, he continues to attack parliamentary ideology:

How many Kings (and those good men too) hath this one errour, That a Tyrant King might lawfully be put to death, been the slaughter of? How many throats hath this false position cut, That a Prince for some causes may by some certain men be deposed? And what blood-shed hath not this erroneous doctrine caused, That Kings are not superiours to, but administrators for the multitude? Lastly, how many rebellions hath this opinion been the cause of, which teacheth that the knowledge whether the commands of Kings be just or unjust, belongs to private men, and that before they yeeld obedience, they not only may, but ought to dispute them?[65]

The political theory that Hobbes had framed before the Civil War could encompass indifference to the personnel of government, but not Ascham's indifference to the constitution of government. Their disagreement goes deeper than a difference of opinion about the constitution of government. They hold fundamentally different outlooks on politics. A sensibility of the loyalist sort, attuned to the suffering of ordinary people in elite political struggles, often issues, as it did for Ascham, in an apolitical disregard for effective differences among kinds of government.[66] But it is also often the accompaniment, as in Hobbesian theory, of a very political concern for the bearing of political institutions on political and social order. Hobbes's analytic focus on the institutional and political causes of civil war, the basis of his absolutist doctrine, is the opposite of Ascham's resigned view of all government.

Nedham and Hobbes simply espoused opposing constitutional doctrines. As its title indicates, *The Case of the Commonwealth of England, Stated* combines arguments for obedience to de facto authority with republican ideology. In chapter 4, for instance, Nedham appeals to the principle of majority rule to justify the title of a conqueror: "A Government Erected by a Prevailing Part of the People Is as Valid *de jure* As If It Had the Ratifying Consent of the Whole."[67] This was a political opinion that Hobbes, it will be recalled from chapter 3 of the present study, was specially concerned to refute.[68] The last chapter of Nedham's work, "A Discourse of the Excellency of a Free State above a Kingly Government," defends the view that a republic is the best form of government and offers the best protection against both tyranny and civil war. It was for this "invaluable jewel of liberty" that the war was fought.[69] *Leviathan's* "Review and Conclusion," alongside the iteration of themes from the Engagers' brief, also reiterates the prescription of an absolutist constitution. "In the 29. Chapter," Hobbes reminds readers, "I have set down for one of the causes of the Dissolutions of Common-wealths, their Imperfect Generation, consisting in the want of an Absolute and Arbitrary Legislative Power."[70]

Hobbes could shift partisan allegiance with regime changes in a loyalist fashion. He could, in the 1647 *De Cive* preface and in *Leviathan's* "Review and Conclusion," accentuate old themes to suit the current mood. But he remained throughout an absolutist, sure that unified and unconditional sovereignty offers the best prescription against civil war and therefore offers the happiest political circumstance for ordinary subjects. The Engagers, making the case for the Commonwealth of England, had concrete political reason for ignoring this other side of Hobbes's political understanding. Some views they held in common, principally a sensitivity to the suffering of ordinary people in the power struggles of the great and an accompanying preoccupation with political ambition. What they did not hold in common was a theory of politics.

CONCLUSION: THE "HOBBESIAN PARADOX"

In a way, Hobbism's fate in the Engagement Controversy presages its fate over a much longer span of history. It is now commonly considered a bifurcated and indeed paradoxical theory of politics. The "paradox of Hobbism" is seen to lie in its derivation of absolutist conclusions from liberal-individualist premises of natural right, consent, and individual self-interest.[71] A summary of the errors in this view is an appropriate note on which to conclude the present study.

Political principles, Ian Shapiro nicely observes, are not "intrinsically radical or conservative: radical ideas in one context become conservative in another and sometimes vice versa."[72] Although the premises of Hobbesian theory, notably the concept of natural right, appear to us as recognizably liberal in character, they were not so in the period. Richard Tuck has shown that at its origin the modern, secular idea of rights was a conservative idea. It was characteristic of conservative Grotian thinkers in the early-modern period to justify absolutism on rights premises. The way in which Hobbes went about doing this (in *De Cive* and *Leviathan*) was unusual in combining recognition of an unalienated individual right of self-defense with the absolutist doctrine of non-resistance. Although he was an iconoclastic Grotian thinker, the enterprise itself of defending absolutism by using rights arguments was a familiar one within the frame of that tradition.[73]

Second, the idea of the "Hobbesian paradox" distorts his argument for absolutism by casting it in abstract and universalistic terms. The Hobbesian argument does not take the form of the proposition that individuals in the abstract should find it in their interest to consent to absolute government. His defense is informed, as individualistic commentaries all too often are not,[74] by a sensitivity to social and political hierarchy. Hobbes distinguishes elite political actors from ordinary subjects, and appeals to the latter to see that they suffer from elite political conflicts and that an absolutist constitution therefore benefits them by inhibiting the ambitions of those who would be sovereign. He did not idealize us, holding "the folly of the common people" as well as "the eloquence of ambitious men" responsible for the Civil War.[75] But he thought absolute monarchy best served the ordinary man's desire for a "retired life."[76]

This last is not a paradoxical argument, only an argument foreign to our own received ideas about the political constitution that offers the most protection for ordinary people. Its plausibility hinges, to begin with, on the diagnosis of the prime threat that the political world holds for ordinary lives. Whereas liberals emphasize endangerment by coercive government and socialists count powerlessness, especially economic, the worst evil, Hobbes focuses on the victimization of common people in the power struggles of political elites. The plausibility of the diagnosis is a function, in turn, of the political context.[77] Hobbes had in view a weak early-modern state lacking in the resources to interfere systematically in the lives of ordinary people.[78] Admittedly he did not see absolutism as a local prescription for a particular kind of state. Within the theory, however, the pertinent political conditions and causal processes are stated with some precision. Hobbes presupposes a world in which generating coercive sovereign authority and controlling elite conflict are the leading political problems. Divided sovereignty, the alternative to an absolutist constitution, carries the twin risks of incapacitating government and exacerbating elite conflict. Divided sovereignty gives rise to civil war, Hobbes explains, because it legitimizes bids for power by ambitious elites. The causal process further requires that elites and masses share the opinion that it is permissible to escalate elite political conflict into armed struggle. The Hobbesian defense of absolutism comes down to the contention that in such circumstances, which are not limited to early-modern Europe, ordinary lives are at greater risk from political ambition than from tyrannous government. Finally, also, there is a commonsense realism of more general currency to Hobbes's understanding that common people are foot soldiers in the world of politics.

Notes

CHAPTER 1. INTRODUCTION

1   Howard Warrender, *The Political Philosophy of Hobbes: His Theory of Obligation* (Oxford: Clarendon Press, 1957), p. vii.
2   Raymond Polin, *Politique et Philosophie chez Thomas Hobbes* (Paris: Presses Universitaires de France, 1953), pp. 240–41 (translation mine).
3   Thomas Hobbes, *Leviathan*, ed. C. B. Macpherson (Harmondsworth: Penguin [Pelican Books], 1968), chapter 17, p. 227.
4   Ibid., p. 226.
5   Ibid. 29, pp. 363–64.
6   Margaret Atwood Judson, "Henry Parker and the Theory of Parliamentary Sovereignty," in *Essays in History and Political Theory in Honor of Charles Howard McIlwain* (Cambridge, Mass.: Harvard University Press, 1936), pp. 138–67; and W. K. Jordan, *Men of Substance: A Study of the Thought of Two English Revolutionaries, Henry Parker and Henry Robinson* (Chicago: University of Chicago Press, 1942).
7   W. H. Greenleaf, "Hobbes: The Problem of Interpretation," in Maurice Cranston and Richard S. Peters (eds.), *Hobbes and Rousseau: A Collection of Critical Essays* (Garden City, N.Y.: Doubleday [Anchor Books], 1972), pp. 6–11.
8   John Plamenatz, *Man and Society*, vol. I, *Political and Social Theory: Machiavelli Through Rousseau* (New York: McGraw-Hill, 1963), p. 147.
9   Greenleaf, "Hobbes: The Problem of Interpretation," pp. 11–17. A. E. Taylor, "The Ethical Doctrine of Hobbes," reprinted in K. C. Brown (ed.), *Hobbes Studies* (Cambridge, Mass.: Harvard University Press, 1965), pp. 35–55. Taylor's Kantian re-

construction of Hobbism, emphasizing the duty of promise keeping, has been argued more recently by D. D. Raphael, *Hobbes: Morals and Politics* (London: Allen & Unwin, 1977), chapter 4. Warrender's reading stresses the place of natural law in Hobbesian theory, natural law being conceived either as a self-evident, axiomatic moral code or as divine law backed by divine sanctions *(The Political Philosophy of Hobbes*, esp. chapters 1, 13–14). The latter, theological, interpretation is put forward by F. C. Hood, *The Divine Politics of Thomas Hobbes* (Oxford: Clarendon Press, 1964).

10 Michael Oakeshott, "Introduction to *Leviathan*," in *Hobbes on Civil Association* (Berkeley: University of California Press, 1975), pp. 64–69. Cf. Warrender, *The Political Philosophy of Hobbes*, chapter 1.

11 C. B. Macpherson, *The Political Theory of Possessive Individualism: Hobbes to Locke* (Oxford: Oxford University Press, 1964), pp. 9–13.

12 Quentin Skinner, "The Ideological Context of Hobbes's Political Thought," *Historical Journal* 9 (1966), p. 314: "If Hobbes intended to ground political obligation on a prior obligation to obey the commands of God, it follows, first, that every contemporary – every follower, opponent, sympathizer – all equally missed the point of his political doctrine. All of them, moreover (a remarkable chance) were mistaken in exactly the same way. For it was Hobbes's theory of obligation which most interested his critics as well as his followers, and all were agreed about the type of theory he was thought to have put forward. All his followers, it has been shown, were concerned to emphasize the obligation to obey any successfully constituted political power [and] cited Hobbes as the authority who had demonstrated that the grounds and the necessity of this obligation lay in man's pre-eminent desire for self-preservation."

13 The generality of a "philosophical outlook" on Hobbes's political theory is remarked by Charles D. Tarlton, "The Creation and Maintenance of Government: A Neglected Dimension of Hobbes's Leviathan," *Political Studies* 26 (1978), pp. 307–8.

14 Michael Oakeshott, "Thomas Hobbes," *Scrutiny* 4 (1935), p. 272: "I think that the true nature of Hobbes's individualism has yet to find its expositor, we have still to wait for the interpreter who will show us that this individualism is based, not upon any foundation in moral opinion at all, but upon a the-

ory of knowledge, upon a thorough-going nominalism and an almost as extreme solipsism." See Greenleaf, "Hobbes: The Problem of Interpretation," pp. 17–24.

15 J. W. N. Watkins, *Hobbes's System of Ideas: A Study in the Political Significance of Philosophical Theories*, 2nd ed. (London: Hutchinson University Library, 1973), p. 43; see also "Philosophy and Politics in Hobbes," *Philosophical Quarterly* 5 (1955), pp. 125–46.

16 Watkins, *Hobbes's System of Ideas*, p. xiii. In a similar vein, Howard Warrender observes (*The Political Philosophy of Hobbes*, p. 102), "The thesis of the present work is tantamount to the assertion that with this account of obligation in the State of Nature, Hobbes's entire theory of moral obligation has now been given in outline, and what remain are matters of explanation or the application of this theory to the affairs of men under various circumstances."

17 Thomas Hobbes, "The Autobiography of Thomas Hobbes," trans. Benjamin Farrington, *The Rationalist Annual, 1958*, ed. by Hector Hawton (London: Watts, 1957), p. 26.

18 Hobbes's idea of a unified science is detailed by M. M. Goldsmith, *Hobbes's Science of Politics* (New York: Columbia University Press, 1966), chapters 1–4. His failure to realize the idea is remarked, e.g., in Macpherson, *The Political Theory of Possessive Individualism*, pp. 10–11; Oakeshott, "Introduction to *Leviathan*," p. 15; Leo Strauss, *The Political Philosophy of Hobbes: Its Basis and Its Genesis*, trans. Elsa M. Sinclair (Chicago: University of Chicago Press [Phoenix ed.], 1963), chapter 1; and Watkins, "Philosophy and Politics in Hobbes," pp. 125–26.

19 Bernard Gert, "Hobbes and Psychological Egoism," *Journal of the History of Ideas* 28 (1967), pp. 503–20. See also F. S. McNeilly, *The Anatomy of Leviathan* (London: Macmillan, 1968), esp. chapters 5–6. Cf. Richard Peters, *Hobbes* (Harmondsworth: Penguin, 1956), chapter 6.

20 Thomas Hobbes, *De Cive: The English Version, entitled in the first edition Philosophicall Rudiments Concerning Government and Society*, ed. Howard Warrender (Oxford: Clarendon Press, 1983), Authors Preface to the Reader, pp. 35–36 (emphasis omitted).

21 Steven Lukes, *Individualism* (Oxford: Basil Blackwell, 1973), pp. 76–77; see generally chapters 11–12.

22 Two recently published commentaries offer reconstructions of Hobbist logic along these lines: Jean Hampton, *Hobbes and the*

Social Contract Tradition (Cambridge: Cambridge University Press, 1986); and Gregory S. Kavka, *Hobbesian Moral and Political Theory* (Princeton, N.J.: Princeton University Press, 1986).

23 Michael Walzer, "The Obligation to Die for the State," in *Obligations: Essays on Disobedience, War, and Citizenship* (Cambridge, Mass.: Harvard University Press, 1970), pp. 77–98.

24 Sheldon S. Wolin, *Politics and Vision* (Boston: Little, Brown, 1960), pp. 281–85.

25 Cf. Hampton, *Hobbes and the Social Contract Tradition*, p. 8. She notices that the use of a "resolutive-compositive" method need not entail individualistic political reasoning. Aristotle, e.g., employs the same methodology but "resolves" the state into constitutive social and political roles. Hampton nonetheless takes the orthodox view that Hobbism represents an individualistic version of the method.

26 *De Cive* Authors Preface to the Reader, p. 32. See also chapter viii, section 1, p. 117 (quoted by Lukes earlier in this section). Hobbes explains in *De Corpore* (*English Works*, vol. I, p. 74) that psychological premises (vs. the first principles of geometry and physics) are sufficient for political analysis: "For if a question be propounded, as, *whether such an action be just or unjust;* if that *unjust* be resolved into *fact against law*, and that notion *law* into the *command* of him or them that have *coercive power*; and that *power* be derived from the *wills* of men that constitute such power, to the end they may live in peace, they may at last come to this, that the appetites of men and the passions of their minds are such, that, unless they be restrained by some power, they will always be making war upon one another; which may be known to be so by any man's experience, that will but examine his own mind."

27 *Leviathan* Introduction, p. 81; see *De Cive* vi, 19, p. 104.

28 The question is the title of Colin Strang's critique of the principle of universalizability, "What if Everyone Did That?" In Judith J. Thomson and Gerald Dworkin (eds.), *Ethics* (New York: Harper & Row, 1968), pp. 151–62.

29 *Leviathan* Review and Conclusion, p. 725; see also Thomas Hobbes, *The Elements of Law: Natural & Politic*, ed. Ferdinand Tönnies (Cambridge: Cambridge University Press, 1928), Part I, chapter i, section 1, p. 1.

30 The dating of the several versions is discussed in Howard Warrender, Editor's Introduction to Thomas Hobbes, *De Cive*

(The Latin Version) (Oxford: Clarendon Press, 1983), pp. 3–16. Regarding the publication of *The Elements of Law*, see also Ferdinand Tönnies, Editor's Preface to *The Elements of Law*, pp. v–viii, xi–xii.

31 *Leviathan* 46, pp. 687–700, offers a sustained critique of Aristotelian philosophy. See also 21, pp. 267–68, and 17, pp. 225–27; and *De Cive* v, 5, pp. 87–88.

32 On "constitutionalism," see, e.g., NOMOS, vol. XX: J. Roland Pennock and John W. Chapman (eds.), *Constitutionalism* (New York: New York University Press, 1979), especially the essays by Pennock, Gordon J. Schochet, and Paul Sigmund. A Straussian version of the orthodoxy that Hobbism is not a constitutional political theory can be found in William Mathie, "Justice and the Question of Regimes in Ancient and Modern Political Philosophy: Aristotle and Hobbes," *Canadian Journal of Political Science* 9 (1976), pp. 449–63.

33 Two contributors to the NOMOS volume remark on the difference between liberal and Aristotelian constitutionalism: Gordon J. Schochet, "Introduction: Constitutionalism, Liberalism, and the Study of Politics," in Pennock and Chapman (eds.), *Constitutionalism*, pp. 1–4; and Nannerl O. Keohane, "Claude de Seyssel and Sixteenth-Century Constitutionalism in France," p. 76.

34 See *Leviathan* 5, 7, and 9; and (discussing the abilities requisite in a political counselor) 25, p. 308. Hobbes states in chapter 7 (p. 131), for instance: "No man can know by Discourse, that this, or that, is, has been, or will be; which is to know absolutely: but onely, that if This be, That is; if This has been, That has been; if This shall be, That shall be: which is to know conditionally; and that not the consequence of one thing to another; but of one name of a thing, to another name of the same thing."

35 E.g., *Leviathan* 5, p. 115: "*Science* is the knowledge of Consequences. . . . Because when we see how any thing comes about, upon what causes, and by what manner; when the like causes come into our power, wee see how to make it produce the like effects." See also 46, p. 682.

36 Richard Ashcraft, "Ideology and Class in Hobbes' Political Theory," *Political Theory* 6 (1978), p. 35. This discussion follows Ashcraft's argument (33–41).

37 E.g., *Leviathan* 4, p. 102: "there being nothing in the world

Universall but Names; for the things named, are every one of them Individuall and Singular."

38 "Methodological structuralism" is inconsistent with the strong methodological individualist position that social phenomena should be explained *solely* in terms of facts about individuals. For a critique of the latter, see Steven Lukes, "Methodological Individualism Reconsidered," in Alan Ryan (ed.), *The Philosophy of Social Explanation* (Oxford: Oxford University Press, 1973), pp. 119–29.

39 The democratic case for taking "amateur" (vs. "professional") social theory seriously is argued by John Dunn, "Social Theory, Social Understanding, and Political Action," in *Rethinking Modern Political Theory: Essays 1979–83* (Cambridge: Cambridge University Press, 1985), pp. 119–38.

40 Cf. Ian Shapiro, "Realism in the Study of the History of Ideas," *History of Political Thought* 3 (1982), pp. 535–78.

41 For opposing views on the merits of the approach generally, cf. E. D. Hirsch, Jr., "Objective Interpretation," *PMLA* 75 (1960), pp. 463–79; and Hans-Georg Gadamer, *Truth and Method*, trans. ed. by Garrett Barden and John Cumming (New York: Seabury Press, 1975), esp. p. 335.

42 *Leviathan* Review and Conclusion, p. 728; see the autobiographical passage describing *The Elements of Law* quoted later in this section (text pertaining to note 54).

43 See Quentin Skinner, "Meaning and Understanding in the History of Ideas," *History and Theory* 8 (1969), pp. 3–53.

44 Ibid., esp. pp. 28–29.

45 R. G. Collingwood, *An Autobiography* (Oxford: Oxford University Press, 1970), p. 39.

46 Ibid., chapter 10.

47 Cf. the appreciative but critical discussion of Collingwood's "logic of question and answer" by Gadamer, *Truth and Method*, pp. 333–41.

48 Collingwood, *An Autobiography*, p. 69.

49 John M. Wallace, *Destiny His Choice: The Loyalism of Andrew Marvell* (Cambridge: Cambridge University Press, 1968), pp. 9–11, discusses the peculiar importance and nature of casuistry in English political thought in the Civil War period.

50 These arguments are discussed in chapters 2 and 5 of the present study. Cf., e.g., Kavka, *Hobbesian Moral and Political Theory*, p. 26: "Hobbes holds that the individual's obligations to the

State are limited only by the right of self-defense. He applies this claim, in complex and inconsistent ways, to persons charged with crimes, battlefield soldiers, prisoners of war, and revolutionaries."

51 Quentin Skinner, "Hobbes's 'Leviathan'," *Historical Journal* 7 (1964), pp. 321–33; and "The Ideological Context of Hobbes's Political Thought," esp. pp. 313–17 (see note 12, this chapter).

52 Quentin Skinner, "Conquest and Consent: Thomas Hobbes and the Engagement Controversy," in *The Interregnum: The Quest for Settlement 1646–1660*, ed. G. E. Aylmer (London: Macmillan, 1972), pp. 96–97 (see also pp. 80–81): "The doctrines of Hobbes's main political works can thus be represented as a somewhat belated though highly important contribution to the lay defence of 'engagement'. It might still be doubted, however, how far this conclusion gives an accurate reflection of Hobbes's *intentions* in writing these works. But there can be no doubt that it does. . . . At the time of publishing *Leviathan* Hobbes made it quite clear that he both saw and intended his great work precisely as a contribution to the existing debate about the rights of *de facto* powers. It goes without saying that *Leviathan* is much else besides."

53 See Skinner, "The Ideological Context of Hobbes's Political Thought," pp. 299, 314.

54 Thomas Hobbes, *Considerations upon the Reputation, Loyalty, Manners, and Religion, of Thomas Hobbes, of Malmesbury, English Works*, vol. IV, p. 414.

55 *Leviathan* Review and Conclusion, pp. 719–21.

56 The continuity in Hobbes's political theory through the three works is remarked, e.g., by Plamenatz, *Man and Society*, vol. I, pp. 117–18; Leslie Stephen, *Hobbes* (Ann Arbor: University of Michigan Press, 1961), pp. 41–42; and Warrender, Editor's Introduction to *De Cive (The Latin Version)*, p. 4.

CHAPTER 2. THE HOBBESIAN COVENANTS: RIGHTS

1 E.g., Steven Lukes, *Individualism* (Oxford: Basil Blackwell, 1973), chapters 11–12; David Gauthier, "The Social Contract as Ideology," *Philosophy and Public Affairs* 6 (1977), pp. 130–64.

2 Henry Parker, *Observations upon some of his Majesties late Answers and Expresses* (London, 1642), p. 16. Richard Tuck, *Natural Rights Theories: Their Origin and Development* (Cambridge:

Cambridge University Press, 1979), chapter 5, pp. 102 and passim, notes the typicality of Parker's argument.

3 Michael Walzer, "The Obligation to Die for the State," in *Obligations: Essays on Disobedience, War, and Citizenship* (Cambridge, Mass.: Harvard University Press, 1970), p. 87.

4 See, e.g., Quentin Skinner, *The Foundations of Modern Political Thought*, vol. II, *The Age of Reformation* (Cambridge: Cambridge University Press, 1978), chapter 7. A modern historian describes Cromwell as "the personification of the Calvinist ideal of the inferior magistrate" (J. H. M. Salmon, *The French Religious Wars in English Political Thought* [Oxford: Clarendon Press, 1959], pp. 106–7).

5 Ian Michael Smart, "The Political Ideas of the Scottish Covenanters. 1638–88," *History of Political Thought* 1 (1980), p. 169.

6 Skinner, *The Foundations of Modern Political Thought*, vol. II, pp. 267–75, 301. See also Julian H. Franklin, "Constitutionalism in the Sixteenth Century: The Protestant Monarchomachs," in David Spitz (ed.), *Political Theory and Social Change* (New York: Atherton, 1967), pp. 117–32; Introduction to *Constitutionalism and Resistance in the Sixteenth Century: Three Treatises by Hotman, Beza, & Mornay* (New York: Pegasus, 1969); and *John Locke and the Theory of Sovereignty: Mixed Monarchy and the Right of Resistance in the Political Thought of the English Revolution* (Cambridge: Cambridge University Press, paperback ed., 1981), pp. 1–3. Illustrations of the equation of parliament and nation, from Henry Parker's *Observations*, are quoted in the next chapter (text pertaining to note 42 of that chapter).

7 Franklin, *John Locke and the Theory of Sovereignty;* Smart, "The Political Ideas of the Scottish Covenanters. 1638–88," pp. 183–93.

8 J. W. Gough, *The Social Contract: A Critical Study of Its Development*, 2nd ed. (1957; reprint, Westport, Conn.: Greenwood, 1978), pp. 94–96, specifically identifies the 1647 Leveller Agreement with the emergence of the idea of a popular "social contract," as opposed to the earlier concept of a "contract of government" (see note 13, this chapter). But Cromwell and Ireton, he notes, preferred that the agreement not be circulated in the country as was planned but rather submitted directly to Parliament. On the Leveller Agreement, see Perez Zagorin, *A History of Political Thought in the English Revolution* (London: Routledge & Kegan Paul, 1954), chapter 3.

9　Charles Herle, *A Fuller Answer to a Treatise Written by Dr. Ferne* (London, 1642), p. 25; quoted in Franklin, *John Locke and the Theory of Sovereignty*, p. 30 (see pp. 28–31).

10　Henry Parker, *Some Few Observations upon his Majesties late Answer to the Declaration, or Remonstrance of the Lords and Commons of the 19. of May, 1642* (London, 1642), p. 3.

11　Tuck, *Natural Rights Theories*, p. 147.

12　A. S. P. Woodhouse (ed.), *Puritanism and Liberty* (Chicago: University of Chicago Press, 1951), pp. 57, 59. Tuck, *Natural Rights Theories*, pp. 147–51, emphasizes the conservatism of the Leveller belief in "society's rights." This contrasts with traditional Whig emphasis on the place of the Levellers in the "history of liberty"; e.g., Donald W. Hanson, *From Kingdom to Commonwealth: The Development of Civic Consciousness in English Political Thought* (Cambridge, Mass.: Harvard University Press, 1970), pp. 322–35.

13　Traditionally, Hobbes's version of the social contract has been contrasted with the dual medieval notions of a *pactum subjectionis*, a constitutional compact between ruler and ruled, and a *pactum unionis*, or contract creating society. The former, a monarchomach idea, buttressed assertions of ultimate popular sovereignty, while the latter concept ran counter to the traditional Aristotelian belief in the natural development of society. The Hobbesian covenants fit in neither category, since they create society and the state simultaneously, and by a pact only among subjects. See Gough, *The Social Contract*, pp. 108–10; and René Gadave, *Un Théoricien Anglais du Droit public au XVIIe siècle: Th. Hobbes* (New York: Arno Press, 1979), pp. 70–76.

14　Tuck, *Natural Rights Theories*, chapter 6.

15　Ibid., pp. 1, 5–7.

16　Ibid., chapter 3, esp. pp. 77–81.

17　Ibid., pp. 101–4, see generally chapters 4 and 5. Selden is an interesting figure, a conservative Grotian thinker and a parliamentarian. Although he thought an absolutist, non-resistance contract possible in principle, he also held that the English constitution did not have this character (pp. 96–100).

18　E.g., Henry Parker, *Observations*, p. 20: "It is unnaturall for any Nation to give away its owne proprietie in it selfe absolutely, and to subject it selfe to a condition of servilitie below men." Richard Tuck discusses this tradition of Grotian natural-rights theory in *Natural Rights Theories*, chapter 7.

19 Tuck, *Natural Rights Theories*, pp. 122–24. For an illustration, see my discussion in chapter 7 of Marchamont Nedham's *Case of the Commonwealth of England, Stated* (1650).

20 *The Elements of Law* I, xix, 10, p. 81.

21 Ibid. II, i, 7, p. 86.

22 Ibid. I, xv, 18, p. 62. According to Tuck, *Natural Rights Theories*, p. 122, this passage did not appear in the original draft of *The Elements of Law*, but was added later to some copies of the manuscript. Parallel passages appear in *De Cive* ii, 14, p. 57, and *Leviathan* 14, pp. 197–98.

23 *The Elements of Law* I, xix, 7, pp. 80–81; see also II, i, 18, p. 90.

24 Sheldon S. Wolin, *Politics and Vision* (Boston: Little, Brown, 1960), p. 285. See also Hanna Pitkin, "Hobbes's Concept of Representation," Part II, *American Political Science Review* 58 (1964), pp. 909–11; and Raymond Polin, *Politique et Philosophie chez Thomas Hobbes* (Paris: Presses Universitaires de France, 1953), pp. 229, 231. But cf. Clifford Orwin, who does not see the problem, "On the Sovereign Authorization," *Political Theory* 3 (1975), p. 29.

25 Henry Hammond, *Works*, vol. I, p. 342; quoted in Tuck, *Natural Rights Theories*, p. 108. The passage reads in full: "The *power* of *violent resisting* invaders, the right of *repelling force by force*, which *God* and *Nature* hath give the *single* man in *community* of *Nature* is now, in case of submission to the *Governour*, parted with, . . . and though it be founded in *self-defence*, he that thus violently resists *the powers*, shall *receive to himself damnation*."

26 *De Cive* v, 7, p. 88. In paragraph 11 (pp. 89–90), Hobbes reiterates that this renunciation of right is the source of sovereign power: "Which *power*, and *Right of commanding*, consists in this, that each Citizen hath conveighed all his strength and power to that man, or Counsell; which to have done (because no man can transferre his power in a naturall manner) is nothing else then to have parted with his Right of resisting."

27 Ibid. v, 7, pp. 88–89.

28 Tuck, *Natural Rights Theories*, pp. 125–29.

29 *De Cive* ii, 18, p. 58. The passage opens, "No man is oblig'd by any *Contracts* whatsoever not to resist him who shall offer to kill, wound, or any other way hurt his Body"; and continues, "Since therefore no man is tyed to *impossibilities*, they who are

threatned either with *death*, (which is the greatest evill to nature) or wounds, or some other bodily hurts, and are not stout
enough to bear them, are not obliged to endure them." As the
discussion strictly parallels *The Elements of Law* (I, xv) the in-
sertion can be precisely located. *De Cive* ii, 17 (the preceding
paragraph) and *The Elements of Law* I, xv, 14, treat compacts
invalid in virtue of earlier promises. In paragraphs 18 and 19
in *De Cive*, Hobbes stipulates that individuals cannot renounce
the right of self-defense against violence nor can they promise
to accuse themselves. Returning to the original outline, paragraph 20 defines an oath; this parallels *The Elements of Law* I,
xv, 15. In *Leviathan*, chapter 14, Hobbes expands on the discussion in chapter ii of *De Cive*. Compare *Leviathan*, p. 192,
with *De Cive* ii, 8, pp. 54–55; and *Leviathan*, pp. 199–200, with
De Cive ii, 18–19, pp. 58–60.

30 *De Cive* ii, 18, p. 59. In a 1641 manuscript of the Latin *De Cive*
(the Chatsworth manuscript) and in the 1642 edition, the passage reads: "They seemed not sufficiently bound, however
much by the pacts they were bound not to resist" (ibid., p.
59n., trans. Warrender).

31 Ibid. ii, 18, p. 59.

32 Hobbes was not unique among early-modern thinkers in distinguishing a private right of self-defense from a public right
of resistance. See Julian H. Franklin, *Jean Bodin and the Rise of
Absolutist Theory* (Cambridge: Cambridge University Press, 1973),
p. 96.

33 *De Cive* ii, 18, p. 59: "In the meer state of nature, if you have a
mind to kill, that state it selfe affords you a Right. . . . But in
a Civill State, where the Right of life, and death, and of all
corporall punishment is with the Supreme; that same Right of
killing cannot be granted to any private person."

34 *De Cive* ii, 18, p. 59. Cf. *Leviathan* 28, p. 353, where Hobbes
stipulates a more strenuous promise: "In the making of a
Common-wealth, every man giveth away the right of defending another; but not of defending himselfe. Also he obligeth
himselfe, to assist him that hath the Soveraignty, in the Punishing of another; but of himselfe not." The promises are compared in chapter 5, in the section entitled "Political Duties: The
Case of Fighting for the State."

35 *Leviathan* notes one exceptional case in which subjects may band
together against the sovereign: when they have "already re-

sisted the Soveraign Power unjustly, or committed some Capitall crime, for which every one of them expecteth death." In
such case, they are only defending their lives, but resistance
becomes unlawful if they are offered pardon (21, pp. 270–71).
This exception casts as right a previous observation about fact.
In *The Elements of Law* (II, viii, 2, p. 134), Hobbes had noticed:
"When a great multitude, or heap of people, have concurred
to a crime worthy of death, they join together, and take arms
to defend themselves for fear thereof."

36 John Plamenatz, *Man and Society*, vol. I, p. 150, observes: "The
merely selfish law-breaker who resists arrest is not particularly
dangerous to society. . . . It is the man who, like John Hamp-
den, defies the sovereign in the name of justice, resisting him
as a matter of principle, who threatens the foundations of social peace."

37 *De Cive* vi, 13, p. 98. Cf. *The Elements of Law* II, i, 5, pp. 85–86,
where Hobbes merely states the general principle: "How far
therefore in the making of a commonwealth, a man subjecteth
his will to the power of others, must appear from the end,
namely security."

38 *De Cive* vi, 13, p. 98.

39 Ibid. The passage continues: "There are many other cases, in
which, since the Commands are shamefull to be done by some,
and not by others, Obedience may, by Right, be perform'd by
these, and refus'd by those." The emphasis on shame fits oddly
with Hobbes's characteristic view that nothing could be worse
than death (e.g., *De Cive* i, 7, p. 47: "Every man . . . shuns
what is evill, but chiefly the chiefest of naturall evills, which is
Death; and this he doth, by a certain impulsion of nature, no
lesse then that whereby a Stone moves downward").

40 *De Cive* vi, 13, p. 98.

41 *Leviathan* 21, p. 264 (margin note). Hobbes explains (p. 265):
"And therefore it may, and doth often happen in Common-
wealths, that a Subject may be put to death, by the command
of the Soveraign Power; and yet neither doe the other wrong."

42 Ibid. 14, p. 189. See note 57, this chapter.

43 Tuck, *Natural Rights Theories*, pp. 1, 5–7. See also Howard
Warrender, *The Political Philosophy of Hobbes: His Theory of Obligation* (Oxford: Clarendon Press, 1957), pp. 18–21, for the
concept of rights, and pp. 192–93 for the asymmetry between
the rights of subject and sovereign.

44 *De Cive* ix, 9, p. 126. See *The Elements of Law* II, iv, 9, p. 105: "Freedom therefore in commonwealths is nothing but the honour of equality of favour with other subjects, and servitude the estate of the rest. A freeman therefore may expect employments of honour, rather than a servant. And this is all that can be understood by the liberty of the subject. For in all other senses, liberty is the state of him that is not subject." See also II, viii, 3, p. 134. But cf. *The Elements of Law* II, ix, 4, p. 143, and *De Cive* xiii, 6, pp. 158–59, where Hobbes includes "harmelesse liberty" in the list of public goods.

45 Chapter 21 collects and supplements discussions in several locales in the earlier versions of the theory. (1) *De Cive* vi (sovereigns' rights), 13, pp. 97–98, details the particular liberties of subjects (cf. *The Elements of Law*, II, i, 5, pp. 85–86). Hobbes also notes the asymmetry between sovereigns' and subjects' rights. See *Leviathan* 21, pp. 268–71. (2) *The Elements of Law* II, ii (comparison of forms of government), 12–16, p. 98, and *De Cive* vii, 18, p. 116, treat the ways in which subjects are discharged of obligation to the sovereign. See *Leviathan* 21, pp. 272–74. (3) *The Elements of Law* II, iv (parental dominion), 9, p. 105, and *De Cive* ix, 9, pp. 125–26, treat the distinction between a "freeman" and a servant. In *De Cive*'s more extended discussion, Hobbes defines liberty, and notes that political liberty consists in exemption from civil law. See *Leviathan* 21, pp. 261–64, 271.

46 Liberty is defined in *De Cive* (ix, 9, p. 125) as "an *absence of the lets, and hinderances of motion.*" See *Leviathan* 21, pp. 261–62. The development in Hobbes's understanding of political liberty can be seen by comparing the statement in *De Cive* that only rulers are exempt from the laws with *Leviathan* 21, p. 271 (margin note): "The Greatest Liberty of Subjects, dependeth on the silence of the Law."

47 *Leviathan* 21, p. 268.

48 *De Cive* xii, 2, p. 147. Cf. *The Elements of Law* II, viii, 4, p. 135; and *De Homine* (1658), trans. Charles T. Wood, T. S. K. Scott-Craig, and Bernard Gert, in Bernard Gert (ed.), *Man and Citizen* (Garden City, N.Y.: Doubleday [Anchor Books], 1972), xv, 2, p. 84.

49 *Leviathan* 21, p. 268. Cf. *De Cive* vi, 13, p. 98 (quoted in this chapter in the text pertaining to note 37).

50 *Leviathan* 21, pp. 268–69.

51 Cf. Warrender, *The Political Philosophy of Hobbes*, pp. 188–94.
52 *Leviathan* 21, p. 269.
53 Cf. *Leviathan*'s "Review and Conclusion," where Hobbes introduces a new law of nature (pp. 718–19): *"That every man is bound by Nature, as much as in him lieth, to protect in Warre, the Authority, by which he is himself protected in time of Peace."* See chapter 5 of the present study, the section entitled "Political Duties: The Case of Fighting for the State."
54 *Leviathan* 21, p. 269.
55 Ibid., p. 270.
56 The logic of Hobbes's argument, which rests on distinguishing prima facie duties from more strenuous obligations to perform, is examined in chapter 5 of the present study.
57 *Leviathan* 14, p. 189; see *The Elements of Law* II, x, 5, p. 148, and *De Cive* xiv, 3, p. 170. The contrast between right and law was a common idea among thinkers in the Tew Circle: see Tuck, *Natural Rights Theories*, pp. 102–3, 111, 120, 130. I have ignored throughout Hobbes's alternate formulation, in *De Cive* and *Leviathan*, limiting natural right to what is necessary to self-preservation (*De Cive* i, 7, p. 47; *Leviathan* 14, p. 189). This formulation is insignificant in his political applications of rights reasoning. Cf. Tuck, *Natural Rights Theories*, pp. 129–32. (Tuck relates the latter definition of natural right to the introduction of the "authorization" version of the covenant in *Leviathan*. The limitation of natural right to what is necessary for self-preservation ties the sovereign's hands. But in turn, the authorization covenant broadens the scope of legitimate uses of power by figuring the sovereign as the agent of the community. See, however, *Leviathan* 28, p. 354, where Hobbes founds the sovereign's right to punish in the natural right of self-preservation. He fails to notice that the limitation of natural right to self-preservation presents a difficulty. "But I have also shewed formerly, that before the Institution of Common-wealth, every man had a right to every thing, and to do whatsoever he thought necessary to his own preservation; subduing, hurting, or killing any man in order thereunto. And this is the foundation of that right of Punishing, which is exercised in every Common-wealth. For the Subjects did not give the Soveraign that right; but onely in laying down theirs, strengthned

him to use his own, as he should think fit, for the preservation of them all: so that it was not given, but left to him, and to him onely; and [excepting the limits set him by naturall Law] as entire, as in the condition of meer Nature, and of warre of every one against his neighbour.")

58 *Leviathan* 27, p. 345.

59 Ibid., see pp. 345–46.

60 T. M. Scanlon, "Rights, Goals, and Fairness," in Stuart Hampshire (ed.), *Public and Private Morality* (Cambridge: Cambridge University Press, 1978), p. 94.

61 *De Cive* xiii, 6, p. 159; *The Elements of Law* II, ix, 4, p. 143.

62 E.g., Scanlon, "Rights, Goals, and Fairness," pp. 95–98.

63 Ronald Dworkin, *Taking Rights Seriously* (Cambridge, Mass.: Harvard University Press, 1977), p. xi.

64 *Leviathan* 21, pp. 268–71. The last is discussed in note 35, this chapter. In chapter 27 (pp. 345–46), as noted previously, self-preservation figures as an excuse for breaking the law, e.g., stealing by the destitute.

65 *The Elements of Law* I, xv, 18, p. 62.

CHAPTER 3. THE HOBBESIAN COVENANTS: POLITICAL AGENCY, REPRESENTATION, AND AUTHORIZATION

1 *Leviathan* 17, p. 227 (emphasis omitted).

2 Ibid.

3 David P. Gauthier, *The Logic of Leviathan: The Moral and Political Theory of Thomas Hobbes* (Oxford: Clarendon Press, 1969), p. 127. Hanna Pitkin describes the significance of the new covenant in similar terms ("Hobbes's Concept of Representation," Part II, *American Political Science Review* 58 [1964], p. 911): "As the representative of them all, the sovereign is then for the first time, in Hobbes's thought, really in a position to use the strength and faculties of any or all of his subjects in a positive way. For they have, by authorizing, made themselves owners of whatever he might do; his acts are their acts, his will is their will, his commitments are their commitments." See also Raymond Polin, *Politique et Philosophie chez Thomas Hobbes* (Paris: Presses Universitaires de France, 1953), chapter 10. In a related vein, Gauthier (chapters 3–4, esp. pp. 110, 124–27) and Pitkin

(pp. 911–13) argue that the authorization covenant, unlike the previous non-resistance formulation, gives the sovereign a new right that he did not possess in the state of nature. This is the right to the assistance of his subjects. Clifford Orwin, "On the Sovereign Authorization," *Political Theory* 3 (1975), pp. 29–31, criticizes both claims concerning the novelty of the authorization formulation. By Orwin's account (pp. 33–38), the key feature of the new covenant is that it relieves subjects of responsibility to God for obedience to political commands. Cf. also Richard Tuck, *Natural Rights Theories: Their Origin and Development* (Cambridge: Cambridge University Press, 1979), pp. 129–30. As previously indicated (chapter 2, note 57), Tuck relates the new covenant to the limitation of natural right, in *De Cive* and *Leviathan*, to what is necessary for self-preservation.

4 Pitkin, "Hobbes's Concept of Representation," Part II, pp. 911, 918. Cf. Gauthier, *The Logic of Leviathan*, pp. 165–66.

5 *Leviathan* 17, pp. 227–28.

6 Henry Parker, *Observations upon some of his Majesties late Answers and Expresses* (London, 1642), pp. 3–4. See James Daly, "The Idea of Absolute Monarchy in Seventeenth-Century England," *Historical Journal* 21 (1978), pp. 235–36.

7 Parker, *Observations*, p. 45.

8 *Leviathan* 16, p. 217. Chapter 16 of *Leviathan*, "Of PERSONS, AUTHORS, and *things Personated*," is a new chapter, inserted just prior to the political covenant in explanation of the terms of that covenant.

9 *Leviathan* 28, p. 354. See also 14, pp. 190–91; *The Elements of Law* I, xv, 3, p. 58, and II, iii, 2, p. 99; *De Cive* ii, 4, pp. 53–54.

10 *The Elements of Law* I, xix, 8, p. 81 (emphasis mine). See also II, viii, 7, pp. 137–38, where the concept is derived from the definition of a corporation ("one person in law"); and II, ii, 11, pp. 97–98. J. H. M. Salmon, *The French Religious Wars in English Political Thought* (Oxford: Clarendon Press, 1959), pp. 114–15, discusses the Roman law background of Hobbes's idea of personification. The development of the concept through the several versions of the political theory is discussed by Pitkin, "Hobbes's Concept of Representation," Part II, pp. 903–7.

11 *De Cive* v, 9, p. 89 (emphasis mine). In an annotation to the second (1647) edition of *De Cive* (vi, 1, pp. 91–92), Hobbes declares that the related distinction between a "city" and a "mul-

titude" is crucial to understanding political authority. See footnote 27, this chapter.

12   *Leviathan* 16, pp. 220–21: "Because the Multitude naturally is not *One*, but *Many*; they cannot be understood for one; but many Authors, of every thing their Representative faith, or doth in their name."

13   Ibid. 17, p. 228 (emphasis omitted).

14   Ibid. 18, p. 232.

15   Pitkin, "Hobbes's Concept of Representation," Part II, pp. 904–5. Cf. Orwin, "On the Sovereign Authorization," pp. 28–29.

16   *Leviathan* 17, p. 227.

17   Howard Warrender, *The Political Philosophy of Hobbes: His Theory of Obligation* (Oxford: Clarendon Press, 1957), pp. 128–30. The affinity between Hobbes's account of authorization and Rousseau's theory is also discussed by René Gadave, *Un Théoricien Anglais du Droit public au XVIIe siècle: Th. Hobbes* (New York: Arno Press, 1979), pp. 48, 100–2, 112, 191–92, 247–55, and by Polin, *Politique et Philosophie chez Thomas Hobbes*, pp. 232–33.

18   R. G. Collingwood, *An Autobiography* (Oxford: Oxford University Press, 1970), p. 39.

19   In the second section of chapter 18, Hobbes defends that second fundamental tenet of an absolutist constitution, unified sovereignty (see chapter 4 of the present study). The *Leviathan* chapter consolidates the first two postcovenant chapters in *The Elements of Law* and *De Cive*. The first chapter of Part II of the former work and chapter 6 of *De Cive* treat rights or powers of sovereignty. Next, *The Elements of Law* (II, ii) and *De Cive* (vii) turn to a formal comparison of the three forms of government – democracy, aristocracy, and monarchy. These comparisons focus on the issue of political accountability. For each form of government, Hobbes reiterates that the terms of its institution, namely, the absence of a covenant between ruler and ruled, preclude sovereign accountability (technically, the sovereign cannot "injure" subjects). See *The Elements of Law* II, ii, 3, p. 93 (democracy); II, ii, 7, p. 94 (aristocracy); and *De Cive* vii, 7, p. 110 (democracy); vii, 9, p. 111 (aristocracy); vii, 12, p. 112 (monarchy).

20   *Leviathan* 18, p. 230.

21   Ibid., p. 232 (the passage is quoted earlier; see text pertaining to note 14).

22 Ibid., pp. 229–32 (margin notes).

23 Ibid., pp. 229, 32.

24 The connection between Hobbesian nominalism and this account of political agency is observed, e.g., by J. A. W. Gunn,
Politics and the Public Interest in the Seventeenth Century (London:
Routledge & Kegan Paul, 1969), pp. 64–65. See also
J. W. N. Watkins, *Hobbes's System of Ideas: A Study in the Political
Significance of Philosophical Theories*, 2nd ed. (London: Hutchinson University Library, 1973), pp. 114–18, and Michael Oakeshott, "Introduction to *Leviathan*," in *Hobbes on Civil Association* (Berkeley: University of California Press, 1975), pp. 60–64.

25 *De Cive* vi, 1, p. 92 (emphasis omitted).

26 Sheldon S. Wolin has described the Hobbesian sovereign as a
"public, institutionalized ego" (*Politics and Vision* [Boston: Little, Brown, 1960], p. 279).

27 *De Cive* vi, 1, p. 92 (emphasis omitted). This passage is an addition to the second (1647) edition of *De Cive*. The distinction
between a "people" and a "multitude" is present from the
beginning in Hobbes's political theory (e.g., *The Elements of
Law* II, ii, 11, pp. 97–98), but it is given special significance in
this edition of *De Cive*. The passage opens: "The Doctrine of
the power of a City over it's Citizens, almost wholly depends
on the understanding of the difference which is between a
multitude of men ruling, and a multitude ruled."

28 *De Cive* (1642 ed.) vii, 11, p. 111.

29 Ibid. xii, 13, p. 151. In addition to previously cited sources, see
Janine Chanteur, "Note sur les Notions de 'Peuple' et de 'Multitude' chez Hobbes," in Reinhart Kosselleck and Roman Schnur
(eds.), *Hobbes-Forschungen* (Berlin: Duncker & Humblot, 1969),
pp. 223–35.

30 *De Cive* vii, 7, p. 110. See also vii, 9, p. 111 (regarding aristocracy), and vii, 12, p. 112 (regarding monarchy), as well as *The
Elements of Law* II, ii, 2, pp. 92–93 (democracy) and 7, p. 94
(aristocracy), and *Leviathan* 18, p. 230.

31 The latter point is made by Terry Heinrichs, "Hobbes & the
Coleman Thesis," *Polity* 16 (1984), p. 658.

32 *The Elements of Law* II, ii, 6, p. 94, and 1, p. 92.

33 Ibid. II, ii, 9, p. 95: "For suppose a decree be made . . . that
such a one shall have the sovereignty for his life; and that
afterward they will choose a new; in this case, the power of
the people is dissolved, or not."

34 Ibid. II, ii, 9–10, pp. 95–97.
35 *De Cive* vii, 5–13, pp. 109–12. With the introduction of the authorization covenant in *Leviathan*, Hobbes eliminated from the political theory the entire chapter describing the process of instituting a government (Part II, chapter ii, in *The Elements of Law*, and chapter vii in *De Cive*). Cf. *Leviathan* 18, pp. 228–29, 231–32 (see text pertaining to note 72, this chapter).
36 *The Elements of Law* II, i, 2, p. 84. See also II, ii, 11, pp. 97–98; II, viii, 9, p. 138; and *De Cive* vi, 1, p. 91, and vii, 13, pp. 151–52.
37 Cf., e.g., Conrad Russell, "The Nature of a Parliament in Early Stuart England," in Howard Tomlinson (ed.), *Before the English Civil War* (London: Macmillan, 1983), pp. 123–50; and J. H. Hexter, "Power Struggle, Parliament, and Liberty in Early Stuart England," *Journal of Modern History* 50 (1978), pp. 1–50.
38 *The Elements of Law* II, ii, 11, p. 97; see *Leviathan* 22, p. 284 (quoted in the text pertaining to note 54, this chapter).
39 The following discussion relies on Salmon, *The French Religious Wars in English Political Thought*, pp. 114–16.
40 Henry Parker, *Observations*, p. 2. See Salmon, *The French Religious Wars in English Political Thought*, p. 82; and Quentin Skinner, *The Foundations of Modern Political Thought*, vol. II, *The Age of Reformation* (Cambridge: Cambridge University Press, 1978), p. 334.
41 *Leviathan* 18, p. 237.
42 Henry Parker, *Observations*, pp. 45, 28, 34; see also p. 5. On the other hand, Parker also asserts (p. 31): "The power of Parliaments is but derivative and depending upon publike consent." Julian H. Franklin (*John Locke and the Theory of Sovereignty: Mixed Monarchy and the Right of Resistance in the Political Thought of the English Revolution* [Cambridge: Cambridge University Press, paperback ed., 1981], pp. 1–2) observes that the identification of representative assemblies with the nation was a characteristic feature of monarchomach theory.
43 Derek Hirst, *The Representative of the People? Voters and Voting in England under the Early Stuarts* (Cambridge: Cambridge University Press, 1975), p. 193, see generally chapters 8–9.
44 *Leviathan* 16, pp. 217–18. See Pitkin, "Hobbes's Concept of Representation," Parts I and II; Gadave, *Un Théoricien Anglais du Droit public au XVIIe siècle: Th. Hobbes*, chapter 3; and Polin, *Politique et Philosophie chez Thomas Hobbes*, chapter 10.

45 Hobbes's conflation of representation and authority is criticized by Pitkin, "Hobbes's Concept of Representation," Part I.

46 *Leviathan* 16, p. 220. See also 26, p. 313: "But the Commonwealth is no Person, nor has capacity to doe any thing, but by the Representative, (that is, the Soveraign;) and therefore the Soveraign is the sole Legislator."

47 Ibid. 22, p. 275.

48 Ibid. 19, pp. 240–41.

49 But cf. *Leviathan* 22, p. 275. At the start of the passage, perhaps unwittingly, Hobbes uses the term "representative" to describe a special variety of political authority: "In Bodies Politique, the power of the Representative is alwaies Limited: And that which prescribeth the Limits thereof, is the Power Soveraign. For Power Unlimited, is absolute Soveraignty. And the Soveraign, in every Commonwealth, is the absolute Representative of all the subjects."

50 Ibid. 19, p. 240.

51 Ibid. See also 22, pp. 275, 284.

52 Ibid. 22, p. 284 (margin note). Cf. Henry Parker's criticism of the royalist view that Parliaments are limited to the function of counseling the king, *Observations*, pp. 5–10.

53 *Leviathan* 22, p. 284; see also 19, p. 240.

54 *Leviathan* 22, p. 284. Subordinate assemblies are limited, Hobbes specifies (pp. 275–76), by "their Writt, or Letters from the Soveraign" and by "the Law of the Common-wealth." In other words, they are governed both by "Letters Patents," instructions concerning their business and terms of assembly, and by the "ordinary Lawes, common to all Subjects."

55 Morton Kaplan, "How Sovereign Is Hobbes' Sovereign?" *Western Political Quarterly* (1956), p. 400; quoted in Pitkin, "Hobbes's Concept of Representation," Part II, p. 917.

56 Pitkin, "Hobbes's Concept of Representation," Part II, p. 917.

57 Pitkin, it should be said, criticizes the "accountability view" of representation in *The Concept of Representation* (Berkeley: University of California Press, paperback ed., 1972), pp. 55–59.

58 *Leviathan* 17, p. 227.

59 Ibid. 18, p. 229.

60 Ibid., pp. 229–30; see also the explanation of the injunction against regicide, p. 232.

61 In addition to the sources cited previously, see Franklin, *John Locke and the Theory of Sovereignty*, pp. 64–65.

62 Jean Hampton, *Hobbes and the Social Contract Tradition* (Cambridge: Cambridge University Press, 1986), pp. 126–27; see also pp. 122–23.

63 See Pitkin, *The Concept of Representation*, pp. 11–12.

64 *Leviathan* 18, p. 230.

65 *De Cive* vi, 20, p. 104.

66 Ibid., pp. 104–5.

67 Ibid., p. 105.

68 Ibid., pp. 104–5. This "false" opinion figures, e.g., in the Engager Nedham's *Case of the Commonwealth of England, Stated* (1650), ed. Philip A. Knachel (Charlottesville: University Press of Virginia, 1969); see chapter 7 of the present study.

69 *De Cive* vi, 20, p. 105.

70 Ibid. vii, 11, p. 111.

71 *Leviathan* 16, pp. 220–21.

72 Ibid. 18, p. 231: "He that dissented must now consent with the rest; that is, be contented to avow all the actions he shall do, or else justly be destroyed by the rest." Cf. *The Elements of Law* II, ii, 6, p. 94: "By plurality of vote," the democratic assembly "transfer[s] that power which before the people had, to the number of men so named and chosen."

73 *The Elements of Law* II, ii, 3, p. 93. See *De Cive* vii, 7, p. 110.

74 *The Elements of Law* II, ii, 4, p. 93.

75 See Warrender, *The Political Philosophy of Hobbes*, pp. 128–30, and, generally, pp. 125–40; as well as Michael Oakeshott, "Introduction to *Leviathan*," pp. 60–62.

76 Jean-Jacques Rousseau, *The Social Contract*, trans. Maurice Cranston (Harmondsworth: Penguin, 1968), book I, chapter 7, p. 63: "Now, as the sovereign is formed entirely of the individuals who compose it, it has not, nor could it have, any interest contrary to theirs; and so the sovereign has no need to give guarantees to the subjects, because it is impossible for a body to wish to hurt all of its members, and, as we shall see, it cannot hurt any particular member. The sovereign by the mere fact that it is, is always all that it ought to be."

CHAPTER 4. HOBBESIAN ABSOLUTISM

1 Leslie Stephen, *The English Utilitarians*, vol. I (New York: G. P. Putnam's Sons, 1900), p. 303. For a survey of Utilitarian readings of Hobbes of the period, see Mark Francis, "The Nineteenth Century Theory of Sovereignty and Thomas Hobbes," *History of Political Thought* 1 (1980), pp. 517–40.

2 John Locke, *The Second Treatise of Government*, in *Two Treatises of Government*, rev. ed., ed. Peter Laslett (New York: New American Library [Mentor Books], 1965), section 93, p. 372.

3 M. M. Goldsmith, "Hobbes's 'Mortall God': Is There a Fallacy in Hobbes's Theory of Sovereignty," *History of Political Thought* 1 (1980), pp. 33–50.

4 See the text pertaining to notes 38–40 of this chapter.

5 Francis, "The Nineteenth Century Theory of Sovereignty and Thomas Hobbes," pp. 520–22 and passim.

6 Ibid., pp. 522, 538.

7 W. H. Greenleaf, "Hobbes: The Problem of Interpretation," in Maurice Cranston and Richard S. Peters (eds.), *Hobbes and Rousseau: A Collection of Critical Essays* (Garden City, N.Y.: Doubleday [Anchor Books], 1972), esp. pp. 6–11.

8 John Plamenatz, *Man and Society*, vol. I, *Political and Social Theory: Machiavelli Through Rousseau* (New York: McGraw-Hill, 1963), pp. 151–52.

9 Ibid., p. 152: "Whether or not there is a sovereign, the common interest of all persons taking part in government is ordinarily that the rules, which make the structure of government what it is, should be respected; because it is on this structure that their power depends."

10 Ibid., p. 147 (quoted in chapter 1, see text pertaining to note 8).

11 Ibid., pp. 136–37. This summarizes a lengthier explanation: "The covenant makes the sovereign powerful, not at all because it involves an immediate keeping of promises, but because it creates a situation in which it becomes everyone's interest that some definite person (the sovereign) should get the better of anyone else he seeks to coerce. I want the sovereign to be able to coerce everyone except me, and everyone else has a desire similar to mine. This is enough to ensure that the covenant makes the sovereign powerful enough to be able to punish anyone who breaks the covenant." See also

John Plamenatz, *The English Utilitarians*, 2nd ed. (Oxford: Basil Blackwell, 1958), chapters 1 and 10.

12   Plamenatz, *Man and Society*, vol. I, p. 152.

13   James Daly, "The Idea of Absolute Monarchy in Seventeenth-Century England," *Historical Journal* 21 (1978), pp. 227–50. It must be said that he thinks "Hobbes's sovereign had far more power than most people had understood by the term 'absolute' " (p. 238); see also "John Bramhall and the Theoretical Problems of Royalist Moderation," *Journal of British Studies* 11 (1971), pp. 26–44.

14   Daly, "The Idea of Absolute Monarchy in Seventeenth-Century England," p. 231.

15   *Leviathan* 20, p. 257. See *The Elements of Law* II, iv, 10, pp. 105–6: "The same family if it grow by multiplication of children, either by generation or adoption; or of servants, either by generation, conquest, or voluntary submission, to be so great and numerous, as in probability it may protect itself, then is that family called a PATRIMONIAL KINGDOM, or monarchy by acquisition; wherein the sovereignty is in one man, as it is in a monarch made by political institution." See also II, iii, 2, pp. 99–100, and *De Cive* ix, 10, p. 126.

16   *Leviathan* 21, pp. 266–68.

17   Ibid., p. 266: "The *Athenians*, and *Romanes* were free; that is, free Common-wealths: not that any particular man had the Liberty to resist their own Representative; but that their Representative had the Libertie to resist, or invade other people. There is written on the Turrets of the city of *Luca* in great characters at this day, the word LIBERTAS; yet no man can thence inferre, that a particular man has more Libertie, or Immunitie from the service of the Commonwealth there, than in *Constantinople*. Whether a Commonwealth be Monarchicall, or Popular, the Freedome is still the same." See *De Cive* x, 8, p. 135.

18   Daly, "The Idea of Absolute Monarchy in Seventeenth-Century England," pp. 240–41 and passim.

19   Ibid., p. 235. Thus, Daly comments: "Their emphasis is not on the lawful scope of the king's power, but on what the subject might do if the king exceeded that scope. They impugned the absoluteness of the king, not so much because he lacked certain powers, but because, whatever power he had, he could be forcibly resisted for exceeding it."

20 The enumeration of essential sovereign powers in *The Elements of Law* is introduced in similar fashion: "How far therefore in the making of a commonwealth, a man subjecteth his will to the power of others, must appear from the end, namely security. For whatsoever is necessary to be by covenant transferred for the attaining thereof, so much is transferred" (II, i, 5, pp. 85–86). See also *De Cive* vi, 13, pp. 97–98.

21 *Leviathan* 18, pp. 229–32 (margin notes). By contrast, the earlier versions of the political theory stipulate only that the sovereign is immune from punishment (*The Elements of Law* II, i, 12, p. 87, and *De Cive* vi, 12, p. 97).

22 In the view of some historians, Daly notes, royalist thinkers in the Stuart period moved from enumerating specific rights of sovereignty to asserting a more general and less defined prerogative power ("The Idea of Absolute Monarchy in Seventeenth-Century England," p. 232).

23 *Leviathan* 18, pp. 233–35 (margin notes): "It is annexed to the Soveraignty," to be (or have): "Judge of what Doctrines are fit to be taught"; "The Right of making Rules, whereby the Subjects may every man know what is so his owne, as no other Subject can without injustice take it from him"; "To him also belongeth the Right of all Judicature and decision of Controversies"; "And of making War, and Peace, as he shall think best"; "And of choosing all Counsellours, and Ministers, both of Peace, and Warre"; "And of Rewarding, and Punishing, and that (where no former Law hath determined the measure of it) arbitrary"; "And of Honour and Order." (The last right, of giving titles of honor, appears only in *Leviathan.*) Cf. *De Cive* vi, 4–11, pp. 93–97, and *The Elements of Law* II, i, 6–13, pp. 86–88.

24 *Leviathan* 18, p. 235 (see the margin note quoted in note 23); also *De Cive* xiii, 16, p. 166.

25 *De Cive* vi, 13, p. 97. See *Leviathan* 42, pp. 576–77.

26 *The Elements of Law* II, i, 14, p. 89: "This device therefore of them that will make civil laws first, and then a civil body afterwards, (as if policy made a body politic, and not a body politic made policy) is of no effect." See also *Leviathan* 46, pp. 699–700.

27 Cf. John Plamenatz, *Man and Society*, vol. I, pp. 150–51. Citing the Constitution of the United States as an example, he contends: "It is possible so to divide authority between dif-

ferent bodies and persons that none is sovereign in Hobbes' sense and yet no dispute can arise which somebody has not the right to settle finally."

28   See, e.g., R. W. K. Hinton, "English Constitutional Theories from Sir John Fortescue to Sir John Eliot," *English Historical Review* 75 (1960), pp. 410–25; Corinne Comstock Weston, "The Theory of Mixed Monarchy under Charles I and After," ibid., pp. 426–43; and Julian H. Franklin, *John Locke and the Theory of Sovereignty: Mixed Monarchy and the Right of Resistance in the Political Thought of the English Revolution* (Cambridge: Cambridge University Press, paperback ed., 1981), chapter 2.

29   Henry Parker, *Observations upon some of his Majesties late Answers and Expresses* (London, 1642), p. 34; see also pp. 22, 45.

30   The just-quoted passage in *Observations* (p. 34) continues: "If the State intrusts this [arbitrary power] to one man, or few, there may be danger in it; but the Parliament is neither one nor few, it is indeed the State it self."

31   Ibid., pp. 40–42.

32   Goldsmith, "Hobbes's 'Mortall God': Is There a Fallacy in Hobbes's Theory of Sovereignty," p. 42; see pp. 42–43. Colwyn Williamson, "Hobbes on Law and Coercion," *Ethics* 80 (1970), pp. 146–55, makes the narrower interpretive argument that legislative and coercive authority are necessarily united.

33   Bodin's *Republique* (1576), which appeared in translation in 1606 with the title *The Six Bookes of a Commonweale*, was an authoritative reference for both sides in the prewar constitutional debates. The influence of Bodin's thought in the period is discussed by Kenneth Douglas McRae, Introduction to Jean Bodin, *The Six Bookes of a Commonweale* (Cambridge, Mass.: Harvard University Press, 1962), pp. A62–A67, and by J. H. M. Salmon, *The French Religious Wars in English Political Thought* (Oxford: Clarendon Press, 1959), chapters 5–6. On Bodinian analytic absolutism, see also Quentin Skinner, *The Foundations of Modern Political Thought*, vol. II, *The Age of Reformation* (Cambridge: Cambridge University Press, 1978), pp. 284–301, esp. 286–89; and Julian H. Franklin, *Jean Bodin and the Rise of Absolutist Theory* (Cambridge: Cambridge University Press, 1973).

34   Bodin's conflation of analytic and prescriptive absolutism is discussed by Plamenatz, *Man and Society*, vol. I, p. 104.

35 *The Elements of Law* II, viii, 7, p. 137. The reference is to Jean Bodin, *The Six Bookes of a Commonweale*, ed. Kenneth Douglas McRae, Book II, chapter 1, p. 194: "Wherefore such states as wherein the rights of soveraigntie are divided, are not rightly to bee called Commonweales, but rather the corruption of Commonweales, as *Herodotus* hath most briefly, but most truely written." See also *The Elements of Law* II, i, 16, pp. 89–90, and 19, p. 91.

36 *De Cive* vii, 4, p. 108: "For example, if the naming of Magistrates, and the arbitration of War, and Peace, should belong to the King, Judicature to the *Lords*, and contribution of Monies to the *People*, and the power of making Lawes too *altogether*, this kind of State would they call a *mixt Monarchie* forsooth. But if it were possible that there could be such a State, it would no whit advantage the liberty of the subject; for as long as they all agree, each single Citizen is as much subject as possibly he can be; but if they disagree, the State returns to a Civill War, and the Right of the *private Sword*, which certainly is much worse than any subjection whatsoever: But that there can be no such kind of Government hath been sufficiently demonstrated in the foregoing Chapter."

37 Ibid. vi, 13, p. 97.

38 *The Elements of Law* II, i, 16, p. 90: "that seeming mixture of several kinds of government, not mixture of the things themselves, but confusion in our understandings, that cannot find out readily to whom we have subjected ourselves."

39 Ibid. II, i, 17, p. 90. See *De Cive* xii, 5, p. 150 (see text pertaining to note 55, this chapter). Franklin, *John Locke and the Theory of Sovereignty*, p. 4n., notes the distinction in Bodinian thought.

40 *De Cive* vi, 18, p. 103.

41 *The Elements of Law* II, i, 17, p. 90.

42 Ibid. II, i, 19, pp. 91–92. The parallel list in *De Cive* (vi, 18, pp. 103–4) differs slightly: "*To make and abrogate Lawes, To* determine *War and Peace*, to know, and judge of all *controversies*, either by himselfe, or by *Judges* appointed by him; to elect all *Magistrates, Ministers*, and *Counsellors*. Lastly, if there be any man who by Right can doe some one action which is not lawfull for any Citizen or Citizens to doe beside himselfe, that man hath obtained *the supreme power*." Bodin's list of the "true markes of Soveraigntie" is similar: see Goldsmith, "Hobbes's

'Mortall God': Is There a Fallacy in Hobbes's Theory of Sovereignty," pp. 36–37. See also René Gadave, *Un Théoricien Anglais du Droit public au XVIIe siècle: Th. Hobbes* (New York: Arno Press, 1979), pp. 134–35.

43 *Leviathan* 18, p. 236.

44 Goldsmith grants this, in apparent contradiction of his main thesis. "Hobbes's 'Mortall God': Is There a Fallacy in Hobbes's Theory of Sovereignty," p. 35: "It seems clear that [Hobbes's] concern in chapter eighteen is not to formulate a complete list of the logically distinguishable rights of sovereignty but rather to justify these rights by showing that they are necessary means to the performance of the state's functions."

45 *Leviathan* 18, pp. 232–33.

46 Ibid. 19, p. 239.

47 *The Elements of Law* II, viii, 7, p. 137. This paraphrases Jean Bodin, *The Six Bookes of a Commonweale*, p. 194: "For the nobilitie which should have the power to make the lawes for all: (which is as much as to say to commaund and forbid what them pleased, without power to appeale from them, or for a man to oppose himselfe against their commaunds) would by their lawes at their pleasure forbid others to make peace or warre, or to levie taxes, or to yeeld fealtie and homage without their leave." See Franklin, *Jean Bodin and the Rise of Absolutist Theory*, p. 30.

48 *De Cive* vi, 7, p. 94; see *The Elements of Law* II, i, 8, p. 86. The medieval language of swords is omitted from *Leviathan*. Cf. 18, pp. 232–33 (quoted in the text pertaining to note 45, this chapter).

49 *De Cive* vi, 8, p. 94. See *The Elements of Law* II, i, 9, pp. 86–87, and *Leviathan* 18, p. 234.

50 *The Elements of Law* II, i, 10, p. 87. See *De Cive* vi, 9, p. 95, and *Leviathan* 18, p. 234.

51 *The Elements of Law* II, i, 11, p. 87; *De Cive* vi, 10, p. 95. In the parallel passage in *Leviathan* (18, p. 235), Hobbes expressly includes under this heading the right to appoint counselors (to wit, Parliament's impeachment in 1640 of Laud and Strafford, principal advisers to Charles I).

52 *Leviathan* 18, p. 233. See *De Cive* vi, 11, pp. 95–96.

53 *The Elements of Law* II, i, 13, p. 88: Some would allot the sovereign "provision limited, as of certain lands, taxes, penalties, and the like, than which (if mis-spent), they shall have

no more, without a new consent of the same men that allowed the former." See *Leviathan* 24, pp. 298–99, and *A Dialogue between A Philosopher and A Student of the Common Laws of England*, *English Works*, vol. VI, pp. 150, 154.

54 *The Elements of Law* II, i, 14, p. 88.

55 *De Cive* xii, 5, p. 150. Cf. *Leviathan* 18, pp. 234–35, where the accent is on military authority. With the Militia Ordinance of 1642 in mind presumably, this being the legislative title for Parliament's army, Hobbes insists that the sovereign must have exclusive authority in this area and also possess the authority to levy the necessary taxes. "Ninthly, is annexed to the Soveraignty, the Right of making Warre, and Peace with other Nations, and Common-wealths; that is to say, of Judging when it is for the publique good, and how great forces are to be assembled, armed, and payd for that end; and to levy mony upon the Subjects, to defray the expenses thereof. For the Power by which the people are to be defended, consisteth in their Armies; and the strength of an Army, in the union of their strength under one Command; which Command the Soveraign Instituted, therefore hath; because the command of the *Militia*, without other Institution, maketh him that hath it Soveraign."

56 An instance of the latter designation is quoted in the preceding note.

57 *De Cive* vi, 17, pp. 102–3. See also vii, 5, p. 109, and 16, pp. 113–15; *The Elements of Law* II, ii, 10, pp. 96–97; and *Leviathan* 19, pp. 246–47. The last-quoted passage from *The Elements of Law* (II, i, 14, pp. 88–89) continues: "Again: supposing those limited forces and revenue, either by the necessary, or negligent use of them, to fail; and that for a supply, the same multitude be again to be assembled, who shall have power to assemble them, that is to compel them to come together? If he that demandeth the supply hath that right (viz.) the right to compel them all; then is his sovereignty absolute: if not, then is every particular man at liberty to come or not; to frame a new commonwealth or not; and so the right of the private sword returneth."

58 *Leviathan* 18, p. 236.

59 Ibid. (emphasis mine).

60 Howard Warrender, *The Political Philosophy of Hobbes: His Theory of Obligation* (Oxford: Clarendon Press, 1957), pp. 179–80,

187, observes the distinction, in Hobbes's analysis, between essential and "expendable" sovereign powers.

61 I am grateful to John Orbell for his comments on the following discussion.

62 *Leviathan* 18, pp. 236–37. See also 29, p. 368: "For what is it to divide the Power of a Common-wealth, but to Dissolve it; for Powers divided mutually destroy each other." In *Behemoth*, Hobbes observes: "They [referring to the common people] dreamt of a mixed power, of the King and the two Houses. That it was a divided power, in which there could be no peace, was above their understanding" (*Behemoth or The Long Parliament*, 2nd ed., ed. Ferdinand Tönnies, with an introduction by M. M. Goldsmith [London: Frank Cass, 1969], p. 125).

63 *Leviathan* 21, p. 261: "But one may ask . . . when, or where has there been a Kingdome long free from Sedition and Civill Warre. In those Nations, whose Common-wealths have been long-lived, and not been destroyed, but by forraign warre, the Subjects never did dispute of the Soveraign Power."

64 Goldsmith, "Hobbes's 'Mortall God': Is There a Fallacy in Hobbes's Theory of Sovereignty," p. 43.

65 *Leviathan* 19, p. 240.

66 *Behemoth*, p. 68; see also pp. 75, 125. Hobbes intended only to tell "the story of their injustice, impudence, and hypocrisy." "For the proceeding of the war, I refer you to the history thereof written at large in English. I shall only make use of such a thread as is necessary for the filling up of such knavery, and folly also, as I shall observe in their several actions" (pp. 119–20).

67 Ibid., p. 70.

68 Ibid., pp. 115–16. See also p. 109: "I understand now, how the Parliament destroyed the peace of the kingdom; and how easily, by the help of seditious Presbyterian ministers, and of ambitious ignorant orators, they reduced this government to anarchy."

69 Ibid., p. 121: "You may see by this, what weak people they were, that were carried into the rebellion by such reasoning as the Parliament used, and how impudent they were that did put such fallacies upon them."

70 Goldsmith, we have seen, actually asserts that Hobbes "needs to prove . . . that disagreement cannot be resolved peacefully – it must always lead to contention" ("Hobbes's 'Mortall

God': Is There a Fallacy in Hobbes's Theory of Sovereignty,"
p. 43). In my view, the opinion that it is permissible to escalate elite conflict into armed struggle is a necessary condition
of the argument, as opposed to an empirical proposition in
need of proof.

71 *Leviathan* 18, p. 233.
72 Plamenatz, *Man and Society*, vol. I, p. 153: "He could not see
that, where there are several final authorities, each in a different field, there may yet be a settled procedure for deciding
any dispute that may arise."
73 See Table 1 in chapter 1.
74 This is the subject of *The Elements of Law* II, vi: "That subjects
are not bound to follow their private judgments in controversies of religion"; *De Cive* xviii: "Concerning those things which
are necessary for our entrance into the Kingdome of Heaven";
and *Leviathan* 43: "Of what is NECESSARY for a Mans Recep-
tion into the Kingdome of Heaven." "The difficulty is this"
(Hobbes puts it in *The Elements of Law*, pp. 113–14): "We have
amongst us the Word of God for the rule of our actions; now
if we shall subject ourselves to men also, obliging ourselves
to do such actions as shall be by them commanded; when the
commands of God and man shall differ, we are to obey God,
rather than man: and consequently the covenant of general
obedience to man is unlawful." See *De Cive* xv, 1, pp. 183–
84, and xviii, 1, p. 250; *Leviathan* 31, p. 395, and 43, p. 609.
75 *The Elements of Law* II, vi, 6, p. 116; *De Cive* xviii, 6, p. 256;
Leviathan 43, pp. 610–11.
76 E.g., *De Cive* vi, 11, p. 96: "No man can serve two Masters:
nor is he lesse, but rather more, a Master, whom we believe
we are to obey for feare of damnation, then he whom we
obey for feare of temporall death."
77 Ibid. xviii, 14, p. 263; see also *The Elements of Law* II, vi, 9, p.
121.
78 *The Elements of Law* II, vi, 14, p. 125; *De Cive* xviii, 13, pp. 262–
63; *Leviathan* 42, pp. 530–31.
79 Although Hobbes knows that "it is not the Romane Clergy
onely, that pretends the Kingdome of God to be of this World,
and thereby to have a Power therein, distinct from that of the
Civill State" (*Leviathan* 47, p. 714).
80 Ibid. 33, p. 427 (emphasis omitted); see *De Cive* xvii, 22, pp.

236–37. Chapter 42 of *Leviathan*, "Of POWER ECCLESIAS-TICALL," is a lengthy refutation of Bellarmine, to Hobbes's mind the most formidable defender of papal supremacy (see esp. pp. 575–76). In *The Elements of Law*, the Erastian doctrine is defended in chapter vii of the second part (the two chapters on religion in this part, vi and vii, carry the overall heading, "That decision of controversies in religion dependeth on the sovereign power"). The parallel chapter in *De Cive*, xi ("Places and Examples of Scripture of the Rights of Government agreeable to what hath beene said before"), presents a Scriptural proof for the necessity of unified sovereignty; compare *Leviathan* 20, pp. 257–60.

81 *Leviathan* 39, p. 499.

82 Ibid. 40, p. 509.

83 *De Cive* xvi, "Of the Kingdome of God under the Old Covenant"; *Leviathan* 40, "Of the RIGHTS of the Kingdome of God, in Abraham, Moses, the High Priests, and the Kings of Judah." "And therefore so far forth as concerneth the Old Testament, we may conclude, that whosoever had the Soveraignty of the Common-wealth amongst the Jews, the same had also the Supreme Authority in matter of Gods externall worship" (*Leviathan* 40, pp. 511–12).

84 *Leviathan* 42, p. 525: "I have shewn already . . . that the Kingdome of Christ is not of this world: therefore neither can his Ministers (unless they be Kings,) require obedience in his name."

85 *The Elements of Law* II, vii, 10–11, p. 132. See *Leviathan* 36, p. 468, and 38, p. 477.

86 E.g., J. W. N. Watkins, *Hobbes's System of Ideas: A Study in the Political Significance of Philosophical Theories*, 2nd ed. (London: Hutchinson University Library, 1973), pp. 1–4 and passim; Richard Ashcraft, "Ideology and Class in Hobbes' Political Theory," *Political Theory* 6 (1978), pp. 27–62; M. M. Goldsmith, Introduction to the Second Edition of *Behemoth*, esp. p. xiii; and Robert P. Kraynak, "Hobbes's *Behemoth* and the Argument for Absolutism," *American Political Science Review* 76 (1982), pp. 837–47. For a somewhat different view, putting more stress on Hobbes's constitutional doctrine, see Royce MacGillivray, "Thomas Hobbes's History of the English Civil War: A Study of *Behemoth*," *Journal of the History of Ideas* 31

(1970), esp. p. 188: "All his causes of the war . . . can be summed up in one: the failure of all manner of men, Royalist and ostensibly loyal as well as seditious, to observe that strict subordination to the King the necessity of which is expounded by Hobbes most forcefully in *Leviathan*."

87 *De Cive* vi, 11, p. 96 (annotation to the 1647 edition, emphasis omitted).

88 The human-science argument that this is always the case is made in Alasdair MacIntyre, "Is a Science of Comparative Politics Possible?" In Alan Ryan (ed.), *The Philosophy of Social Explanation* (Oxford: Oxford University Press, 1973), esp. pp. 174–75.

89 E.g., Ashcraft, "Ideology and Class in Hobbes' Political Theory," p. 50: "Hobbes' socioeconomic explanation of the Civil War was, in the end, placed within the framework of an ideological conflict over principles of theology and political philosophy."

90 *De Cive* vi, 13, p. 97. Further illustrations of the same point include the following. Under a popular government, Hobbes observes in *Leviathan* (18, p. 231), no one imagines that sovereignty is conditional: "That men see not the reason to be alike in a Monarchy . . . proceedeth from the ambition of some, that are kinder to the government of an Assembly, whereof they may hope to participate, than of Monarchy, which they despair to enjoy." And in the same work (12, p. 182), he asks: "Who is there that does not see, to whose benefit it conduceth, to have it believed, that a King hath not his Authority from Christ, unlesse a Bishop crown him?" See also *The Elements of Law* II, vi, 9, p. 121: "And they who strive concerning such [religious] questions and divide themselves into sects, are therefore to be accounted zealous of the faith, their strife being but carnal. . . . For they are not questions of faith, but of wit, wherein, carnally, men are inclined to seek the mastery of one another."

91 *De Cive* vi, 11, p. 96 (annotation to the 1647 edition, emphasis omitted). In *Behemoth* (p. 193), Hobbes observes: "I believe it is the desire of most men to bear rule; but few of them know what title one has to it more than another, besides the right of the sword."

92 *De Cive* Authors Preface to the Reader, p. 37.

93 See John M. Wallace, *Destiny His Choice: The Loyalism of An-*

drew Marvell (Cambridge: Cambridge University Press, 1968), chapter 1; and the discussion in chapter 7 of the present study.

94 *De Cive* x, 18, p. 140.

95 This is remarked, e.g., by Jean Hampton, *Hobbes and the Social Contract Tradition* (Cambridge: Cambridge University Press, 1986), pp. 105–6. Cf. Susan Moller Okin, " 'The Soveraign and his Counsellours': Hobbes's Reevaluation of Parliament," *Political Theory* 10 (1982), pp. 49–75, who argues that Hobbes expresses a mellower view of Parliament in the later (posthumously published) *Dialogue . . . of the Common Laws.*

96 Hobbes conceptualizes the issue in traditional fashion as a comparison of monarchy, aristocracy, and democracy; his arguments, however, principally contrast monarchy and parliamentary government (see, e.g., *The Elements of Law* II, v, 3, p. 110, and *De Cive* x, 19, p. 140). In the first two versions of the political theory, there are two chapters devoted to the comparison of forms of government. The first treats the process by which the several forms are instituted, to the point that, whichever the form of government, sovereignty is unconditional (*The Elements of Law* II, ii, and *De Cive* vii). This chapter is omitted from *Leviathan;* the functional equivalent is the contractarian defense of unconditional sovereignty that appears at the beginning of chapter 18 on sovereigns' rights. The second chapter on the topic in *The Elements of Law* (II, v) and *De Cive* (x) compares the inconveniences of various forms of government; this corresponds to chapter 19 of *Leviathan.*

97 *Leviathan* 19, p. 241.

98 *The Elements of Law* II, v, 3, p. 110; *De Cive* x, 3, p. 131; *Leviathan* 22, pp. 279–80.

99 Cf. *De Cive* v, 10, p. 89, where Hobbes distinguishes subordinate associations, such as companies of merchants, from states by the scope of their authority and the liberties of membership: "*Cities* they are not, because they have not submitted themselves to the will of the company simply, and in all things, but in certain things onely determined by the City; and on such termes as it is lawfull for any one of them to contend in judgement against the *body it selfe of the sodality;* which is by no means allowable to a *Citizen* against the *City.*" A prudential argument for the expediency of dissent in subordinate political bodies (so members may avoid responsibility for their fellows' debts and crimes) appears in *Leviathan*

22, pp. 278–79. The distinction between sovereign and non-sovereign associations based on the legality of dissent was a Grotian theme; see Richard Tuck, *Natural Rights Theories: Their Origin and Development* (Cambridge: Cambridge University Press, 1979), pp. 65–66.

100 *Leviathan* 22, pp. 282–83.

101 Ibid. 19, p. 241.

102 *The Elements of Law* II, v, 4, pp. 110–11.

103 Ibid., p. 111. See *De Cive* x, 11, p. 137.

104 *Leviathan* 19, p. 243. See *The Elements of Law* II, v, 5, p. 111, and *De Cive* x, 6, p. 133.

105 *The Elements of Law* II, v, 6, p. 112; see *Leviathan* 19, p. 243.

106 *De Cive* x, 13, p. 138; see *The Elements of Law* II, v, 7, p. 112, and *Leviathan,* 19, p. 242.

107 *Leviathan* 19, pp. 244–45; cf. *De Cive* x, 16, p. 139.

108 *Leviathan* 19, p. 245.

109 In addition to the passage from *The Elements of Law* quoted in the last paragraph, see *De Cive* x, 11, p. 137; *Leviathan* 19, p. 242, and 25, pp. 309–10.

110 *Leviathan* 25, p. 310.

111 *De Cive* x, 10, pp. 136–37.

112 *The Elements of Law* II, v, 8, p. 112.

113 *Leviathan* 19, p. 243; see also *De Cive* x, 12, p. 137.

114 *De Cive* x, 12, p. 138.

115 *The Elements of Law* II, v, 8, p. 112.

116 *De Cive* x, 7, p. 134.

117 James Harrington, *Oceana*, p. 175; quoted in Perez Zagorin, *A History of Political Thought in the English Revolution* (London: Routledge & Kegan Paul, 1954), pp. 134–35.

CHAPTER 5. HOBBESIAN ROLES

1 J. W. N. Watkins, "Philosophy and Politics in Hobbes," *Philosophical Quarterly* 5 (1955), p. 142. See also *Hobbes's System of Ideas: A Study in the Political Significance of Philosophical Theories,* 2nd ed. (London: Hutchinson University Library, 1973), chapter 6, section 20, pp. 72–74.

2 M. M. Goldsmith, *Hobbes's Science of Politics* (New York: Columbia University Press, 1966), pp. 63–66.

3 C. B. Macpherson, *The Political Theory of Possessive Individual-*

ism: Hobbes to Locke (Oxford: Oxford University Press, 1964), p. 45.

4 Michael Oakeshott, "The Moral Life in the Writings of Thomas Hobbes," in *Hobbes on Civil Association* (Berkeley: University of California Press, 1975), pp. 119–31.

5 The Hobbesian state of nature is not therefore a moral vacuum. See Howard Warrender, *The Political Philosophy of Hobbes: His Theory of Obligation* (Oxford: Clarendon Press, 1957), p. 41 (and generally, the Introduction and Part I). For the distinction between grounds and "validating conditions" of obligation, see pp. 14–17. Part III makes the case that Hobbes grounds obligation in natural – finally divine – law.

6 Ibid., p. 63.

7 David P. Gauthier, *The Logic of Leviathan: The Moral and Political Theory of Thomas Hobbes* (Oxford: Clarendon Press, 1969), p. 139.

8 They are chapters iii and iv in Part II of *The Elements of Law;* and *De Cive* viii and ix.

9 *The Elements of Law* II, iii, 8, p. 101; cf. *De Cive* viii, 9, p. 20. The following is another example: "And if it happen, that the master himself by captivity or voluntary subjection, become servant to another, then is that other master paramount" (*The Elements of Law* II, iii, 6, p. 101; see *De Cive* viii, 8, p. 119).

10 Compare *Leviathan* 20, p. 256, with the passages from *The Elements of Law* and *De Cive* cited in the preceding note.

11 *Leviathan* 22, pp. 274–75, 285.

12 Regarding merchant companies, see text pertaining to note 100, chapter 4.

13 *Leviathan* 22, pp. 274–84.

14 Ibid., pp. 275–76.

15 Ibid., p. 284.

16 Ibid., pp. 285–87. See *De Cive* xiii, 13, p. 163: "A faction [is] a multitude of subjects gathered together, either by mutuall *contracts* among themselves, or by the power of some one, without his or their [authority] who bear the supreme Rule."

17 *Leviathan* 22, pp. 286–87. See *De Cive* xiii, 13, pp. 163–64: "Those Princes who permit factions, doe as much as if they received an enemy within their walls."

18 *De Cive* xii, 13, p. 155.

19 Ibid.

20 *Leviathan* 23, p. 289: "A PUBLIQUE MINISTER, is he, that by the Soveraign . . . is employed in any affaires, with Authority

to represent in that employment, the Person of the Common-wealth."

21 Ibid., pp. 289–90.
22 E.g. (ibid., p. 293): "An Ambassador sent from a Prince, to congratulate, condole, or to assist at a solemnity, though Authority be Publique; yet because the businesse is Private . . . is a Private person."
23 Ibid., pp. 293–94.
24 E.g., regarding provincial governors (ibid., p. 290): "For such Protectors, Vice-Roys, and Governors, have no other right, but what depends on the Soveraigns Will."
25 E.g., Henry Parker, *Observations upon some of his Majesties late Answers and Expresses* (London, 1642), p. 32, and *Some Few Observations upon his Majesties late Answer to the Declaration, or Remonstrance of the Lords and Commons of the 19. of May, 1642* (London, 1642), pp. 13–14.
26 Cf. *The Elements of Law* II, x, 4, pp. 147–48, and *De Cive* xiv, 1, p. 168.
27 *Leviathan* 30, p. 391.
28 Ibid. 25, pp. 306–8.
29 Ibid., pp. 308–10.
30 Ibid. 26, pp. 327–29.
31 Ibid. 28, p. 361.
32 Macpherson, *The Political Theory of Possessive Individualism*, pp. 62–67. Macpherson specifically argues that Hobbes has a market concept of justice.
33 Ibid., pp. 97–99, and passim.
34 *Leviathan* 28, p. 361; see also 23, pp. 290–91.
35 Ibid. 28, p. 361.
36 Ibid. 17, p. 228 (emphasis omitted); see *The Elements of Law* I, xix, 7, pp. 80–81, and *De Cive* v, 9, p. 89.
37 Ronald Hutton, *The Royalist War Effort 1642–1646* (London: Longman, 1982), chapters 15–18; and J. S. Morrill, *The Revolt of the Provinces: Conservatives and Radicals in the English Civil War 1630–1650* (London: Allen & Unwin, 1976), pp. 98–111.
38 *Leviathan* Review and Conclusion, pp. 718–19 (emphasis omitted). See also 29, pp. 375–76: A subject "is obliged . . . to protect his Protection as long as he is able."
39 *De Cive* ii, 18, p. 59. See chapter 2, text pertaining to note 34.
40 *De Cive* vi, 5, p. 93.
41 *Leviathan* 28, p. 353.

42 *The Elements of Law* I, xv, 18, p. 62.

43 See also *De Cive* vii, 18, p. 116.

44 *Leviathan* 21, p. 270.

45 Ibid. Review and Conclusion, p. 719.

46 Ibid., p. 720.

47 Ibid.

48 Ibid. 20, p. 257.

49 Warrender, *The Political Philosophy of Hobbes*, pp. 5–7, 41, 75–77.

50 Ibid., pp. 13–17.

51 Ibid., p. 16. Warrender illustrates (p. 15): "Sanity or maturity
. . . operate in most ethical systems, as they do in that of
Hobbes, as validating conditions for obligations deriving from
another source; or, to convert to the negative form, insanity or
immaturity operate as invalidating principles for such obligations."

52 "Suspended" and "prima facie" obligations are distinguished,
ibid., pp. 26–28. Obligations are "suspended" in the absence
of validating conditions, whereas Warrender applies the label
"prima facie" to instances in which it is not specified whether
the validating conditions pertain. I use the term "prima facie
obligation" in a looser sense to refer simply to weak obligations.

53 Ibid., p. 102 (the passage is quoted in chapter 1, note 16). Warrender discusses dangerous duties in chapter 8, pp. 188–95.

54 Ibid., pp. 190–91. For pertinent passages in *De Cive* and *Leviathan*, see chapter 2, text pertaining to notes 37 and 52.

55 Warrender, *The Political Philosophy of Hobbes*, p. 192.

56 Ibid.

57 Ibid., p. 118. In Warrender's view (pp. 192–93), it must also
be left to the individual to assess the need to perform lesser
duties.

58 Ibid., p. 118, see generally, pp. 63–67, 115–18.

59 *Leviathan* 28, p. 361. On the idea of prima facie obligation, see
Colin Strang, "What if Everyone Did That?" In Judith J. Thom-
son and Gerald Dworkin (eds.), *Ethics* (New York: Harper &
Row, 1968), pp. 151–62.

60 *De Cive* vi, 13, pp. 97–98; cf. *Leviathan* 21, p. 268.

61 *Leviathan* 21, p. 270; see also 28, p. 361.

62 Ibid. Review and Conclusion, p. 728.

63 *The Elements of Law* II, iii, 1, p. 99; *De Cive* viii, 1, pp. 117–18;
Leviathan 20, p. 256.

64 *Leviathan* 20, p. 256: "In summe the Rights and Consequences of both *Paternall* and *Despoticall* Dominion, are the very same with those of a Soveraign by Institution."

65 Ibid. 21, p. 262. Thus, with regard to promising, it is a basic stipulation that "covenants entred into by fear, in the condition of meer Nature, are obligatory. . . . And even in Commonwealths, if I be forced to redeem my selfe from a Theefe by promising him mony, I am bound to pay it, till the Civill Law discharge me" (ibid. 14, p. 198).

66 Ibid. 20, p. 252.

67 Ibid., p. 255.

68 Ibid. Review and Conclusion, pp. 720–21. Elsewhere, Hobbes emphasizes that receipt of benefits entails tacit consent; see the discussions regarding servants and children later in this chapter.

69 *The Elements of Law* II, iii, 2, pp. 99–100; *De Cive* viii, 1, pp. 117–18; cf. *Leviathan* 20, pp. 252–53.

70 Michael J. Sandel, *Liberalism and the Limits of Justice* (Cambridge: Cambridge University Press, 1982), p. 58.

71 *De Cive* viii, 2–3, p. 118. See *The Elements of Law* II, iii, 2–3, pp. 99–100; and *Leviathan* 20, p. 255.

72 *De Cive* viii, 3, p. 118 (margin note).

73 Ibid. Cf. *The Elements of Law* II, iii, 3, p. 100, and *Leviathan* 20, pp. 255–56.

74 *The Elements of Law* II, iii, 7, p. 101; *De Cive* viii, 9, p. 120. See also *Leviathan* 20, p. 255.

75 *The Elements of Law* II, iii, 3, p. 100.

76 *De Cive* viii, 1, p. 117.

77 *Leviathan* 20, p. 256. See also *De Cive* viii, 1, p. 117. The latter (just quoted) passage, describing the exchange of benefits between master and servant, begins: "If a man taken Prisoner in the Wars . . . promises the Conquerour, or the stronger Party, *his Service, i.e.* to do all whatsoever he shall command him . . .''

78 *Leviathan* 20, p. 256.

79 *De Cive* viii, 5, pp. 118–19: "The *Lord* therefore hath no less Dominion over a Servant that *is not*, then over one that *is bound*, for he hath a *Supreme Power* over both." See *The Elements of Law* II, iii, 5, p. 100. In *De Cive* viii, 7, p. 119, and *Leviathan* 20, p. 256, Hobbes applies the concept of authorization to the master-servant relationship.

80 *Leviathan* 20, p. 255; see *The Elements of Law* II, iii, 3, p. 100,

and *De Cive* viii, 3–4, p. 118. *De Cive* (viii, 9, p. 120) stipulates that masters ought "in equity" to protect their servants.

81 Gilbert Meilaender, " 'A Little Monarchy': Hobbes on the Family," *Thought* 53 (1978), pp. 402–3.

82 Cf. Warrender, *The Political Philosophy of Hobbes*, pp. 235–36, who argues that childrens' obligations are best understood as falling under the heading of natural-law obligations.

83 *Leviathan* 20, p. 253. See *The Elements of Law* II, iv, 3, pp. 103–4. The parallel passage in *De Cive* (ix, 1–2, pp. 121–22) omits the imputation of consent.

84 *The Elements of Law* II, iv, 3, pp. 103–4. See *Leviathan* 20, p. 254. *De Cive* links obligation directly to benefit (ix, 4, p. 123).

85 *The Elements of Law* II, iv, 3, pp. 103–4. See *De Cive* ix, 3, p. 122, and *Leviathan* 30, p. 382.

86 *The Elements of Law* II, iv, 1–7, pp. 102–4; *De Cive* ix, 2–6, pp. 122–24; *Leviathan* 20, pp. 253–55.

87 *Leviathan* 20, p. 253. See *The Elements of Law* II, iv, 2, p. 103, and (on the topic of political conquest) II, ii, 15, p. 98.

88 *Leviathan* 30, p. 382; see *De Cive* ix, 8, pp. 124–25.

89 *De Cive* ix, 8, p. 124; see *Leviathan* 30, p. 382.

90 *De Cive* ix, 8, p. 124: "The *enfranchised son*, or *released servant*, doe now stand in lesse fear of their *Lord* and *Father*, being deprived of his naturall and lordly power over them, and (if regard be had to true and inward *Honour*) doe *Honour* him lesse, then before. For *Honour* . . . is nothing else but the estimation of anothers power; and therefore he that hath least power, hath alwayes least *Honour*."

91 Ibid.

92 Cf. John Dunn, *The Political Thought of John Locke: An Historical Account of the Argument of the 'Two Treatises of Government'* (Cambridge: Cambridge University Press, 1969), p. 236: "Like any moral brief, it [the *Two Treatises of Government*] contains implicit terms which constitute a hypothetical moral rationale for a social structure. But it is a moral rationale of the duties of the tenants of the various roles, not a rationale of the relationships between the roles themselves. Macpherson misunderstands the extent to which Locke treats the social structures in which men live as data, as social facts, which cannot be explained as the immediate products of intentional actions and which cannot be effectively manipulated by individuals, which constitute in fact the context of their lives." See also John Dunn,

"Individuality and Clientage in the Formation of Locke's Social Imagination," in *Rethinking Modern Political Theory: Essays 1979–83* (Cambridge: Cambridge University Press, 1985), p. 33.

93 The last right of sovereignty detailed in chapter 18 of *Leviathan* (pp. 235–36) is that of establishing "Lawes of Honour": "to appoint what Order of place, and dignity, each man shall hold; and what signes of respect, in publique or private meetings, they shall give to one another."

94 Parliament's Militia Ordinance and Charles I's Commissions of Array, the formal instruments by which the armies were raised, are discussed by Morrill, *The Revolt of the Provinces*, pp. 39–40. See also Hutton, *The Royalist War Effort 1642–46*, and Mark A. Kishlansky, *The Rise of the New Model Army* (Cambridge: Cambridge University Press, 1979).

95 *De Cive* ix, 3, p. 122. See also i, 14–15, p. 50.

96 *Leviathan* 15, p. 211. Cf. *The Elements of Law* I, xvii, 1, p. 68; and *De Cive* iii, 13, p. 68.

97 *De Cive* vi, 13, pp. 97–98. See also *The Elements of Law* II, i, 5, pp. 85–86.

CHAPTER 6. THE ART OF GOVERNMENT

1 For a survey of commentaries of the interwar period associating Hobbism with totalitarianism, see Deborah Baumgold, "Political Commentary: Interpretation of the Tradition of Political Theory as a Mode of Political Inquiry; An Examination of Leo Strauss's Hobbes Commentaries" (Ph.D. dissertation, Princeton University, 1980), chapter 2.

2 *Leviathan* 19, pp. 239–40. According to John M. Wallace, *Destiny His Choice: The Loyalism of Andrew Marvell* (Cambridge: Cambridge University Press, 1968), p. 14, it was typical for royalists to deny the distinction between king and tyrant in connection with discussions of obedience.

3 Susan Moller Okin, " 'The Soveraign and his Counsellours': Hobbes's Reevaluation of Parliament," *Political Theory* 10 (1982), p. 72.

4 E.g., Michael Oakeshott, "Introduction to *Leviathan*," in *Hobbes on Civil Association* (Berkeley: University of California Press, 1975), pp. 62–63; Howard Warrender, *The Political Philosophy of Hobbes: His Theory of Obligation* (Oxford: Clarendon Press, 1957), pp. 180–88; A. E. Taylor, "The Ethical Doctrine of

Hobbes," in K. C. Brown (ed.), *Hobbes Studies* (Cambridge, Mass.: Harvard University Press, 1965), pp. 45–49; René Gadave, *Un Théoricien Anglais du Droit public au XVIIe siècle: Th. Hobbes* (New York: Arno Press, 1979), pp. 215–36; M. M. Goldsmith, *Hobbes's Science of Politics* (New York: Columbia University Press, 1966), chapter 6.

5 E.g., David P. Gauthier, *The Logic of Leviathan: The Moral and Political Theory of Thomas Hobbes* (Oxford: Clarendon Press, 1969), pp. 138–39.

6 Mario A. Cattaneo, "Hobbes Théoricien de l'Absolutisme Eclairé," in Reinhart Kosselleck and Roman Schnur (eds.), *Hobbes-Forschungen* (Berlin: Duncker & Humblot, 1969), p. 209, translation mine. See also "Hobbes's Theory of Punishment," trans. J. M. Hatwell, in K. C. Brown (ed.), *Hobbes Studies* (Cambridge, Mass.: Harvard University Press, 1965), pp. 275–97, esp. p. 276.

7 Only two duties do not refer to previously specified rights of sovereignty: public charity and policies to deter idleness (*Leviathan* 30, p. 387). Warrender, *The Political Philosophy of Hobbes*, p. 87, remarks the equation of sovereigns' rights with their duties in *Leviathan*.

8 E.g., Jean Hampton, *Hobbes and the Social Contract Tradition* (Cambridge: Cambridge University Press, 1986), p. 193: "Unfortunately, Hobbes never gives a fully developed argument explaining why a self-interested sovereign's rule would be so 'enlightened.' "

9 *De Cive* vi, 13, p. 99 (annotation to the 1647 edition, emphasis omitted). See *Leviathan* 18, p. 238.

10 *Leviathan* 18, p. 238 (emphasis mine).

11 *De Cive* vi, 13, p. 99 (annotation to the 1647 edition, emphasis omitted): "But it cannot be deny'd but a Prince may sometimes have an inclination to doe wickedly; but grant then that thou hadst given him a power which were not absolute, but so much onely as suffic'd to defend thee from the injuries of others, which, if thou wilt be safe, is necessary for thee to give; are not all the same things to be feared? for he that hath strength enough to protect all, wants not sufficiency to oppresse all. Here is no other difficulty then, but that humane affaires cannot be without some inconvenience. And this inconvenience it self is in the Citizens, not in the Government; for if men could rule themselves, every man by his own com-

mand, that's to say, could they live according to the Lawes of Nature, there would be no need at all of a City, nor of a common coercive power."

12 *De Cive* xiii, 1, p. 156. The historical point – that Englishmen in the period did not typically equate absolutism with arbitrary rule – is argued by James Daly, "The Idea of Absolute Monarchy in Seventeenth-Century England," *Historical Journal* 21 (1978), esp. p. 242.

13 *The Elements of Law* II, ix, 1, p. 142; *De Cive* vi, 13, p. 99; *Leviathan* 30, p. 376. The sovereign's natural-law duties are emphasized by Taylor, "The Ethical Doctrine of Hobbes," pp. 45–49; and by Warrender, *The Political Philosophy of Hobbes*, pp. 109–10, 178–79, and passim.

14 *De Cive* vi, 13, p. 99 (annotation to the 1647 edition, emphasis omitted).

15 See *A Dialogue . . . of the Common Laws of England*, pp. 33–34 (the passage is quoted later in this section).

16 *The Elements of Law* II, ix, 1, p. 142; see *De Cive* xiii, 2, p. 157.

17 *Leviathan* 19, p. 241.

18 *The Elements of Law* II, v, 4, p. 111. See also *De Cive* x, 4 and 7, pp. 132, 133; and *Leviathan* 19, p. 241.

19 *Leviathan* 19, p. 241.

20 *De Cive* x, 18, p. 140.

21 *Leviathan* 11, p. 161: "I put for a generall inclination of all mankind, a perpetuall and restlesse desire of Power after power, that ceaseth onely in Death."

22 *A Dialogue . . . of the Common Laws of England*, pp. 33–34.

23 Niccolo Machiavelli, *The Prince*, trans. George Bull (Harmondsworth: Penguin, 1961), chapter 17.

24 The statement is quoted, e.g., in J. A. W. Gunn, *Politics and the Public Interest in the Seventeenth Century* (London: Routledge & Kegan Paul, 1969), p. 68.

25 *The Elements of Law* II, ix, 1, p. 142. See *De Cive* xiii, 2, p. 157, and *Leviathan* 30, p. 376. In *The Elements of Law* (II, ix, 3, p. 143), Hobbes defines the "temporal good[s] of [the] people" as: "1. Multitude. 2. Commodity of living. 3. Peace amongst ourselves. 4. Defence against foreign power." The list in *De Cive* (xiii, 6, pp. 158–59) varies slightly: "1. That they be defended against forraign enemies. 2. That Peace be preserved at home. 3. That they be enrich't as much as may consist with publique security. 4. That they enjoy a harmelesse liberty."

Gunn, *Politics and the Public Interest in the Seventeenth Century*, pp. 61–82, discusses the concept of the public interest in Hobbesian theory.

26   *Leviathan* 19, pp. 241–42. See also 30, p. 388; *The Elements of Law* II, v, 1, p. 108; *De Cive* x, 2 and 18, pp. 130–31, 140. Hobbes's identification of the power of the sovereign with the power of his subjects is treated by Gadave, *Un Théoricien Anglais du Droit public au XVIIe siècle: Th. Hobbes*, pp. 233–36.

27   *The Elements of Law* II, v, 1, p. 108. See *De Cive* x, 2, pp. 130–31.

28   Chapters viii and ix in Part II of *The Elements of Law* treat the causes of rebellion and the duties of rulers; they are chapters xii and xiii in *De Cive*.

29   *De Cive* xiii, 9, p. 160. See *The Elements of Law* II, ix, 5, p. 144: "For maintaining of peace at home, there be so many things necessarily to be considered, and taken order in, as there be several causes concurring to sedition."

30   Accurately, there are three Hobbesian categories. *The Elements of Law* (II, viii, 1, p. 133) lists: (1) discontent, encompassing popular fear of punishment and burdensome taxation, as well as political ambition (2–3, pp. 133–35); (2) pretense of right, referring to seditious opinions (4–10, pp. 135–38); and (3) hope of success (11–14, pp. 138–41). Cf. the more abstract categories in *De Cive* (xii, 1, pp. 145–46): (1) "internall disposition," meaning seditious opinions (1–8, pp. 146–52); (2) "externall Agent," or popular and elite discontent (9–10, pp. 152–53); and (3) the "action it selfe," i.e., the organization of a seditious "faction" (11–13, pp. 153–56).

31   *The Elements of Law* II, ix, 5, p. 144; *De Cive* xiii, 10–11, pp. 161–62.

32   *De Cive* xiii, 12, pp. 162–63. See *The Elements of Law* II, ix, 7, p. 145.

33   *The Elements of Law* II, ix, 8, pp. 145–46; *De Cive* xiii, 9 and 13, pp. 160–61, 163–64.

34   E.g., *De Cive* xiii, 8, pp. 159–60.

35   See esp. *Leviathan* 26, pp. 315–17. The common-law tradition is treated by J. G. A. Pocock, *The Ancient Constitution and the Feudal Law: A Study of English Historical Thought in the Seventeenth Century* (1957; reprint, New York: Norton, 1967), chapter 2, and (on Hobbes's critique) chapter 7, pp. 162–71.

36   *Leviathan* 26, p. 316.

37 Hobbes denies the force of legal precedents, ibid., pp. 323–25.

38 *The Elements of Law* II, x, 8, p. 150. See *Leviathan* 26, p. 317, and *A Dialogue . . . of the Common Laws of England*, p. 5.

39 *A Dialogue . . . of the Common Laws of England*, p. 26: "A law is the command of him or them that have the sovereign power, given to those that be his or their subjects, declaring publicly and plainly what every of them may do, and what they must forbear to do." See also p. 24; *De Cive* xiv, 1, p. 168; and *Leviathan* 26, p. 312.

40 *A Dialogue . . . of the Common Laws of England*, pp. 36–68, esp. pp. 50–54, and p. 118.

41 Ibid., pp. 68–121, esp. pp. 70, 91–92, 96–97, and 118–19.

42 Ibid., pp. 121–37, esp. pp. 121–22.

43 Ibid., p. 122: "Now the person to whom this authority of defining punishments is given, can be no other, in any place of the world, but the same person that hath the sovereign power. . . . For it were in vain to give it to any person that had not the power of the militia to cause it to be executed." See, generally, pp. 121–26.

44 *Leviathan* 28, p. 353 (emphasis omitted); see *De Cive* xiii, 16, p. 166.

45 *Leviathan* 18, p. 235 (margin note), and 27, pp. 338–39; *De Cive* xiii, 16, p. 166. Cf. *Leviathan* Review and Conclusion, p. 721, where Hobbes speaks of "Absolute and Arbitrary Legislative Power" (the passage is quoted in note 83, this chapter). Warrender, *The Political Philosophy of Hobbes*, p. 261, emphasizes the distinction in Hobbes's thought between arbitrary government and absolute government conducted according to law.

46 *The Elements of Law* II, x, 8, p. 150. Hobbes's descriptions of the state of nature are pertinent: *The Elements of Law* I, xix, 5, pp. 79–80; *De Cive* v, 5, pp. 87–88; *Leviathan* 17, pp. 225–26.

47 *De Cive* vi, 9, p. 95 (emphasis omitted). The passage continues with this definition of civil law: "the commands of him who hath the *chiefe authority* in the City, for direction of the future actions of his Citizens." See *The Elements of Law* II, i, 10, p. 87. The parallel passage in *Leviathan* (18, p. 234) emphasizes the need for laws governing property: "Seventhly, is annexed to the Soveraigntie, the whole power of prescribing the Rules, whereby every man may know, what Goods he may enjoy and what Actions he may doe, without being

molested by any of his fellow Subjects: And this is it men call *Propriety*. For before constitution of Soveraign Power . . . all men had right to all things; which necessarily causeth Warre: and therefore this Proprietie, being necessary to Peace, and depending on Soveraign Power, is the Act of that Power, in order to the publique peace. These Rules of Propriety (or *Meum* and *Tuum*) and of *Good*, *Evill*, *Lawfull*, and *Unlawfull* in the actions of Subjects, are the Civill Lawes."

48   *De Cive* vi, 11, p. 95 (the topic of the paragraph is political education). See also v, 1, p. 85; *The Elements of Law* I, xix, 1, p. 77. The nature of deliberation and willing is treated in *Leviathan* 6, pp. 126–28.

49   Goldsmith, *Hobbes's Science of Politics*, observes (p. 202): "Although the sovereign need not act by law, law will usually be the best means of action available to him – it conforms others' actions to the rules by the threat of physical coercion or punishment rather than by the use of force."

50   *Leviathan* 30, p. 376, summarizes the sovereign's duties: "a generall Providence, contained in publique Instruction, both of Doctrine, and Example; and in the making, and executing of good Lawes, to which individuall persons may apply their own cases." More attention is paid to political education in *Leviathan* than in the earlier versions of the political theory; cf. the just-quoted passage with *De Cive* xiii, 3, pp. 157–58 (the latter is quoted at the beginning of this section). One paragraph is devoted to the topic in the chapters on sovereigns' duties in the first two versions (*The Elements of Law* II, ix, 8, pp. 145–46; *De Cive* xiii, 9, pp. 160–61); this expands into eight pages in *Leviathan* (30, pp. 377–85).

51   *The Elements of Law* II, x, 2, p. 147.

52   Ibid. II, viii, 6, p. 136. See also the distinction between law and counsel, II, x, 4, p. 148: "In counsel the expression is, Do, because it is best; in a law, Do, because I have right to compel you; or Do, because I say, do: when counsel which should give the reason of the action it adviseth to, becometh the reason thereof itself, it is no more counsel, but a law." See *De Cive* xiv, 1, p. 168, and *Leviathan* 25, p. 303.

53   *De Cive* xiv, 2, p. 169. See *The Elements of Law* II, x, 2, p. 147 ("a law bindeth by a promise of obedience in general"), and *Leviathan* 25, p. 303, and 26, p. 312.

54   *De Cive* xiv, 2, p. 170 (annotation to the 1647 edition, empha-

sis omitted). See *The Elements of Law* I, xix, 1, p. 77, and *Leviathan* 27, pp. 338, 343. The distinction between formal and prudential motives for obedience to law was commonly drawn by Protestant thinkers in the sixteenth and early seventeenth centuries, according to Richard Tuck, *Natural Rights Theories: Their Origin and Development* (Cambridge: Cambridge University Press, 1979), p. 93. For an interpretation of the role of the distinction in Hobbesian theory, see Warrender, *The Political Philosophy of Hobbes*, chapter 9, esp. p. 205.

55 Tuck, *Natural Rights Theories*, p. 91, quoting John Selden, *Opera*, I, col. 106. Selden's association with the Tew Circle is discussed, p. 101.

56 *Leviathan* 27, p. 343.

57 *De Cive* xiv, 7, p. 172. Cf. *The Elements of Law* II, x, 6, p. 149, where Hobbes distinguishes between "simple" and "penal" law; and *Leviathan* 26, p. 331 ("these Penal Lawes are for the most part written together with the Lawes Distributive").

58 *De Cive* vi, 4, p. 93. Cf. *The Elements of Law* II, i, 6, p. 86, and *Leviathan* 18, p. 231.

59 *De Cive* xiv, 7, pp. 172–73; see *Leviathan* 27, pp. 338–39.

60 *Leviathan* 30, pp. 387–88.

61 Warrender discusses these topics, *The Political Philosophy of Hobbes*, pp. 183–85.

62 *Leviathan* 30, p. 388.

63 *De Cive* xiii, 15, pp. 165–66; *Leviathan* 30, p. 388.

64 *De Cive* xiii, 15, p. 165.

65 *Leviathan* 30, pp. 388–89.

66 Ibid., p. 388.

67 *De Cive* xiii, 17, p. 167. See Cattaneo, "Hobbes's Theory of Punishment," pp. 275–97.

68 *Leviathan* 28, p. 353; see *De Cive* xiii, 16, p. 166.

69 *Leviathan* 28, p. 355. Other distinctions follow from the requirements that punishments be inflicted by public authorities, for the transgression of law. E.g., "private injuries, and revenges," "pain inflicted without publique hearing," or by "Usurped power" are acts of hostility because they are not public acts carried out by public authorities (pp. 354–55). See also *De Cive* xiii, 16, p. 166.

70 *Leviathan* 18, p. 235, and *De Cive* xiii, 16, p. 166.

71 *The Elements of Law* II, ix, 7, p. 145. See *De Cive* xiii, 12, pp. 162–63, and *Leviathan* 30, pp. 385–86.

72 *De Cive* xiii, 12, p. 163; see *Leviathan* 27, pp. 342–43.
73 *Leviathan* 30, pp. 390–91, and 28, pp. 361–62.
74 Ibid. 30, p. 386.
75 Ibid. 27, p. 342.
76 Ibid. 30, p. 389.
77 Ibid., pp. 389–90. Indeed, extreme destitution totally excuses stealing, as necessary for self-preservation (27, p. 346).
78 *Leviathan* 30, p. 390.
79 Ibid., pp. 385–86. See also 27, p. 347.
80 Ibid. 27, pp. 350–51.
81 Ibid., p. 350.
82 Ibid., pp. 344–45: "For though all Crimes doe equally deserve the name of Injustice . . . yet it does not follow that all Crimes are equally unjust, no more than that all crooked lines are equally crooked; which the Stoicks not observing, held it as great a Crime, to kill a Hen, against the Law, as to kill ones Father."
83 Ibid. Review and Conclusion, p. 721: "I have set down for one of the causes of the Dissolutions of Common-wealths, their Imperfect Generation, consisting in the want of an *Absolute and Arbitrary Legislative Power*" (emphasis mine).
84 *The Elements of Law* II, viii, 2, p. 134, gives several examples: "As in the time of Henry VII. the seditions of the Cornish men that refused to pay a subsidy, and, under the conduct of the Lord Audley, gave the King battle upon Blackheath; and that of the northern people, who in the same king's time, for demanding a subsidy granted in parliament, murdered the Earl of Northumberland in his house." See II, ix, 5, p. 144; *De Cive* xii, 9, p. 152, and xiii, 10, p. 161.
85 *De Cive* xiii, 10, p. 161.
86 *The Elements of Law* II, ix, 5, p. 144.
87 Ibid. II, viii, 8, p. 138. See *De Cive* xii, 7, pp. 150–51, and *Leviathan* 29, pp. 367–68, 373.
88 *Leviathan* 29, pp. 367–68.
89 Ibid., p. 373. In a similar vein, see *De Cive* xiii, 8, p. 160, where Hobbes stresses the need to make provision for continuing supply: "We must . . . for fear of War, in time of Peace hoord up good summs, if we intend the safety of the Common-weal."
90 *The Elements of Law* II, ix, 5, p. 144; *De Cive* xii, 9, p. 152, and xiii, 10, pp. 161–62; *Leviathan* 30, p. 386.

91 *Leviathan* 30, p. 386. The passage concludes with this exception: "saving that the rich, who have the service of the poor, may be debtors not onely for their own persons, but for many more."

92 Hobbes's taxation policy is discussed by Dudley Jackson, "Thomas Hobbes's Theory of Taxation," *Political Studies* 21 (1973), pp. 175–82, and by Aaron Levy, "Economic Views of Thomas Hobbes," *Journal of the History of Ideas* 15 (1954), pp. 589–95.

93 *Leviathan* 30, pp. 386–87; see *The Elements of Law* II, ix, 5, p. 144, and *De Cive* xiii, 11, p. 162. In a related vein, Hobbes also recommends legislation to encourage those who can to work (*Leviathan* 30, p. 387). See also *The Elements of Law* II, ix, 4, p. 143, and *De Cive* xiii, 14, pp. 164–65.

94 *The Elements of Law* II, ix, 5, p. 144. Jackson, "Thomas Hobbes's Theory of Taxation," pp. 179–80, finds this an odd assertion considering that in the period the imposition of excise taxes occasioned popular riots. He hypothesizes that Hobbes was rather more appreciative of the opposition from men of property to taxing wealth.

95 *De Cive* vi, 17, p. 102 (the latter emphasis – from "partly" to "lust" – is mine).

96 *Leviathan* 31, pp. 406–7.

97 Ibid. 30, p. 390 (the passage is quoted earlier; see text pertaining to note 78).

98 Ibid. 27, pp. 348–49.

99 *De Cive* xiii, 16, p. 166.

100 *Leviathan* 27, p. 339.

101 Colin Strang, "What if Everyone Did That?" In Judith J. Thomson and Gerald Dworkin (eds.), *Ethics* (New York: Harper & Row, 1968), pp. 155–56. In the continuation of the passage, the "Defaulter" announces: The principle of universalization "doesn't impress me as a reason why *I* should [pay, etc.], however many people do or don't." See pp. 159–60 for the argument that responsibility for public goods is shared between ruler and ruled.

102 *Leviathan* Introduction, p. 81.

103 Cf., e.g., *De Cive* vi, 13, p. 99 (annotation to the 1647 edition, emphasis omitted): "Although they, who have the chief Command, doe not all those things they would, and what they know profitable to the City," it is also the case that "Cit-

izens, who busied about their private interest, and carelesse
of what tends to the publique, cannot sometimes be drawn
to performe their duties without the hazard of the City."

104 " 'The proportions and relations of things are just as much
facts as the things themselves; and if you get those wrong,
you falsify the picture really seriously.' " Dorothy L. Sayers,
Gaudy Night (New York: Avon Books, 1968), p. 21.

105 Cf. Hampton, *Hobbes and the Social Contract Tradition,* p. 194.

106 *De Cive* x, 7, p. 133.

107 On the importance of the translation, see Maurice Mandelbaum, "Societal Facts," in Alan Ryan (ed.), *The Philosophy of
Social Explanation* (Oxford: Oxford University Press, 1973), esp.
p. 113.

CHAPTER 7. HOBBES'S POLITICAL SENSIBILITY

1 The title "Leviathan" may have been used in connection with
The Elements of Law. There seems to have existed a manuscript,
dated May 1640, with the title *Leviathan, principles of law and
policy,* which likely was a copy of *The Elements of Law.* Whether
this was Hobbes's title or a later addition is unknown. See
W. H. Greenleaf, "A Note on Hobbes and the Book of Job,"
Anales de la Catedra Francisco Suarez 14 (1974), p. 23.

2 E.g., Robert Sanderson, *XXXV Sermons* (London, 1681), p. 310
(second pagination), quoted in Greenleaf, "A Note on Hobbes
and the Book of Job," p. 22: "So can the Lord deal, and often
doth, with the great *Behemoths* and *Leviathans* of the world."

3 The mood is described by John M. Wallace, *Destiny His Choice:
The Loyalism of Andrew Marvell* (Cambridge: Cambridge University Press, 1968), chapter 1.

4 *Leviathan* Introduction, p. 81.

5 Ibid. 17, p. 227.

6 Ibid. 28, p. 362. The reference is Job 41: 33–34: "Upon earth
there is not his like, who is made without fear. He beholdeth
all high *things:* he *is* a king over all the children of pride."

7 Royce MacGillivray, "Thomas Hobbes's History of the English
Civil War: A Study of *Behemoth," Journal of the History of Ideas*
31 (1970), pp. 184–85, raises the possibility that Hobbes did
not so name the work. The early editions of the work do not
include "Behemoth" in the title. On the other hand, the work
is so titled in the manuscript on which the Tönnies edition is

based, a manuscript apparently written by Hobbes's amanuensis.

8 *Behemoth*, pp. 119–20. Hobbes comments in similar vein on the Long Parliament in *A Dialogue . . . of the Common Laws of England*, pp. 13–14. The passage is quoted in note 21, this chapter.

9 Cf. the genre of Hobbes interpretation emphasizing the moral-psychological significance of pride. E.g., Leo Strauss, *The Political Philosophy of Hobbes: Its Basis and Its Genesis*, trans. Elsa M. Sinclair (Chicago: University of Chicago Press [Phoenix ed.], 1963), and *Natural Right and History* (Chicago: University of Chicago Press, 1953), chapter 5; Michael Oakeshott, "The Moral Life in the Writings of Thomas Hobbes," in *Hobbes on Civil Association* (Berkeley: University of California Press, 1975), pp. 75–131.

10 *Leviathan* 29, p. 374. Compare the passage from Anthony Ascham's *Of the Confusions and Revolutions of Governments*, ed. G. W. S. V. Rumble (Delmar, N.Y.: Scholars' Facsimiles & Reprints, 1975), p. 144 (see text pertaining to note 42).

11 *De Cive* v, 5, p. 88.

12 *Leviathan* 29, p. 374.

13 Ibid. 31, p. 398 (emphasis omitted). See also 33, p. 420, and *De Cive* xv, 6, pp. 186–87.

14 *Leviathan* 31, p. 398.

15 Ibid., pp. 397–98; *De Cive* xv, 5, pp. 185–86. See also *Of Liberty and Necessity*, *English Works*, vol. IV, p. 249. Bishop Bramhall criticized Hobbes for ascribing irresistible power to political authority, *The Questions Concerning Liberty, Necessity, and Chance, Clearly Stated and Debated between Dr. Bramhall . . . and Thomas Hobbes*, *The English Works of Thomas Hobbes*, vol. V, p. 133.

16 *De Cive* xv, 6, p. 186; see *Leviathan* 31, p. 398.

17 Aubrey records that he heard Hobbes "inveigh much against the Crueltie of Moyses for putting so many thousands to the Sword for Bowing to the Golden Calf." Oliver Lawson Dick (ed.), *Aubrey's Brief Lives* (Ann Arbor: University of Michigan Press, 1962), p. 157.

18 *De Cive* Authors Preface to the Reader, p. 36 (emphasis omitted): "I have not yet made it out of a desire of praise . . . but for your sakes Readers, who I perswaded my selfe, when you should rightly apprehend and thoroughly understand this Doctrine I here present you with, would rather chuse to brooke

with patience some inconveniences under government (because humane affairs cannot possibly be without some) then selfe opiniatedly disturb the quiet of the publique."

19 Ibid.

20 *Leviathan* Review and Conclusion, p. 728. See also 21, pp. 267–68, where Hobbes charges that ancient political theory, meaning specifically Aristotelianism, encourages bloodshed. "By reading of these Greek, and Latine Authors, men . . . have gotten a habit . . . of favouring tumults, and of licentious controlling the actions of their Soveraigns; and again of controlling those controllers, with the effusion of so much blood; as I think I may truly say, there was never any thing so deerly bought, as these Western parts have bought the learning of the Greek and Latine tongues."

21 *A Dialogue . . . of the Common Laws of England*, p. 13. In the continuation of the passage (pp. 13–14), Hobbes reiterates his attack on the Long Parliament: "And when there is a Parliament, if the speaking and leading men should have a design to put down monarchy, as they had in the Parliament which began to sit the third of November, 1640, shall the King . . . be disabled to perform his office, by virtue of these acts of Parliament which you have cited? If this be reason, it is reason also that the people be abandoned, or left at liberty to kill one another."

22 *De Cive* x, 7, p. 134.

23 Earlier, in February 1649, a similar oath had been put to the Council of State. For the history of the Engagement Oath, see John M. Wallace, "The Engagement Controversy 1649–1652: An Annotated List of Pamphlets," *Bulletin of the New York Public Library* 68 (1964), pp. 384–87.

24 According to Wallace, ibid., p. 386, passage of the oath was probably occasioned by the unrest surrounding the trial of Lilburne, the Leveller leader, in October 1649.

25 This point is emphasized by Quentin Skinner, "Conquest and Consent: Thomas Hobbes and the Engagement Controversy," in G. E. Aylmer (ed.), *The Interregnum: The Quest for Settlement 1646–1660* (London: Macmillan, 1972), p. 94. Howard Warrender notes (Editor's Introduction to the Latin *De Cive*, pp. 14–16) that in this period existing censorship laws were temporarily allowed to lapse (as of September 1651).

26 Hobbes's assertion that irresistible power confers dominion was

cited approvingly by Ascham, although he also criticized Grotius and Hobbes for supposing that men could renounce all natural rights (Ascham, *Of the Confusions and Revolutions of Governments*, pp. 108, 119–21). This was the second edition of Ascham's work. The first edition appeared in July 1648, with the title, *A Discourse, wherein is examined what is particularly lawfull during the Confusions and Revolutions of Goverment*. See G. W. S. V. Rumble, Introduction to *Confusions and Revolutions*, pp. 1–2; and Wallace, *Destiny His Choice*, p. 30.

27 Marchamont Nedham, *The Case of the Commonwealth of England, Stated*, ed. Philip A. Knachel (Charlottesville: University Press of Virginia, 1969), pp. 129–30. The excerpts are characterized by Nedham as arguments for submission to the present powers and against continued royalist resistance (pp. 135–36). In the same vein, he also ran lengthy, unsigned passages from *De Corpore Politico* in several issues of *Mercurius Politicus* of January 1651. This was the official newspaper of the Commonwealth, which Nedham edited. See Quentin Skinner, "The Ideological Context of Hobbes's Political Thought," *Historical Journal* 9 (1966), p. 311.

28 *Leviathan* Review and Conclusion, p. 719.

29 Ibid., p. 728.

30 Skinner, "The Ideological Context of Hobbes's Political Thought"; "Conquest and Consent: Thomas Hobbes and the Engagement Controversy." See also Wallace, *Destiny His Choice*, chapter 1; and Perez Zagorin, *A History of Political Thought in the English Revolution* (London: Routledge & Kegan Paul, 1954), chapter 5.

31 Zagorin, *A History of Political Thought in the English Revolution*, chapters 6 and 9; Wallace, "The Engagement Controversy 1649–1652," pp. 384–89.

32 Although Anthony Ascham and Marchamont Nedham are known for making the case for obedience to de facto authority on secular grounds, their tracts include providential appeals. E.g., *Confusions and Revolutions*, p. 98: "God sayes, *By me Princes raigne; For the governing Powers which are, are of God.*" See also pp. 109–10, 148. Providence figures in Nedham's *Case of the Commonwealth of England, Stated*, pp. 13, 18, 32, 46–49.

33 Rous and Dury also drew a distinction between the legality of authority and the legality of commands; i.e., the lawful commands of de facto rulers must be obeyed (Zagorin, *A History*

of Political Thought in the English Revolution, pp. 67–70). The contrast between providential and secular engagement arguments is Quentin Skinner's theme in "Conquest and Consent: Thomas Hobbes and the Engagement Controversy." See also Rumble, Introduction to *Confusions and Revolutions*, pp. 2–10, and Wallace, "The Engagement Controversy 1649–1652," pp. 384–89.

34 Warrender, Editor's Introduction to *De Cive (The Latin Version)*, pp. 10–11. For information on Ascham's *Discourse*, see note 26, this chapter.

35 *De Cive* Authors Preface to the Reader, pp. 30–31 (see text pertaining to note 65, this chapter), p. 36.

36 *The Elements of Law* II, v, 8, p. 112.

37 *De Cive* Authors Preface to the Reader, pp. 37–38 (emphasis omitted).

38 Rumble, Introduction to *Confusions and Revolutions*, pp. 1–2.

39 Ascham was anxious to establish this point. A statement prefacing the work notes that it was first published in the summer of 1648, well before Cromwell's victory: "The Reader may be pleased to understand, that this Discourse was made Publique, long before any change of Governement was undertaken here, and therefore could not by any obliquity point at that, which it could not then by any meanes see." *Confusions and Revolutions*, n.p.

40 Ibid., pp. 1–2.

41 Ibid., Preface to the Reader, n.p.; see also p. 91. At the beginning of the work (p. 2), in one of its better-known passages, Ascham says he speaks to "the rank of the people": "These are the Anvill on which all sorts of Hammers discharge themselves; they seldome or never begin a Warre, but are all concern'd in it after it is begun." Compare the passage from *Leviathan* quoted earlier in this chapter: By Hobbes's description, the people "receive their motion" from the sovereign or from ambitious rivals (see text pertaining to note 10).

42 Ascham, *Confusions and Revolutions*, p. 144; see also p. 117. The calamity of civil war is described on pp. 137, 146, and 200.

43 Wallace, *Destiny His Choice*, p. 37: "He [Marvell] captured in some of his graphic sentences the sadness with which many people watched the King's sun decline, and he caught the elegiac mood which was to sweep the country on the publication of the *Eikon Basilike*. It is no accident, I believe, that Marvell's

poems in 1648–49 are either elegies or lamentations. The civil war and the King's execution enhanced as nothing else was ever to do again in English history a general sense of the world's mutability."

44 Ibid., pp. 1–8.

45 Hobbes described the circumstances of his homecoming in "The Autobiography of Thomas Hobbes," p. 28. For differing estimations of Ascham, cf. Irene Coltman, *Private Men and Public Causes: Philosophy and Politics in the English Civil War* (London: Faber & Faber, 1962), Part III; and John Wallace's critical review, "The Cause Too Good," *Journal of the History of Ideas* 24 (1963), pp. 150–54. See also Wallace, *Destiny His Choice*, pp. 36–37.

46 Among the arguments against engagement, critics noted the obvious objection that the principle licenses political ambition. It encourages "daring and ambitious spirits to attempt continual innovations with this confidence, that if they can by anyways (how unjust soever) possess themselves of the supreme power, they ought to be submitted unto." [Robert Sanderson], *A Resolution of Conscience* (1649), pp. 5–6, quoted in Philip A. Knachel, Introduction to Nedham, *The Case of the Commonwealth of England, Stated,* pp. xxx–xxxi.

47 Ascham, *Confusions and Revolutions*, p. 92; see also pp. 146, 159. Nedham, *The Case of the Commonwealth of England, Stated,* p. 30. *Leviathan* Review and Conclusion, p. 728.

48 We know that Hobbes was keenly aware of Ascham. The assassination of Ascham contributed to the fear for his own safety that led Hobbes to come home in 1651. In "The Autobiography of Thomas Hobbes" (pp. 27–28), he reports: "When these scholars read that book of mine *[Leviathan]*, the gates of the temple of Janus flew open. I was falsely accused to the King of supporting the impious deeds of Cromwell and justifying crime. . . . I could not but think of Dorislaus and Ascham. . . . So I returned to my native land, not well assured of safety, but because there was nowhere else I could be safer."

49 Ascham, *Confusions and Revolutions*, p. 82. The passage continues: "And though the oath for the right magistrate be taken in the strictest terms of undergoing death and danger, yet it is to be understood always conditionally, as most promises are." This stipulation in Hobbesian theory is discussed in chapter 2, in the section entitled "Self-defense and a right of resistance."

50 Ibid., p. 82. The passage continues: "They who live under the full power of the unjust party may be said to take quarter, and to be in the same condition with the former: and so have the liberty to oblige themselves to that which the Prince may now expect from them, *viz.* to swear to those under whose power they live, that they will not attempt any thing against them."

51 *Leviathan* Review and Conclusion, p. 720. Compare Ascham, *Confusions and Revolutions*, p. 4: "And he must be a rare Example who makes not his last resolution for his owne life, or subsistence, which is equivalent to life; And therefore the valiantest and most strictly oblig'd Troops stick not to aske quarter, when they cannot defend themselves any longer, and are justified for it, even by those for whom they swore to die."

52 *Leviathan* Review and Conclusion, p. 719. The point is also discussed in Hobbes's autobiographical letter, *Considerations upon the Reputation, Loyalty, Manners, and Religion, of Thomas Hobbes,* pp. 423–24. His employer, the third earl of Devonshire, had come home from the Continent in 1645 and submitted to Parliament. See Leslie Stephen, *Hobbes* (Ann Arbor: University of Michigan Press, 1961), pp. 36, 43.

53 Ascham, *Confusions and Revolutions*, p. 46.

54 Ibid., pp. 138–39, 83, 43–44. In the first passage, Ascham observes that active obedience to a usurping power may actually be morally preferable to passive obedience: "For he who executes actively the Office of a Justice of Peace, or of another Inferiour Magistracy, by Virtue of a Commission sent to him by a suppos'd Illegall Magistrate, and thereby doth good to his poore Neighbours, doth not a thing so bad, as he doth, who even under his Legall Magistrate is prest out to warre against those, whom his Conscience cannot condemne, nor designe to death; yea or pay Taxes to be imployd against those whom his Conscience justifies."

55 Ascham, *Confusions and Revolutions*, p. 109. See also p. 138: "Besides into what Condition would we put our selves if we will not obey? in a State there can be no such thing as *Nonobedience:* Every man must either Command or obey, or else live by himselfe, by his owne Lawes and his owne Militia." Compare, e.g., *Leviathan* 17, pp. 227–28, and 21, pp. 268–69.

56 Nedham, *The Case of the Commonwealth of England, Stated,* p. 51. In the appendix, Nedham observes that Hobbesian principles

counsel against diehard loyalty to the Stuarts (p. 136): "From whence may plainly be inferred that since no security for life, limbs, and liberty (which is the end of all government) can now be had here by relinquishing our right of self-protection and giving it up to any other power beside the present, therefore it is very unreasonable in any man to put himself out of the protection of this power by opposing it and reserving his obedience to the King of Scots or any other power whatsoever; it being clear that neither he, nor any other, can now protect us by affording any possible security from violence and injury."

57 Ascham, *Confusions and Revolutions*, pp. 31–32, 115–17, 141 ("our obeying such in Lawfull things, is no assertion of their right"), 148, 159.

58 Nedham, *The Case of the Commonwealth of England, Stated*, p. 40; see also pp. 19, 27, 35–36, 39, 129.

59 *Leviathan* Review and Conclusion, p. 720. Nedham appeals to tacit consent to justify the title of the victor in a civil war, *The Case of the Commonwealth of England, Stated*, pp. 38–40. Both *Leviathan's* "Review and Conclusion" and Nedham's *Case* also observe that conquest is the foundation of most governments, and cite the example of William the Conqueror (*Leviathan* Review and Conclusion, pp. 721–22; Nedham, *Case*, pp. 25–26, 27–28, 37–38). Regarding the importance of conquest theory in seventeenth-century political thought, cf. J. G. A. Pocock, *The Ancient Constitution and the Feudal Law: A Study of English Historical Thought in the Seventeenth Century* (1957; reprint, New York: Norton, 1967), chapter 2, pp. 42–45, 53–55, and (on Hobbes) chapter 7, pp. 162–70; Wallace, *Destiny His Choice*, pp. 22–28; and Quentin Skinner, "History and Ideology in the English Revolution," *Historical Journal* 8 (1965), pp. 151–78.

60 *Behemoth*, pp. 135, 180.

61 Ascham, *Confusions and Revolutions*, p. 76 (also pp. 131–33). See Wallace, *Destiny His Choice*, pp. 56–58.

62 Ascham, *Confusions and Revolutions*, p. 158.

63 *De Cive* Authors Preface to the Reader, p. 36 (emphasis omitted).

64 Ibid., p. 37.

65 Ibid., pp. 30–31.

66 Cf. *Confusions and Revolutions*, p. 75, where Ascham suggests that the fundamental laws and parliaments characteristic of

republican governments offer protection against the outbreak of political ambition.

67 Marchamont Nedham, *The Case of the Commonwealth of England, Stated,* p. 34. He goes on to equate the majority, i.e., the "prevailing" part, with the whole people (p. 36): "By right of war, the whole must needs reside in that part of the people which prevailed."

68 Chapter 3, section titled "Authorization."

69 Nedham, *The Case of the Commonwealth of England, Stated,* p. 111. The chapter formed the basis for a 1656 Nedham treatise, *The Excellency of a Free State* (see Knachel, Introduction to *Case,* pp. xxxix–xl).

70 *Leviathan* Review and Conclusion, p. 721.

71 E.g., C. B. Macpherson, *The Political Theory of Possessive Individualism: Hobbes to Locke* (Oxford: Oxford University Press, 1964), p. 106. Cf. Michael Oakeshott, "Introduction to *Leviathan,*" in *Hobbes on Civil Association,* pp. 60–64.

72 Ian Shapiro, *The Evolution of Rights in Liberal Theory* (Cambridge: Cambridge University Press, 1986), p. 304.

73 This discussion follows Richard Tuck, *Natural Rights Theories: Their Origin and Development* (Cambridge: Cambridge University Press, 1979), pp. 2–4.

74 John Plamenatz's reading is a notable exception to this generalization. See, e.g., the passage from *Man and Society,* vol. I, *Political and Social Theory: Machiavelli Through Rousseau* (New York: McGraw-Hill, 1963), quoted in chapter 2, note 36.

75 *De Cive* xii, 13, p. 155 (margin note). See *Behemoth,* pp. 115–16, 144, 158.

76 *De Cive* x, 7, p. 134 (the passage is quoted in chapter 4; see text pertaining to note 116).

77 See R. G. Collingwood, *An Autobiography* (Oxford: Oxford University Press, 1970), p. 61: "Take Plato's *Republic* and Hobbes's *Leviathan,* so far as they are concerned with politics. Obviously the political theories they set forth are not the same. But do they represent two different theories of the same thing? Can you say that the *Republic* gives one account of 'the nature of the State' and the *Leviathan* another? No; because Plato's 'State' is the Greek πόλις, and Hobbes's is the absolutist State of the seventeenth century."

78 For a poignant description of the difficulties of early-modern rulers, which concludes with the poignant reminder that sub-

jects in this century suffer the historical solution of the problem of state power, see Howell A. Lloyd, *The Rouen Campaign 1590–1592: Politics, Warfare and the Early-Modern State* (Oxford: Clarendon Press, 1973), esp. pp. 196–97.

Bibliography

WORKS BY THOMAS HOBBES

"The Autobiography of Thomas Hobbes." Translated by Benjamin Farrington. In *The Rationalist Annual: 1958*, pp. 22–31. Edited by Hector Hawton. London: Watts, 1957.

Behemoth or The Long Parliament, 2nd ed. Edited by Ferdinand Tönnies. Introduction by M. M. Goldsmith. London: Frank Cass, 1969.

Considerations upon the Reputation, Loyalty, Manners, and Religion, of Thomas Hobbes. In *The English Works of Thomas Hobbes*, vol. IV, pp. 409–40. Edited by Sir William Molesworth. London: John Bohn, 1840.

De Cive: The English Version, entitled in the first edition Philosophicall Rudiments Concerning Government and Society. Edited by Howard Warrender. Oxford: Clarendon Press, 1983. References to *De Cive* cite the chapter (lowercase roman numeral), section (arabic numeral), and the page number in this edition.

[De Corpore] Elements of Philosophy. The First Section, Concerning Body. In *The English Works of Thomas Hobbes*, vol. I. Edited by Sir William Molesworth. London: John Bohn, 1839.

De Homine. Translated by Charles T. Wood, T. S. K. Scott-Craig, and Bernard Gert. In *Man and Citizen*, pp. 33–85. Edited by Bernard Gert. Garden City, N.Y.: Doubleday (Anchor Books), 1972.

A Dialogue between A Philosopher and A Student of the Common Laws of England. In *The English Works of Thomas Hobbes*, vol. VI, pp. 3–160. Edited by Sir William Molesworth. London: John Bohn, 1840.

The Elements of Law: Natural & Politic. Edited by Ferdinand Tönnies. Cambridge: Cambridge University Press, 1928. References to *The Elements of Law* cite the part (uppercase roman numeral), chapter (lowercase roman numeral), section (arabic numeral), and the page number in this edition.

The English Works of Thomas Hobbes, 11 vols. Edited by Sir William Molesworth. London: John Bohn, 1839–45.

Leviathan. Edited by C. B. Macpherson. Harmondsworth: Penguin (Pelican Books), 1968. References to *Leviathan* cite the chapter (arabic numeral) and the page numer in this edition.

Of Liberty and Necessity. In *The English Works of Thomas Hobbes*, vol. IV, pp. 229–78. Edited by Sir William Molesworth. London: John Bohn, 1840.

OTHER WORKS

Ascham, Anthony. *Of the Confusions and Revolutions of Governments.* Edited by G. W. S. V. Rumble. Delmar, N.Y.: Scholars' Facsimiles & Reprints, 1975.

Ashcraft, Richard. "Ideology and Class in Hobbes' Political Theory." *Political Theory* 6 (1978): 27–62.

Baumgold, Deborah. "Political Commentary: Interpretation of the Tradition of Political Theory as a Mode of Political Inquiry; An Examination of Leo Strauss's Hobbes Commentaries." Ph.D. dissertation, Princeton University, 1980.

Bodin, Jean. *The Six Bookes of a Commonweale*. Edited by Kenneth Douglas McRae. Cambridge, Mass.: Harvard University Press, 1962.

Brown, K. C., ed. *Hobbes Studies*. Cambridge, Mass.: Harvard University Press, 1965.

Cattaneo, Mario A. "Hobbes Théoricien de l'Absolutisme Eclairé." In *Hobbes-Forschungen*, pp. 199–210. Edited by Reinhart Kosselleck and Roman Schnur. Berlin: Duncker & Humblot, 1969.

Cattaneo, Mario A. "Hobbes's Theory of Punishment." Translated by J. M. Hatwell. In *Hobbes Studies*, pp. 275–97. Edited by K. C. Brown. Cambridge, Mass.: Harvard University Press, 1965.

Chanteur, Janine. "Note sur les Notions de 'Peuple' et de 'Multitude' chez Hobbes." In *Hobbes-Forschungen*, pp. 223–35. Edited by Reinhart Kosselleck and Roman Schnur. Berlin: Duncker & Humblot, 1969.

Collingwood, R. G. *An Autobiography*. Oxford: Oxford University Press, 1970.

Coltman, Irene. *Private Men and Public Causes: Philosophy and Politics in the English Civil War*. London: Faber & Faber, 1962.

Daly, James. "The Idea of Absolute Monarchy in Seventeenth-Century England." *Historical Journal* 21 (1978): 227–50.

Daly, James. "John Bramhall and the Theoretical Problems of Royalist Moderation." *Journal of British Studies* 11 (1971): 26–44.

Dick, Oliver Lawson, ed. *Aubrey's Brief Lives*. 1949. Reprint. Ann Arbor: University of Michigan Press, 1962.

Dunn, John. "Individuality and Clientage in the Formation of Locke's Social Imagination." In *Rethinking Modern Political Theory: Essays 1979–83*, pp. 13–33. Cambridge: Cambridge University Press, 1985.

Dunn, John. *The Political Thought of John Locke: An Historical Account of the Argument of the 'Two Treatises of Government.'* Cambridge: Cambridge University Press, 1969.

Dunn, John. "Social Theory, Social Understanding, and Political Action." In *Rethinking Modern Political Theory: Essays 1979–83*, pp. 119–38. Cambridge: Cambridge University Press, 1985.

Dunn, John. *Western Political Theory in the Face of the Future*. Cambridge: Cambridge University Press, 1979.

Dworkin, Ronald. *Taking Rights Seriously*. Cambridge, Mass.: Harvard University Press, 1977.

Francis, Mark. "The Nineteenth Century Theory of Sovereignty and Thomas Hobbes." *History of Political Thought* 1 (1980): 517–40.

Franklin, Julian H., ed. *Constitutionalism and Resistance in the Sixteenth Century: Three Treatises by Hotman, Beza, & Mornay*. New York: Pegasus, 1969.

Franklin, Julian H. "Constitutionalism in the Sixteenth Century: The Protestant Monarchomachs." In *Political Theory and Social Change*, pp. 117–32. Edited by David Spitz. New York: Atherton, 1967.

Franklin, Julian H. *Jean Bodin and the Rise of Absolutist Theory*. Cambridge: Cambridge University Press, 1973.

Franklin, Julian H. *John Locke and the Theory of Sovereignty: Mixed Monarchy and the Right of Resistance in the Political Thought of the English Revolution*. Cambridge: Cambridge University Press, paperback ed., 1981.

Gadamer, Hans-Georg. *Truth and Method*. Translation edited by Garrett Barden and John Cumming. New York: Seabury Press, 1975.

Gadave, René. *Un Théoricien Anglais du Droit public au XVIIe siècle: Th. Hobbes*. New York: Arno Press, 1979; reprint of the 1907 edition, titled *Th. Hobbes et ses Theories du Contrat Social et de la Sou-verainete.*

Gauthier, David P. *The Logic of Leviathan: The Moral and Political Theory of Thomas Hobbes.* Oxford: Clarendon Press, 1969.

Gauthier, David [P.]. "The Social Contract as Ideology." *Philosophy and Public Affairs* 6 (1977): 130–64.

Gert, Bernard. "Hobbes and Psychological Egoism." *Journal of the History of Ideas* 28 (1967): 503–20.

Goldsmith, M. M. "Hobbes's 'Mortall God': Is There a Fallacy in Hobbes's Theory of Sovereignty." *History of Political Thought* 1 (1980): 33–50.

Goldsmith, M. M. *Hobbes's Science of Politics.* New York: Columbia University Press, 1966.

Goldsmith, M. M. Introduction to the Second Edition of *Behemoth or The Long Parliament,* by Thomas Hobbes, pp. v–xiv. Edited by Ferdinand Tönnies. London: Frank Cass, 1969.

Gough, J. W. *The Social Contract: A Critical Study of Its Development,* 2nd ed. 1957. Reprint. Westport, Conn.: Greenwood, 1978.

Greenleaf, W. H. "Hobbes: The Problem of Interpretation." In *Hobbes and Rousseau: A Collection of Critical Essays,* pp. 5–36. Edited by Maurice Cranston and Richard S. Peters. Garden City, N.Y.: Doubleday (Anchor Books), 1972.

Greenleaf, W. H. "A Note on Hobbes and the Book of Job." *Anales de la Catedra Francisco Suarez* 14 (1974): 9–34.

Gunn, J. A. W. *Politics and the Public Interest in the Seventeenth Century.* London: Routledge & Kegan Paul, 1969.

Hampton, Jean. *Hobbes and the Social Contract Tradition.* Cambridge: Cambridge University Press, 1986.

Hanson, Donald W. *From Kingdom to Commonwealth: The Development of Civic Consciousness in English Political Thought.* Cambridge, Mass.: Harvard University Press, 1970.

Heinrichs, Terry. "Hobbes & the Coleman Thesis." *Polity* 16 (1984): 647–66.

Hexter, J. H. "Power Struggle, Parliament, and Liberty in Early Stuart England." *Journal of Modern History* 50 (1978): 1–50.

Hinton, R. W. K. "English Constitutional Theories from Sir John Fortescue to Sir John Eliot." *English Historical Review* 75 (1960): 410–25.

Hirsch, E. D., Jr. "Objective Interpretation." *PMLA* 75 (1960): 463–79.

Hirsch, E. D., Jr. *Validity in Interpretation*. New Haven, Conn.: Yale University Press, 1967.

Hirst, Derek. *The Representative of the People?: Voters and Voting in England under the Early Stuarts*. Cambridge: Cambridge University Press, 1975.

Hood, F. C. *The Divine Politics of Thomas Hobbes*. Oxford: Clarendon Press, 1964.

Hutton, Ronald. *The Royalist War Effort 1642–1646*. London: Longman, 1982.

Jackson, Dudley. "Thomas Hobbes's Theory of Taxation." *Political Studies* 21 (1973): 175–82.

Jordan, W. K. *Men of Substance: A Study of the Thought of Two English Revolutionaries, Henry Parker and Henry Robinson*. Chicago: University of Chicago Press, 1942.

Judson, Margaret Atwood. *The Crisis of the Constitution: An Essay in Constitutional and Political Thought in England 1603–1645*. New Brunswick, N.J.: Rutgers University Press, 1949.

Judson, Margaret Atwood. "Henry Parker and the Theory of Parliamentary Sovereignty." In *Essays in History and Political Theory in Honor of Charles Howard McIlwain*, pp. 138–67. Cambridge, Mass.: Harvard University Press, 1936.

Kavka, Gregory S. *Hobbesian Moral and Political Theory*. Princeton, N.J.: Princeton University Press, 1986.

Keohane, Nannerl O. "Claude de Seyssel and Sixteenth-Century Constitutionalism in France." In *Constitutionalism*, pp. 47–83. Edited by J. Roland Pennock and John W. Chapman. New York: New York University Press, 1979.

Kishlansky, Mark A. *The Rise of the New Model Army*. Cambridge: Cambridge University Press, 1979.

Kosselleck, Reinhart, and Roman Schnur, eds. *Hobbes-Forschungen*. Berlin: Duncker & Humblot, 1969.

Kraynak, Robert P. "Hobbes's *Behemoth* and the Argument for Absolutism." *American Political Science Review* 76 (1982): 837–47.

Levy, Aaron. "Economic Views of Thomas Hobbes." *Journal of the History of Ideas* 15 (1954): 589–95.

Lloyd, Howell A. *The Rouen Campaign 1590–1592: Politics, Warfare and the Early-Modern State*. Oxford: Clarendon Press, 1973.

Locke, John. *The Second Treatise of Government*. In *Two Treatises of Government*, rev. ed., pp. 305–541. Edited by Peter Laslett. New York: New American Library (Mentor Books), 1965.

Bibliography

Lukes, Steven. *Individualism*. Oxford: Basil Blackwell, 1973.

Lukes, Steven. "Methodological Individualism Reconsidered." In *The Philosophy of Social Explanation*, pp. 119–29. Edited by Alan Ryan. Oxford: Oxford University Press, 1973.

MacGillivray, Royce. "Thomas Hobbes's History of the English Civil War: A Study of *Behemoth*." *Journal of the History of Ideas* 31 (1970): 179–98.

Machiavelli, Niccolo. *The Prince*. Translated by George Bull. Harmondsworth: Penguin, 1961.

MacIntyre, Alasdair. "Is a Science of Comparative Politics Possible?" In *The Philosophy of Social Explanation*, pp. 171–88. Edited by Alan Ryan. Oxford: Oxford University Press, 1973.

McNeilly, F. S. *The Anatomy of Leviathan*. London: Macmillan, 1968.

Macpherson, C. B. *The Political Theory of Possessive Individualism: Hobbes to Locke*. Oxford: Oxford University Press, 1964.

McRae, Kenneth Douglas. Introduction to Jean Bodin, *The Six Bookes of a Commonweale*, pp. A3–A67. Cambridge, Mass.: Harvard University Press, 1962.

Mandelbaum, Maurice. "Societal Facts." In *The Philosophy of Social Explanation*, pp. 105–18. Edited by Alan Ryan. Oxford: Oxford University Press, 1973.

Mathie, William. "Justice and the Question of Regimes in Ancient and Modern Political Philosophy: Aristotle and Hobbes." *Canadian Journal of Political Science* 9 (1976): 449–63.

Meilaender, Gilbert. " 'A Little Monarchy': Hobbes on the Family." *Thought* 53 (1978): 401–15.

Morrill, J. S. *The Revolt of the Provinces: Conservatives and Radicals in the English Civil War 1630–1650*. London: Allen & Unwin, 1976.

Nedham, Marchamont. *The Case of the Commonwealth of England, Stated*. Edited by Philip A. Knachel. Charlottesville: University Press of Virginia, 1969.

Oakeshott, Michael. "Introduction to *Leviathan*." In *Hobbes on Civil Association*, pp. 1–74. Berkeley: University of California Press, 1975.

Oakeshott, Michael. "The Moral Life in the Writings of Thomas Hobbes." In *Hobbes on Civil Association*, pp. 75–131. Berkeley: University of California Press, 1975.

Oakeshott, Michael. "Thomas Hobbes." *Scrutiny* 4 (1935): 263–77.

Okin, Susan Moller. " 'The Soveraign and his Counsellours': Hobbes's Reevaluation of Parliament." *Political Theory* 10 (1982): 49–75.

Bibliography

Orwin, Clifford. "On the Sovereign Authorization." *Political Theory* 3 (1975): 26–44.

Parker, Henry. *Observations upon some of his Majesties late Answers and Expresses.* London, 1642.

Parker, Henry. *Some Few Observations upon his Majesties late Answer to the Declaration, or Remonstrance of the Lords and Commons of the 19. of May, 1642.* London, 1642.

Pennock, J. Roland, and John W. Chapman, eds. *Constitutionalism.* NOMOS, vol. XX. New York: New York University Press, 1979.

Peters, Richard. *Hobbes.* Harmondsworth: Penguin, 1956.

Pitkin, Hanna Fenichel. *The Concept of Representation.* Berkeley: University of California Press, paperback ed., 1972.

Pitkin, Hanna [Fenichel]. "Hobbes's Concept of Representation." Parts I, II. *American Political Science Review* 58 (1964): 328–40; 902–18.

Plamenatz, John. *The English Utilitarians,* 2nd ed. Oxford: Basil Blackwell, 1958.

Plamenatz, John. *Man and Society.* Vol. I, *Political and Social Theory: Machiavelli Through Rousseau.* New York: McGraw-Hill, 1963.

Pocock, J. G. A. *The Ancient Constitution and the Feudal Law: A Study of English Historical Thought in the Seventeenth Century.* 1957. Reprint. New York: Norton, 1967.

Polin, Raymond. *Politique et Philosophie chez Thomas Hobbes.* Paris: Presses Universitaires de France, 1953.

Raphael, D. D. *Hobbes: Morals and Politics.* London: Allen & Unwin, 1977.

Rousseau, Jean-Jacques. *The Social Contract.* Translated by Maurice Cranston. Harmondsworth: Penguin, 1968.

Rumble, G. W. S. V. Introduction to Anthony Ascham, *Of the Confusions and Revolutions of Governments.* Delmar, N.Y.: Scholars' Facsimiles & Reprints, 1975.

Russell, Conrad. "The Nature of a Parliament in Early Stuart England." In *Before the English Civil War,* pp. 123–50. Edited by Howard Tomlinson. London: Macmillan, 1983.

Ryan, Alan, ed. *The Philosophy of Social Explanation.* Oxford: Oxford University Press, 1973.

Ryan, Alan. *The Philosophy of the Social Sciences.* New York: Random House (Pantheon Books), 1970.

Salmon, J. H. M. *The French Religious Wars in English Political Thought.* Oxford: Clarendon Press, 1959.

Bibliography

Sandel, Michael J. *Liberalism and the Limits of Justice*. Cambridge: Cambridge University Press, 1982.

Sayers, Dorothy L. *Gaudy Night*. New York: Avon Books, 1968.

Scanlon, T. M. "Rights, Goals, and Fairness." In *Public and Private Morality*, pp. 93–111. Edited by Stuart Hampshire. Cambridge: Cambridge University Press, 1978.

Schochet, Gordon J. "Introduction: Constitutionalism, Liberalism, and the Study of Politics." In *Constitutionalism*, pp. 1–4. Edited by J. Roland Pennock and John W. Chapman. New York: New York University Press, 1979.

Shapiro, Ian. *The Evolution of Rights in Liberal Theory*. Cambridge: Cambridge University Press, 1986.

Shapiro, Ian. "Realism in the Study of the History of Ideas." *History of Political Thought* 3 (1982): 535–78.

Skinner, Quentin. "Conquest and Consent: Thomas Hobbes and the Engagement Controversy." In *The Interregnum: The Quest for Settlement 1646–1660*, pp. 79–98. Edited by G. E. Aylmer. London: Macmillan, 1972.

Skinner, Quentin. *The Foundations of Modern Political Thought*. Vol. II, *The Age of Reformation*. Cambridge: Cambridge University Press, 1978.

Skinner, Quentin. "History and Ideology in the English Revolution." *Historical Journal* 8 (1965): 151–78.

Skinner, Quentin. "Hobbes's 'Leviathan'." *Historical Journal* 7 (1964): 321–33.

Skinner, Quentin. "The Ideological Context of Hobbes's Political Thought." *Historical Journal* 9 (1966): 286–317.

Skinner, Quentin. "Meaning and Understanding in the History of Ideas." *History and Theory* 8 (1969): 3–53.

Smart, Ian Michael. "The Political Ideas of the Scottish Covenanters. 1638–88." *History of Political Thought* 1 (1980): 167–93.

Stephen, Leslie. *The English Utilitarians*, 3 vols. New York: G. P. Putnam's Sons, 1900.

Stephen, Leslie. *Hobbes*. 1904. Reprint. Ann Arbor: University of Michigan Press, 1961.

Strang, Colin. "What if Everyone Did That?" In *Ethics*, pp. 151–62. Edited by Judith J. Thomson and Gerald Dworkin. New York: Harper & Row, 1968.

Strauss, Leo. *Natural Right and History*. Chicago: University of Chicago Press, 1953.

Strauss, Leo. *The Political Philosophy of Hobbes: Its Basis and Its Gene-*

sis. Translated by Elsa M. Sinclair. Chicago: University of Chicago Press (Phoenix ed.), 1963.

Tarlton, Charles D. "The Creation and Maintenance of Government: A Neglected Dimension of Hobbes's Leviathan." *Political Studies* 26 (1978): 307–27.

Taylor, A. E. "The Ethical Doctrine of Hobbes." In *Hobbes Studies*, pp. 35–55. Edited by K. C. Brown. Cambridge, Mass.: Harvard University Press, 1965; reprint of the 1938 *Philosophy* article.

Tuck, Richard. *Natural Rights Theories: Their Origin and Development*. Cambridge: Cambridge University Press, 1979.

Wallace, John [M.]. "The Cause Too Good." *Journal of the History of Ideas* 24 (1963): 150–54.

Wallace, John M. *Destiny His Choice: The Loyalism of Andrew Marvell*. Cambridge: Cambridge University Press, 1968.

Wallace, John M. "The Engagement Controversy 1649–1652: An Annotated List of Pamphlets." *Bulletin of the New York Public Library* 68 (1964): 384–405.

Walzer, Michael. "The Obligation to Die for the State." In *Obligations: Essays on Disobedience, War, and Citizenship*, pp. 77–98. Cambridge, Mass.: Harvard University Press, 1970.

Warrender, Howard. Editor's Introduction to Thomas Hobbes, *De Cive (The Latin Version)*. Oxford: Clarendon Press, 1983.

Warrender, Howard. *The Political Philosophy of Hobbes: His Theory of Obligation*. Oxford: Clarendon Press, 1957.

Watkins, J. W. N. *Hobbes's System of Ideas: A Study in the Political Significance of Philosophical Theories*. 2nd ed. London: Hutchinson University Library, 1973.

Watkins, J. W. N. "Philosophy and Politics in Hobbes." *Philosophical Quarterly* 5 (1955): 125–46.

Weston, Corinne Comstock. "The Theory of Mixed Monarchy Under Charles I and After." *English Historical Review* 75 (1960): 426–43.

Williamson, Colwyn. "Hobbes on Law and Coercion." *Ethics* 80 (1970): 146–55.

Wolin, Sheldon S. *Politics and Vision*. Boston: Little, Brown, 1960.

Woodhouse, A. S. P., ed. *Puritanism and Liberty*. Chicago: University of Chicago Press, 1951.

Zagorin, Perez. *A History of Political Thought in the English Revolution*. London: Routledge & Kegan Paul, 1954.

Index

absolutism, 2–3; analytic, 56–57, 61–66, 69; benefits ordinary people, 78–79, 120, 123–24, 133–35; complemented by "art of government," 5, 75, 102, 106; contemporary connotations of, 60–61, 159n13, 178n12; defined, 62; Grotian arguments and, 26; ignored by Engagers, 127; prescriptive, 57–58, 63–66, 78–79; and unconditional sovereignty, 40–41, 57, 60–61, 102–4, 169n96; and unified sovereignty, 57–69 passim, 72–73, 78, 153n19, 167n80; *see also* arbitrary rule; civil war, absolute monarchy deters; supreme authority

accountability, 39–42, 49, 53–54, 117, 153n19; as constitutionalist tenet, 104; and representation, 47–48; *see also* absolutism, and unconditional sovereignty; parliamentary constitutional doctrine

agency: corporate, 84; political, 4, 38–45 passim, 48–55 passim, 57, 98, 154n26

ambition, political, 2–3, 60, 71–72, 74–75, 78, 108, 109, 113, 122–24, 127–28, 133–35, 168nn90–91, 179n30, 190n46

arbitrary power, 61, 180n45; Henry Parker on, 62, 161n30

arbitrary punishment, 112, 113

arbitrary rule, 109, 114; and absolutism, 60, 104, 114, 178n12, 180n45; theory licenses, 5, 57, 101–2; *see also* tyranny

Aristotle, 11, 60, 83, 100, 187n20

Ascham, Anthony, 90, 125–32, 188n26, n32, 189n39, n41, 191nn50–51, n55, 192n66; Hobbes aware of, 190n48

Ashcraft, Richard, 14, 168n89

Austin, John, 56

authorization: and account of household authority, 174n79; contemporary connotations of, 24, 49; covenant of, 3–4, 17, 20, 36–41 passim, 48–55 passim, 150n57, 151n3, 152n8, 155n35; public, 84

Behemoth, 71, 73, 120, 121, 131, 165n62, n66, 185n7

behemoth in story of Job, 120

Bellarmine, Cardinal, 167n80

Bentham, Jeremy, 56

Bodin, Jean, 57, 63, 65, 66, 161n33, 162n35, n42, 163n47

Bramhall, Bishop, 186n15

Index

mixed constitution, 57, 62–66 passim, 71, 162n36; *see also* divided sovereignty
Molesworth, William, 56
monarchomach constitutional theory, 22, 44, 49, 145n13, 155n42
monarchy, 41, 42, 44, 52, 168n90; English, 45–46; preference for, 3, 75–79, 105, 118, 124, 131, 134; representative assemblies under, 20, 46–47, 80, 84, 156n54
Morrill, J. S., 176n94

natural law, 178n11; and duty of sovereigns, 104; interpretation of, 81, 90
natural rights, *see* rights, natural; self-defense
Nedham, Marchamont, 125–26, 128, 130–33, 188n32, 191n56, 193n69; published extracts from *The Elements of Law*, 188n27
Nero, 118
nominalism, 6, 14, 39–40, 139n14; political application of, 41, 43–44, 46, 55, 154n24
non-resistance, doctrine of, 23, 25, 126; espoused by Hobbes, 24, 26–28, 134; parliamentarians denied, 60–61; theological justification of, 72; *see also* covenant, non-resistance formulation of

Oakeshott, Michael, 6, 81, 138n14
obligation: Ascham's view of, 127, 129–30; attaches to role, 87, 92–93; of children, *see* parental authority; distinguished from performance, 81, 87; and employment, 87–88; as interpretive theme, 2, 5–6, 19, 58, 81, 83, 102; prima facie, 18, 32, 81, 83, 90–94, 130, 173n52, n59; of servants, *see* household authority relationships; significance of, in theory,

82; and taxation, 115–16; Warrender's interpretation of, 81, 90–91; *see also* military service; subjects
Okin, Susan Moller, 169n95
Orwin, Clifford, 152n3
ownership concept of authority, 48–49

Papacy, 60, 73, 74, 167n80
parental authority, 83, 94, 97–99, 174n64
Parker, Henry, 4, 21–25, 27, 38, 39, 44, 62, 64, 155n42, 156n52, 161n30
Parliament: conceptions of, 43–45, 155n42; Hobbes's view of, 169n95; *see also* Long Parliament; Rump Parliament; Short Parliament
parliamentary constitutional doctrine: and accountability, 4, 24, 38, 44, 126; and common law, 108–9; and military authority, 21–22; and representation, 24, 38, 54; and *rex singulis major, universis minor,* 44; and right of resistance, 3–4, 21–26 passim, 60, 127, 159n19; and taxation, 67; *see also* constitutional debates; divided sovereignty; mixed constitution
parliamentary government, 168n90; criterion of, 68; criticized, 75–78; *see also* representative assemblies
patrimonial kingdom, 159n15
personification, 152n10
Pitkin, Hanna Fenichel, 37, 47, 151n3, 152n10, 156n45, n57
Plamenatz, John, 5–6, 58–59, 71, 148n36, 158n9, n11, 160n27, 166n72
Pocock, J. G. A., 179n35, 192n59
Polin, Raymond, 2, 153n17

209